'Personally and professionally loss and ber[...] D1141546 not least acknowledging our common hu[...] while at the same time recognising individual experiences. In presenting theory and exploring its application to individualised support this book responds to this challenge making a timely and helpful contribution to supporting people with intellectual disabilities in an often neglected area of practice.'

— Ruth Northway, Professor of Learning Disability
Nursing, University of South Wales

'Loss and death are inescapable parts of life's rich tapestry; and it is a sad reality that people with intellectual disabilities are often excluded from exploring sensitive issues that surround loss and death. This is why, for me, this book is so valuable, for we are slowly but surely moving to a new era as to how this group of people make sense of loss and death and how we can support them. Through a series of well-constructed chapters that consolidate issues surrounding loss for people with intellectual disabilities, the book moves on to provide a unique evidence-based text that will be of considerable value to all those who work with people with intellectual disabilities, so that they might be helped to better understand loss and death as inescapable parts of life; in much the same ways as other citizens. The editor has successfully brought together a range of eminent and authoritative contributors who present a range of issues from the broad based nature of loss, particularly in relation to this population, and the contextual nature of appropriate care and support. I believe that this ground breaking and unique book will be of considerable value as a resource to practitioners and students alike who seek to support people with intellectual disabilities with compassion through their experiences of loss.'

— Bob Gates, Professor of Learning Disabilities, University of West
London, Institute for Practice, Interdisciplinary Research and Enterprise
(INSPIRE), Editor of the British Journal of Learning Disabilities,
Emeritus Professor, the Centre for Learning Disability Studies, University
of Hertfordshire, and Honorary Professor of Learning Disabilities,
Hertfordshire Partnership University NHS Foundation Trust

'This work, edited by Professor Read, does not shrink from addressing challenging topics including a person's sense of being deprived of rights and journeying through life's transitions. Some journeys are planned while others are unexpected or unwelcome, but all need to be sensitively addressed. Every health, social and educational professional/carer should read this text so as to be able to effectively support people with intellectual disabilities through life defining and shaping times.'

— Jim Blair, Consultant Nurse Intellectual Disabilities, Great
Ormond Street Hospital, Associate Professor Kingston and
St George's Universities, and BILD Health Advisor

Sheffield Hallam University
Learning and Information Services
Withdrawn From Stock

Supporting People with Intellectual Disabilities Experiencing Loss and Bereavement

of related interest

Bereavement, Loss and Learning Disabilities
A Guide for Professionals and Carers
Robin Grey
ISBN 978 1 84905 020 3
eISBN 978 0 85700 363 8

How to Break Bad News to People with Intellectual Disabilities
A Guide for Carers and Professionals
Irene Tuffrey-Wijne
Foreword by Professor Baroness Sheila Hollins
ISBN 978 1 84905 280 1
eISBN 978 0 85700 583 0

Autism and Loss
Rachel Forrester-Jones and Sarah Broadhurst
ISBN 978 1 84310 433 9
eISBN 978 1 84642 715 2

Living with Learning Disabilities, Dying with Cancer
Thirteen Personal Stories
Irene Tuffrey-Wijne
Foreword by Professor Baroness Sheila Hollins
ISBN 978 1 84905 027 2
eISBN 978 0 85700 200 6

Intellectual Disability and Dementia
Research into Practice
Edited by Karen Watchman
Foreword by Diana Kerr
ISBN 978 1 84905 422 5
eISBN 978 0 85700 796 4

SUPPORTING PEOPLE
with INTELLECTUAL
DISABILITIES
EXPERIENCING LOSS
and BEREAVEMENT

Theory and Compassionate Practice

EDITED BY SUE READ

FOREWORD BY OWEN BARR

Jessica Kingsley *Publishers*
London and Philadelphia

Epigraph (p.15 and 48), copyright © G. Bonanno 2009, reprinted with permission of Basic Books, a member of the Perseus Books Group. FICA Spiritual History (p.73), copyright © C. Puchalski 1996, reprinted with permission of C Puchalski. Table 5.1, copyright © G Fitchett 2002, reprinted with permission of Academic Renewal Press. Fig. 5.1, copyright © J Manson 2012, reprinted with permission of J Manson. Fig. 6.1 and Case Study (p.88), copyright © H Priest 2012, adapted with permission of Routledge/Taylor and Francis Group. Epigraph (p.104), copyright © J. Light, reprinted with permission of Informa Healthcare. 'Perceptions of a Grandaughter', copyright © E Jennings, reprinted with permission of David Higham Associates Limited. Figs 18.2 and 18.2a, copyright © S Read, reprinted with permission of Quay Books.

First published in 2014
by Jessica Kingsley Publishers
73 Collier Street
London N1 9BE, UK
and
400 Market Street, Suite 400
Philadelphia, PA 19106, USA

www.jkp.com

SHEFFIELD HALLAM UNIVERSITY
WL
155.937087
SU
LEARNING AND INFORMATION SERVICES

Copyright © Jessica Kingsley Publishers 2014
Foreword copyright © Owen Barr 2014

All rights reserved. No part of this publication may be reproduced in any material form (including photocopying or storing it in any medium by electronic means and whether or not transiently or incidentally to some other use of this publication) without the written permission of the copyright owner except in accordance with the provisions of the Copyright, Designs and Patents Act 1988 or under the terms of a licence issued by the Copyright Licensing Agency Ltd, Saffron House, 6–10 Kirby Street, London EC1N 8TS. Applications for the copyright owner's written permission to reproduce any part of this publication should be addressed to the publisher.

Warning: The doing of an unauthorised act in relation to a copyright work may result in both a civil claim for damages and criminal prosecution.

Library of Congress Cataloging in Publication Data
A CIP catalog record for this book is available from the Library of Congress

British Library Cataloguing in Publication Data
A CIP catalogue record for this book is available from the British Library

ISBN 978 1 84905 369 3
eISBN 978 0 85700 726 1

Printed and bound by Bell & Bain Ltd, Glasgow

MIX
Paper from responsible sources
FSC
www.fsc.org   FSC® C007785

This book is dedicated to my sister, Lynn.

Mother, wife, daughter, sister, aunt, nurse and friend to so many. The first link in our sibling chain is irretrievably broken, and somehow it just feels like the family will never be the same again. Sleep well 'til next time...

Contents

Foreword

Owen Barr

Over the 30 years I have been working with services for people with intellectual disabilities the life expectancy of this group of people has increased considerably and it is now common that people with intellectual disabilities will outlive their parents, siblings, members of their extended families and close friends. Recognition of the range of losses people with intellectual disabilities may experience in their lives and the potential impact these losses may have on the person with intellectual disabilities, their opportunity for activities, living arrangements, friendships and relationships, are important aspects of any service that claims to be person-centred and provides holistic and compassionate support.

Internationally, the need to recognise and respect people's individuality is integral to stated aims and policies of all services for people with intellectual disabilities. Despite this at times myths still exist about how people with intellectual disabilities may not understand or indeed realise that someone has died. Whilst the communication abilities of some people may make it difficult for them to fully articulate a detailed understanding of the nature of death, it is my experience that all people with intellectual disabilities do know when people and activities important to them in their lives are no longer present or have changed. This for me is not in question.

This excellent book brings together contributions from experienced and international practitioners who have worked with people with intellectual disabilities across a wide range of settings. The important theoretical perspectives which underpin the work of supporting people who are experiencing loss to continue having fulfilling lives are clearly presented in an accessible manner. Through the use of case studies, real meaning is given to the stories people have shared, in particular the detail and impact of their personal recollections.

In keeping with the recognition of individuality among all people, including people with intellectual disabilities, it is necessary to take time to try to understand what the loss means to the person who has experienced it, and in doing so, to remember that even the apparently same loss can have very different short and longer term impacts for people. Experiencing a loss is challenging for everyone, including families and professional carers, but it does not automatically necessarily result in major pathology for people with or without intellectual disabilities. The chapters within the book provide clear and realistic information that focuses on people as individuals.

The wide variety of chapters within this book provide a balanced perspective of the challenges people may encounter and practical, creative suggestions from experienced practitioners on what actions may be supportive to people with intellectual disabilities. Real insights that take into account the potential relevance of particular clinical conditions that individuals may have (or settings in which people may live) are explored.

I commend the authors on the insights and practical suggestions, underpinned by theoretical explanations and the use of evidence-based research. This book should be a valuable resource to practitioners and students in services that seek to compassionately support people with intellectual disabilities to continue to grow and have fulfilling lives after experiences of loss.

Owen Barr,
Head of School of Nursing,
University of Ulster

Acknowledgements

I personally know every author who has contributed to this book, and it gladdened my heart that everyone found the time in their busy schedules to contribute. Each author was deliberately chosen because of their unique expertise and the bringing together of such an expert group in one volume makes for a truly inspirational read.

I owe a huge debt of gratitude to each and every author, for their patience and for giving their time, energy and expertise. Special thanks to Emily McClave, Commissioning Editor at Jessica Kingsley Publishers, for her encouragement and wisdom and for having faith in the success of the book. A special thank you to my dear friend and colleague, Dr Helena Priest, for help with the final editing.

Finally, personal thanks (again) to my husband, Robin, and my son, Chris, for recognising how important my work remains to me and for not complaining too much when I vanished for endless hours to my study. Behind every successful book lies an understanding, forgiving and supportive family.

Thank you.

Introduction

Sue Read

> *If we understand the different ways people react to loss,
> we understand something about what it means to be
> human…something about the way we experience life
> and death, love and meaning, sadness and joy.*

> *(Bonanno 2009, p.3)*

Life is characterised by movement and constant change and therefore by its very nature, by transitions, losses and grief (Thompson 2002). There is a wealth of literature around loss, death and bereavement generally, to help us understand the nature of loss and its prevailing and varied impact on individuals. Similarly, there is a steady, developing body of knowledge around this topic in relation to people with an intellectual disability (PWID). However, there is limited exploration about the continuum of personal and diverse experiences of loss across this population, and much of the existing texts are dated and narrowly focused.

The inevitability of death is a constant reminder of the fragility of life. Such concepts remain important but become more complex when a person struggles to make sense of abstract concepts, and is often protected from the stark realities of loss and grief by well-meaning, protective professional carers and family members. Although loss and death are embedded threads woven into the very fabric of life itself, people with an intellectual disability (ID) rarely get constructive opportunities to learn (or talk) about such sensitive issues. Subsequently, successfully accommodating loss can be difficult for many people with an ID. Whether the person is coping with general loss (such as transition), dealing with the death of others (family and friends), or is facing their own impending death (due to deteriorating health conditions or ageing), it may result in disenfranchised grief (Doka 1989, 2002) and disenfranchised death (Read 2006). People experiencing disenfranchised loss will inevitably require additional help and support to manage their grief and ultimately accommodate their loss.

This unique book will consolidate contemporary issues surrounding loss for people with ID providing an evidence-based resource with flexible usage. Each chapter theme has been carefully selected in recognition of the broad based nature of loss, particularly in relation to this population, and the contextual nature of appropriate care and support. A case study approach has been encouraged throughout to ground the chapters in the reality of practice issues, to nurture reader reflection and to maximise the application of theory to practise in transparent and meaningful ways. Each chapter will capture historical and contemporary challenges, integrate evidence to support best practice approaches, and suggest constructive ways of providing future loss support in a dynamic, ever-changing health and social care context.

Initially adopting a broad approach to loss, this book will then identify, introduce and consolidate a range of contemporary loss themes that often present specific challenges, some of which are new and have received scant attention up until now. For ease of access, the book is divided into three parts:

Part I: Theoretical Perspectives
Part II: Contemporary Practice Issues
Part III: Specialist Contexts and Considerations

Such focused approaches gently translate directly into ID practice, highlighting and redressing the challenges of care and support in relation to existing theoretical components. Part I provides the theoretical basis and framework for subsequent sections and chapters, with care and compassion as recurrent threads.

In Chapter 1 Read introduces the concept of loss, defining its nature and exploring its impact across various loss experiences in addition to the most commonly known form: death as loss. The chapter incorporates a range of contemporary approaches in relation to loss, bereavement and compassionate care which are introduced, defined and critically explored. Introducing the client population, defining and exploring loss in its broadest sense, and identifying the potential for loss from an ID perspective, the chapter presents a contextual backcloth against which all the chapters will ably sit.

Chapter 2 introduces a personal, lived experience of what it's like to experience loss, and the factors that helped in the struggle to accommodate that loss. Death is perceived by many to be the ultimate loss, and the co-author of this chapter is a woman with an ID who shares her story to encapsulate some of the challenges and issues experienced, and ultimately what helped her to cope with her loss. Read and Carr will embed this lived experience into a wider context, critically exploring the challenges to meaningful support, all of which is underpinned by the notion of compassion. Mary's story will continue in Chapter 7 but with a different dimension: a counselling perspective using a resilience framework.

There are a considerable number of texts around loss, grief and bereavement, but few that focus specifically around this marginalised group. Chapter 3 provides an overview of contemporary grief theories and integrates a range of models in relation to support for this population. Read will focus particularly on the concept of disenfranchised death and grief in relation to people with an ID, and ways of addressing the impact of this, with suggestions for future care, compassion and support.

Some people with an ID may not receive the help and support they need at the time they need it the most or indeed may not be included in customary rituals surrounding loss. In Chapter 4, Dodd and Blackman sensitively introduce and define the concept of complicated grief, explore the impact of this on individuals and introduce ideas to address complicated grief in meaningful ways.

Spirituality and faith can play an important role for many people within the loss, death and dying context. In this inspiring chapter (5), Bill Gaventa carefully defines and critically explores the nature of spirituality and ways of integrating meaning (i.e. making sense of spirituality) in the loss context with people who have an ID. Chapter 5 firmly establishes the foundations for understanding the nature of spirituality and identifies strategies for support.

Holistic approaches to contemporary healthcare recognise that psycho/social and emotional support is a fundamental aspect when meeting the needs of the patient in any context. The aim of Chapter 6 is to introduce, define and describe psychological support within the caring context generally. Priest then goes on to integrate these ideas and concepts into care and support models for PWID. This is an important chapter, establishing compassion as an integral part of the caring role and providing the theoretical thread that will weave its way throughout the text.

As the title suggests, **Part II: Contemporary Practice Issues**, highlights issues of loss, death and dying from within a number of focused practical perspectives. Drawing on the first section, here authors explore the impact of loss in relation to PWID from the multidimensional perspectives of parents, professional carers and advocacy viewpoints.

Traditional literature on grief and bereavement has been particularly concerned with maladaptation to loss and its pathological variants but there is an emergent direction that centres around positive psychology. Researchers and practitioners have recalibrated their understanding of grief to include resilience as both a natural capacity to emerge from loss and as a goal for therapy. In Chapter 7, Machin introduces the concept of resilience and describes a unique model that she has developed over a number of years that helps practitioners to explore resilience within loss and grief. A case study is then used to illustrate how the model has been used to support a bereaved woman with an ID.

Many people with an ID have communication impairments and may feel uncomfortable with verbal communication as the main vehicle. The aim of Chapter 8 is to explore a range of creative approaches that can help others to engage with people with ID in meaningful ways. Read introduces and clarifies approaches such as life story work, memory boxes, using photographs, storytelling, art work and films that can help individuals to explore loss in constructive ways, which are captured in mediums that can be stored and kept over time. Thus creating long term continuing bonds with the deceased.

Caring for people with an ID who are dealing with loss can be extremely challenging and sometimes difficult, particularly so if the carers themselves are also sharing the loss (as in families). In Chapter 9, Bowman introduces the concept of carer fatigue, explores the potential enduring impact of caring, identifies how to recognise fatigue illustrating how organisations can deal with it, and ultimately defines proactive ways of coping with this in the caring context.

With increased life expectancy, many PWID are expected to outlive their parents, previously the predominant providers of care. End-of-life care is becoming an important, inherent feature of care provision of PWID, and professional carers have a crucial role to play when loss permeates into their end-of-life care. Wiese has vast experiences of supporting professional carers in end-of-life situations, and in Chapter 10, explores this in relation to adults with ID within a community setting.

Specialist Contexts and Considerations is the final section of this book, providing an opportunity to critically explore a range of contexts that have particular loss implications from a rich, diverse and eclectic mix of authors.

Advocates can provide crucial support for the person with an ID, particularly during difficult times in their lives. In Chapter 11, Corcoran explores the potential for advocacy to empower individuals with ID during times of loss and bereavement. The purpose of advocacy is explained, and challenges and responses to disempowerment are explored. Examples of case-focused and cause-focused advocacy are provided to give an overview of independent advocacy, the process and the skill set of the advocate and advocacy facilitator.

This powerful chapter centres around loss with five PWID (three individuals and a married couple) who have been involved in advocacy partnerships with a voluntary organisation in Stoke, Staffordshire UK. Corcoran worked alongside the five people to establish the focus and content for this chapter, to ensure it is grounded in the reality of the lived experiences of others and to give 'voice' to PWID within the loss context.

Loss never occurs in a vacuum but within a social context, and this context can often shape how survivors can accommodate their loss. Since the majority of people with ID live at home and not in professional care settings, the family will play a pivotal role in supporting loss, particularly transitional loss. In Chapter 12, Gibbs defines the family, explores the demographical changing shape of the family and introduces the importance of loss from a parent and sibling perspective.

People within the autistic spectrum have a range of differing needs and complex communication challenges. In Chapter 13, Forrester-Jones defines what constitutes the autistic spectrum and describes associated key characteristics of such conditions. A case study is embedded in the chapter as a vehicle to explore how loss can be sensitively supported when individuals have specific communication and cognitive impairments.

The losses associated with restricted environments are anticipated to be vast, but there is limited empirical research that explores the loss experiences of PWID themselves within this particular context. Chapter 14 introduces a unique perspective on loss, as Hobson, Read and Priest describe a small, qualitative research study that captured the lived experiences of loss for PWID within a medium secure environment in England. This chapter probably raises more questions than it provides answers regarding loss in restrictive environments for this marginalised population.

A significant proportion of children diagnosed with a life limited condition also have an ID. In Chapter 15, drawing on a lifetime's career as a practitioner and academic, Brown critically explores the meaning and understanding of loss that children and young people hold, describes the holistic approach to caring with compassion and identifies good practice initiatives within this particular caring context.

Holistic support at the end-of-life is fundamental to the potential for a peaceful or easeful death. In Chapter 16, Ryan, Guerin and Larkin introduce key factors to end-of-life care and support when the patient has an ID. They identify the factors that may inhibit such care and support and explore best practice initiatives for effective management.

Parks is the parent of a teenager who has cytomegalovirus, and has previously written her story around living with a daughter with significant, complex needs and its effect on the family. In Chapter 17, Parks adds a further dimension to the themes of loss in this book by exploring the impact of loss from within the family environment itself. The prevailing impact on the family dynamics are catalogued as the whole family constantly adjusts to the variable demands when a loved family member has a deteriorating health condition in this incredibly powerful reminder of the realities of family life.

Research involving people with ID cannot be described as easy because it has not been done enough as yet. In Chapter 18, Read provides a brief introduction to the research process, identifies the inherent challenges to meaningfully engaging marginalised groups across the research continuum, and identifies particular research methodologies conducive to inclusive research. As a fitting end to this book, she concludes by highlighting potential research opportunities within the loss context.

The authors for this book have been carefully selected from across the world, in recognition of their notable expertise and to provide an international flavour to the topic. Many are established researchers and authors who bring a unique, established renown and expertise around loss and ID. Some are neophyte researchers and authors with a fresh, eager and developing interest in the field of loss. Some have an ID themselves, or have children with an ID, and therefore have huge personal experiences of loss. Such an eclectic combination of contributors will ensure variety and provide a unique rich tapestry from which to explore the journeys of loss for PWID.

Whilst the primary audience for this text is professionals specialising in ID health and social care, it will also be of interest to generic healthcare providers and those offering psychological support across generic services since many PWID will be accessing various mainstream services. This audience will include general nurses, palliative and end-of-life care practitioners, medical personnel, social workers, counsellors, psychologists and students across all fields of nursing within the international arena.

> *People with a learning disability [sic] are a part of us rather than being apart from us.*
>
> *(Todd 2006, p.23)*

PART I
THEORETICAL PERSPECTIVES

Chapter 1

Loss in the caring context

Sue Read

SUMMARY

The aim of this introductory chapter is to provide a contextual backcloth against which all the subsequent chapters will sit. Introducing death as the ultimate loss, it will then define and explore loss in its broadest sense. The client population will be introduced and the potential for loss from an intellectual disability (ID) perspective will be identified. Loss can affect people with an intellectual disability (PWID) across the lifespan, and issues related to this potential for loss across the lifespan will be highlighted.

Introduction

> *The terrible, dreadful act of his dying was, he could see, reduced*
> *by all those round him to the level of a chance unpleasantness,*
> *something indecent in part (rather like the way people treat*
> *a man who, upon entering a drawing room, gives off a bad*
> *smell), reduced with that same 'decency' that he had served*
> *all his life; he could see that no-one would take pity on him*
> *because no-one wanted even to understand his situation.*
>
> *(Tolstoy 2005, pp.42–3)*

The Death of Ivan Ilyich (2005) is regarded by many as one of Tolstoy's classics, a search for the meaning of death. In this short story, when confronted with his own impending death, only by reflecting on his life (and his life through the eyes of others around him) can Ilyich fully come to terms and accept his own pending mortality. It is a timeless, carefully crafted narrative of humanity, mystery and meaning around death and dying.

Everyone will come to a dying part in their lives, whether it be a sudden death, or a protracted one borne out over months or years. Whilst death is recognised as the only certainty within life itself, it is rarely openly discussed and such discussions are often frowned upon in our contemporary society. For many, death can be perceived as a sense of failure: a failure by medical professionals and scientists who cannot stop the disease from advancing; a failure by parents from protecting their child from contracting life limiting conditions; a failure by the patient themselves in not wanting to fight their illness anymore; a failure by the nurses who try constantly to minimise pain and suffering; a failure by some religious faith leaders who try to rationalise and explain why the person is dying and loved ones are taken from their family and friends. But for others death becomes a time of reflection and celebration: of a life once lived, however long or short; of a person's achievement in surviving for days, weeks, months or even years; of a person's determination to live well until dying. It becomes a celebration of a person's varied contributions to their family, friends and wider circles; of loving and being loved; of a life once lived; and the reality of the fragility of life itself and the need to embrace every precious, living moment. Death is usually perceived as the hardest, greatest loss to accommodate, perhaps because of its finality, permanence and irreversibility. But perhaps it's also a reminder of our own pending mortality that naturally grows ever closer with increasing age.

Read (2011) describes death as having a number of roles: as a regular or constant companion or as a sudden and unexpected visitor, when it arrives without warning or time to prepare and is perceived as untimely. Death can be a welcomed friend after times of enduring pain and no expectation of release. Death can also be a stranger, when, for example, death and loss are shrouded in secrecy and individuals are not allowed to know about death and loss until absolutely necessary, for example when the person involved has an ID (Read 2011). Whilst 'death is inevitable, the experience of death and dying may not be universal' (Todd 2009, p.245), particularly if you have an ID.

Having an ID can mean so many different things to different people. It may mean that you struggle with abstract concepts, or might need variable care and support to help you to do the everyday things that people ordinarily enjoy in life. You may struggle with conventional communication. What all this means is that you may be routinely in difficult conversations around loss, dying and death. People with IDs are frequently actively and deliberately excluded from any death and dying processes (Read and Elliott 2003). Family, friends and well-meaning professional carers often seek to protect PWID from the stark reality of sadness and loss, as if by protecting them and not talking about it, loss simply won't happen, or the person with an ID will not express reactions to loss. As Conboy-Hill realistically identified:

> Failure to recognise the impact of loss on people with learning disabilities [sic] arises from our need to see such people as lacking in effective emotional apparatus...this conveniently feeds our own need to avoid discussion of pain and grief and so the cycle of ignorance and inaction has been perpetuated. (Conboy-Hill 1992, p.151)

In other words, sometimes carers shield people and protect them because they are really shielding and protecting themselves from the sad reality of loss, dying and death.

It also seems like a factorial affect emerges, where the more complex the needs of a person, the less is the likelihood of PWID being involved in this sensitive but important area of their life (Read and Elliott 2003) for a whole host of reasons (see Chapter 3). For example, having an ID itself means you are unlikely to be actively involved in loss, dying and death issues. Having an ID and communication impairments means that you are even less likely to be actively involved and having an ID, communication impairments and challenging behaviours means that your are much less likely to be involved. Consequently, PWID are particularly vulnerable from a loss, dying and death perspective (Read and Elliott 2003).

For those professionals caring and supporting people exposed to loss or experiencing dying and death, it can be most stressful (Hackett and Palmer 2010) and challenging but equally incredibly rewarding. It has often been described as a privileged position from which to travel along the lonely paths with people experiencing such pain, whether physical, psycho-social, emotional or spiritual. Jeffreys (2011) describes such a person as an 'exquisite witness' (Jeffreys 2011, p.3), signifying anyone who steps in to help (for example) a grieving person.

However, loss, dying and death experiences are unique to the individual, as people all grieve in different ways (Worden 2009) and such responses are dependent on many factors (see Chapter 3). Death never occurs in a vacuum but within a social context and the nature of that context can influence greatly how the person faces the end of their life and how others accommodate the death of their friend/family member (Read 2008). That social context can have a huge impact on how the experience is lived, where patients receive their care and support, when they can expect care and support and indeed who they receive this care and support from. Whilst death is a tangible loss, and generally the most difficult of losses to accommodate, people experience many other losses throughout their lives that can feel equally painful, but may be less tangible or visible, and subsequently not be as easily acknowledged or constructively and consistently supported.

A sense of loss

Loss can be described as a sense of being deprived or being without, and as such can be expected or unexpected. For example, the student who does not revise for an exam will not be surprised when they fail; but the student who does revise, but perhaps unwittingly revises the wrong topics, will be both surprised and disappointed at failing their exam.

Life is characterised by movement and change and therefore by its very nature, by transitions, losses and grief (Thompson 2002), and Oswin succinctly reminds us of the importance of loss when she described how 'it sometimes seems as if all our lives we are trying to cope with loss – either the fear of it, or the memory of it or its raw immediate presence' (Oswin 1991, p.15). Subsequently loss remains omnipresent (Read 2011). For the majority of people, loss is dealt with within the individual's immediate social context, with help and support sought from family, friends and work colleagues (Worden 2009), but others may need specific help to adapt to the changes incurred through that loss.

Loss is about journeys, and such journeys can be planned, unexpected, educational, instantly forgettable and similarly forever memorable. Loss is universal and can have a profound impact on individuals throughout life and across other journeys. There are many different types of loss, which Schultz and Harris (2011) describe as either being *common* loss (such as losses experienced through growing up and growing old); *uncommon* loss (such as abandonment, abuse, migration, violent death); or *non-finite* loss (Schultz and Harris 2011). They describe non-finite loss as a continuing presence of the loss, which, because it may not necessarily involve death, may go unrecognised and difficult to articulate and explain (Schultz and Harris 2011, p.239). Similarly, Machin (2009, pp.13–31) identifies three distinct types of loss:

- **Developmental** loss and change, which occur across the life course.

- **Circumstantial** loss and change, unpredictable, and incorporating changes in relationships, ill health and disability and death.

- **Invisible** grief and undervalued people, where marginalised communities rarely receive the support they need following a loss.

Interestingly, there are close similarities between the first two types, and likewise the third (whether termed 'invisible' or 'non-finite'), which relates to losses that aren't tangible and often aren't easily identifiable or recognised by others and subsequently aren't appropriately supported.

This book has been written to address the needs of one particular marginalised and stigmatised population which has often been denied the opportunity to routinely be involved in loss, dying and death: namely PWID. Not only do PWID experience non-finite loss, they are often exposed to the invisibility of grief following loss and bereavement. They can also be treated as invisible patients when diagnosed with a life limiting condition and throughout their palliative care journey. This first chapter will provide a contextual backcloth for this text, introducing the population which is the predominant focus of the book, and providing a gentle introduction and rationale as to why the topics within this text have been included. It will introduce, define and clarify terms that will be used throughout the book, explore the probable contexts in which PWID will be supported and identify the range of potential losses that this group may experience.

Defining the population

Across the world there are various terms used to collectively refer to people with an intellectual disability/learning disability/mental retardation. However, most people with an ID distinctly dislike the use of any specific, collective term or label; they just want to be known by their name. The World Health Organisation (WHO 2001) defined learning disabilities as 'a state of arrested or incomplete development of mind', whereas the UK Department of Health (DH) defines it as 'the presence of a significantly reduced ability to understand new or complex information, to learn new skills (impaired intelligence), with a reduced ability to cope independently (impaired social functioning), which started before adulthood, with a lasting effect on development' (DH 2001a, p.14). Clearly such definitions describe individuals who may have a whole range of presenting competencies in communication, social skills, social functioning and/or behaviour, but who nonetheless remain 'amongst the most socially excluded and vulnerable groups in Britain today' (DH 2001a, p.14). This UK definition is broadly consistent with that used in the current version of the World Health Organisation's International Classification of Disease (ICD-10), which includes the rather outdated term 'mental retardation'.

The typical way of defining learning/intellectual disability, is by measuring the IQ (Intelligent Quotient) of less than 70. The IQ levels associated with ID are: for mild ID, IQ levels 50–69; moderate, 35–49; severe, 20–34; and profound, IQ levels below 20 (WHO 2001, p.35). Some differentiate between levels of disability due to low IQ plus additional significant disabilities, neurological damage and physical and/or sensory disabilities (Emerson, Moss and Kiernan 1995). However, often IQ measurements alone may not present a complete picture, and some question the accuracy, validity and reliability of this measurement in favour of clinical judgement (Webb and Whitaker 2012). Mencap (a UK national charity, described as the voice of learning disability in the UK) define a learning disability simply as 'a reduced intellectual ability and difficulty with everyday activities – for example household tasks, socialising or managing money – which affects someone for their whole life' (Mencap 2013a).

The following people are *not* included in the accepted definition of learning/intellectual disability: people who develop an intellectual disability after the age of 18; people who suffer brain injury in accidents after the age of 18; people with complex medical conditions which affected their intellectual abilities and were developed after the age of 18 (e.g. Alzheimer's disease); people with specific learning difficulties such as dyslexia (Luckerson *et al.* 1992, pp.4–5). Emerson *et al.* (2011, p.2) estimate that there are approximately 1,198,000 PWID in England, of which 298,000 are children and young people under the age of 17. They state that 14.9 per cent of carers in England care for someone with an ID, with 1.9 per cent of these carers having an ID themselves. Globally it is estimated that approximately 1–3 per cent of the worldwide population has an ID, with the rate for moderate, severe and profound ID being around 0.3 per cent (WHO 2001, p.35).

The term learning disability was introduced in the UK to replace 'mental handicap', but outside the UK the most favoured term appears to be intellectual disability. Since this book is an international resource, the term intellectual disability (ID) is used throughout to represent all other global terminology used to describe this population.

Similarities and differences

Whilst PWID are likely to 'function on a developmental level that is inconsistent with their chronological age' (Lavin 2002, p.314), they carry an associated history of marginalisation, devaluation and stigma. However it is worth remembering that PWIDs have more similarities to us than differences from us, particularly within the loss, death and bereavement context (Cartlidge and Read 2010; Read 2005a). There are three key times when any similarities are likely to be particularly apparent:

- **At birth:** All babies require fundamental care and support, i.e. feeding, changing, nurturing, regardless of presenting obvious disabilities.

- **As old age approaches:** As the body ages and body parts begin to weaken and don't function as well as they have previously done, society may become more tolerant of people of advancing age, and be more patient.

- **As death approaches:** Most people want similar things as the end-of-life approaches – choice and autonomy, to die in a place of their choosing, to have people they love and care about around them and to have an easeful death, free from pain and discomfort.

PWID are reliant on so many people for so much throughout their lives, and hence have the same, if not more, potential for loss experiences. The important point to note is that if those gatekeepers around them don't recognise the importance of loss, and the key features of support and compassion (see Chapter 6) when supporting loss, then the person with an ID is unlikely to receive the support they need at the time they most need it.

Potential for loss

In a world where differentness is not always positively valued, PWID remain one of the most socially disadvantaged groups of people within society (Disability Rights Commission 2006). Historically, PWID have lived through a troubled past of marginalisation, stigma and segregation, traditionally cloistered away in large, long stay institutions, secreted away from the rest of society. Following a raft of public enquiries around their care and support in such environments, and more recently around healthcare treatment and access, one has to wonder how this has impacted upon the individuals of this distinct but unique community.

The Ely Report of 1969 was the first of a number of shocking indictments around institutionalised treatment of PWID, alleging abuse in a long stay hospital near Cardiff (Socialist Health Association 1969). More recently, the Cornwall investigation (Healthcare Commission 2006), the Sutton Merton investigation (Healthcare Commission 2007), the Winterbourne Review (DH 2012a) and a series of critical health reports (Heslop *et al.* 2013; Mencap 2004; Mencap 2007; Mencap 2012) all illustrate that PWID are still vulnerable from a health and social care perspective.

PWID are likely to experience profound and multiple losses across the lifespan, many of which are invisible, and therefore go unnoticed, unrecognised and unsupported. The impact of these losses may be variable and far reaching, the potential for which may exist even before the person has been born or diagnosed as having an ID. Prevailing negative attitudes, low expectation and stereotyping, myths and stigmas surrounding disability and disabling conditions, fears and misguided assumptions surround people with an ID in abundance, influencing societal expectations for people deemed 'different'. Imagine being born into a world where everything you did was judged and everything you tried to do met resistance and barriers, because of the practicalities, misconstrued preconceived ideas, stereotypes and ideals of others. Consequently, people with an ID face a number of obvious losses associated with their disability from the day they are born. The remainder of this chapter will briefly introduce a number of particular losses which have shaped the development (and informed the content) of this book.

Loss across the lifespan

Some children with an ID may attend a specialist school, travelling on specially adapted transport; some may be integrated into ordinary schools with additional specialist support as necessary. Many children and young people born with life-limiting conditions also have an associated ID, and because of advances in medical therapeutic interventions, fortunately are now surviving into adulthood. Transition from child to adult health and social care services can incur numerous losses as the young person and their supporting parents have to learn to navigate new systems and processes to access the necessary support. Professionals in palliative care services and hospices play a pivotal role in anticipating and responding to the losses associated with transition.

Although most people continue to live within the family home, a proportion of PWID will live in various supportive housing, independently or with other people who have an ID. Some may still live in large institutions specifically designed for groups of similarly disabled people, although the existence of these is (thankfully) diminishing. The enduring impact on the family (including siblings) of having a child with an ID is well documented, and often the feelings of loss associated with this are huge. As PWID are living longer, the longer term impact on the families will require much empirical exploration, particularly around loss, dying and death.

In the UK, in 2010/11, only 6.6 per cent of adults with ID were reported to be in some form of paid employment, although it is estimated that 65 per cent of PWID would like a paid job (DH 2009). Work can boost self-esteem, make life much more interesting, introduce people to different social groups and opportunities and promote independence. That sense of not being employable can incur an inherent sense of abandonment and uselessness and all that this entails.

As PWID live longer, they are experiencing the range of malignant and non-malignant conditions that accompany such longevity. Hospitals, hospices and other generic support services are slowly beginning to recognise the need to make reasonable adjustments to their organisations in order to ensure they are fully accessible to people who struggle with the written (and spoken) word and have problems with cognition. With the demise of institutionalised care for PWID in favour of more socially integrated models, a range of professionals across health and social care will be confronted by PWID accessing their generic services, and education and training around what it means to live (and die) with an ID is fundamental to effective and consistent support.

Conclusion

Loss permeates throughout everyone's lives, but for some communities it may be harder to express feelings of loss in meaningful, socially acceptable ways and individuals may not be given the appropriate support they need at the time they need it the most. Having an ID means different things to different people, and the impact of the disability may be multiple, varied and wide ranging. However, for some individuals, getting the help they require may prove difficult. The following chapter topics were deliberately selected to address a wealth of issues in relation to loss, dying and death in the lives of PWID. Whether it is loss of autonomy and choice, or loss related to transition, self-esteem end-of-life care or bereavement, readers should find help, support and direction within the following pages. An underpinning theme in these chapters is the need for compassion integrated within a collaborative approach to maximise appropriate care and support, whatever the loss.

People with an ID continue to teach families and professionals so much about loss, death and dying, we just need to afford them opportunities to help us to learn from them. Such opportunities have been deliberately woven throughout this book as PWID were invited to co-author chapters and share their stories of loss to help others to learn.

CHAPTER 2

Living with loss

Sue Read and Mary Carr

SUMMARY

Death is perceived by many to be the ultimate loss, and the aim of this chapter is to introduce and critically explore death as loss from a personal perspective. Mary is a woman with intellectual disabilities (IDs), and has agreed to tell her story of loss to encapsulate some of the challenges and issues experienced throughout her journey. She wanted to share with others what helped her to cope with her loss, and what became important to her throughout her grief work. The co-authors will embed this lived experience in a wider context, critically exploring the challenges to meaningful support and exploring the notion of compassion in relation to grief work.[1]

Introduction

As stated previously, death never occurs in a vacuum but within a social context (Read 2008) and the nature of that social context will define and shape how individuals with an ID deal with their loss and accommodate the void in their lives when grief steps in. Sometimes it feels like people with an ID have to 'make sense of nonsense' as they struggle to understand the meaning behind the death when sometimes there appears to be no logical meaning at all.

For those who struggle with cognition and comprehension challenges, abstract issues like death can feel overwhelming, and the

---

1   Editor's note: Sadly, Mary died following a short illness after having completed this chapter, but was determined that her legacy lived on in this book. A truly remarkable, selfless woman.

fundamental characteristics of death (such as finality and irreversibility) difficult to understand and grasp. Additionally, communication impairments can compound the issue as carers struggle to find the words to convey the sensitive messages around (for example) breaking bad news, truth telling and simplifying complex terms. Simultaneously, people with an ID (PWID) may not be able to find the words that well describe how they are feeling and what they subsequently need. Indeed, some people might not know exactly what they need or how to get it, or what usual behaviour is after a loved one dies.

Sometimes there is a decision not to involve people associated with marginalised groups (including PWID) in the bereavement process for a whole host of reasons (see Chapter 1), and this can result in disenfranchised grief (see Chapter 3) and complicated grief (see Chapter 4).

In this chapter, Mary Carr shares her story of grief following the death of her mother, to illustrate helpful strategies that she encountered in her grief journey. Mary lives independently, with support from regular carers, in a bungalow in a busy town where she has lived all her life. She attends a day centre for people with an ID, and is a member of Reach, an advocacy organisation in Stoke (UK) that works (among other issues) proactively to champion the rights of people with an ID, particularly around health access issues. Mary has many friends, and talks freely and candidly about her loss, what helped and what could have been different.

CASE STUDY: MARY'S STORY

Losses and changes

I have had several bereavements. I lost my nan and granddad Milner; my granddad Frost (but didn't particularly like him); my dad (he lived with my sister so I only saw him when I visited my sister usually each week); my step dad (Peter); my uncle Sid; and my mum. I never went to my nan and granddad's funeral, 'cause I was at boarding school (aged 11/12 years then) and my mum said I was too young. I didn't go to my step dad's funeral, it was too far away. Someone at the school told me that Peter was ill, but when I got home mum said that he had 'passed away'. When I went back to school I ran away, I hated that school! I got punished too, so mum said I didn't have to go back again. Although I didn't go to the funerals, I do know where they are all buried.

Mum dying was the hardest thing. I was very close to my mum, I looked after her and she looked after me. Mum gave up in the end, because she wanted to be with Peter again. My biggest regret is that she didn't manage to see me get married, she would have liked that.

Figure 2.1 Mary and her mother

She died on the 12th May, 2008, so it's been five years now. She was very ill at home, she couldn't walk, and kept falling off the settee where she slept. She was a large lady, 32 stones she weighed. We had to call the fire brigade to help pick her up when she fell. She had gout in her foot, and when the GP visited he recommended she go straight to hospital. I didn't like the doctor because he said my mum was fat and couldn't look after herself. When she went to hospital, the fire men had to carry her through a window, she couldn't fit through the door way. She was in the hospital for a long time before she died.

The day she died I can remember well. I was having lunch out with an advocate friend, Andrew, in town. My sister rang to say that mum had died and Andrew took me to the hospital, where my brother was waiting for me and we went to see my mum's body. Mum was still in a bed and I cried. We went into a quiet room with the nursing staff, and they told me what had happened. Afterwards I went to see my friends at the advocacy organisation. It's so good having friends to talk to.

My sister arranged the funeral, and my brother paid for it. Mum was cremated and we had a service at the Salvation Army. Mum's funeral was exactly what she wanted. I started smoking again then, but I've stopped now. I can't understand why I didn't cry at the funeral, when everyone else did. My brother, sister and nephew cried. Perhaps I was trying to be strong...

What helped

Talking to a bereavement counsellor was really helpful – it gets it off your back. Anniversaries and birthdays are bad, even now. I still wish she was here. She knows I love her. I'd give her a hug. Sometimes I wish I was with her as I feel very lonely now. A family friend still visits on a Saturday and Monday. He helps me with my bills. I go to the Day Services five days each week; the people there provide company and friendship.

Sometimes talking to other people who have had a bereavement can help. It can remind you that death happens everywhere, not just to you. It just feels like that. Bereaved people can sometimes help each other. Help and support can come from all different places and people. Having lots of friends is good, and having long term support is useful.

Christmas is hard, I stay at home on my own, but I do get a present off my friend who visits. It feels good to tell my story, easier somehow. I like to paint, some of my paintings have been in a museum, many are on the walls of my home. Talking is the best way.

What do I miss the most? Loving and caring for my mum. We went everywhere together. I don't know what I'd do without my dog 'Lucky'. I had two dogs but 'Dylan' died.

Happy memories

Figure 2.2 Mary's mother and father

My happiest memories are when I think about going out and about with mum. When mum got married to Peter – I was a bridesmaid. July 15th 1983, it was, and then Peter died suddenly in September 1983, of a heart attack, just a few months after they were wed.

Talking to a professional helps, sometimes I talk and cry with friends. Sharing your sad story with others helps. I don't worry about dying; I want to be with my mum in heaven. I don't go to church. Sometimes it just feels like people don't care. All the people I really cared about have died. My advice to others would be to find professional help. Talk to people who can help you, don't bottle up your feelings.

Mary is able to clearly articulate her experiences, thoughts and feelings. She initially dictated her story and the co-author transcribed it, then Mary reviewed it several times to ensure accuracy and that the sentiment was portrayed as she intended.

Learning from loss

Meaningful involvement

Talking about loss and death may generally be a socially and culturally taboo subject, but when asked about loss and its impact, many people automatically trace their history of loss and want to share their whole life experience of loss with the person who asked. Mary was much the same, as she automatically catalogued a whole family history incorporating grandparents and her stepfather who had died. Mary had predominantly lived at home (with the exception of a relatively short early period spent at a boarding school) and this may have positively influenced how she had knowledge and understanding of all the family bereavements. However, Mary still did not attend any of the early funerals of her family, perhaps because her parents wanted to protect her as a young person, but she still knew where everyone was buried so was able to take flowers or visit when she wanted to. Not being allowed to attend funerals or participate in other rituals following a death is described as disenfranchised grief, and is common for people with an ID. This is explored further in Chapter 3.

A continuum of support

As a fairly autonomous person, networking remains important to Mary and her ability to access various support networks across her circle of support provided her with a range of avenues within which individuals could support her with her loss. Circles of support have been recognised in end-of-life care (O'Kelly and O'Kelly 2006) and such frameworks are easily transferable to other sensitive aspects of life including bereavement, incorporating a range of different people available to the person (see Figure 2.3).

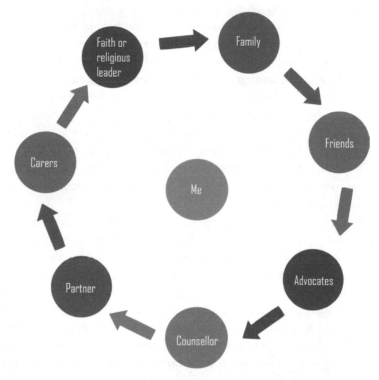

Figure 2.3 Circle of support (after O'Kelly and O'Kelly 2006)

Mary specifically identified the feelings of isolation and perceived loneliness often associated with loss, as bereaved people feel the uniqueness of grief and rightly believe that their loss is unlike anyone else's. However, for people who have limited social networks, and few family members, the lack of meaningful support systems may compound the reactions to loss as they struggle to find people to tell their story to. Similarly, telling a story requires a certain level of verbal skill, and some people may not have the ability to vocalise their experiences in this way.

Support and support systems are highlighted as being particularly crucial to Mary and came in many different forms as Mary recognised the need to talk about her loss. Some five years after the death of her mother Mary still welcomes the opportunity to share her story with others, and this may be in keeping with maintaining continuing bonds with those she loved (Klass *et al.* 2006) and keeping those cherished memories alive. Or it may simply be a constructive and welcomed response to those who demonstrate interests in her life, life history and heritage.

Peer support was also highlighted as being helpful to Mary, as she recognised how people with IDs could effectively help each other. Being able to seek the solace of others who had experienced similar losses redressed the thoughts that loss only happens to you, and may lessen the inherent sense of isolation. Mary also accessed longer term, regular support in the form of advocates and professional counsellors, which she positively valued. The role of advocacy and support is clarified in Chapter 11 and Mary's experience of counselling is explored further in Chapter 7, under the theme of resilience. In this chapter, Mary's story of loss and grief is revisited but from a bereavement counselling perspective specifically.

Whatever avenue was accessed, the *need* to talk about loss was evident throughout Mary's account, whether this was informally with friends or carers, or formally through advocates, counsellors or Day Service staff. 'Communication is the essence of human life' (Light 1997, p.61), and talking and communicating is not simply about one person's ability to understand and be understood effectively by other people. The ability and willingness of other people to take time to interpret, respond and ensure their responses have been heard and understood is equally important. Having people around you who really want to talk with you (even about sensitive topics) and communicate with you in a way that you understand, is fundamental to effective and meaningful support for those experiencing loss.

It is also important that such support people are *comfortable* talking about issues surrounding loss and grief, which some people may not be. If talking about difficult topics is obviously uncomfortable for a carer or support person, then bereaved people may intuitively or physically observe this and will avoid talking about such issues because of the effect it has on others. Carers who do find talking about death and loss difficult (and it may be perhaps because of events happening in their personal lives around loss), should acknowledge this with their manager and peers and ensure other carers are available instead. Unlike other skills associated with caring, support for loss and death is demanding and can take its toll on those doing the caring resulting in carer fatigue (see Chapter 9).

Gaventa argues that *everyone* has a spiritual dimension to their lives (see Chapter 5), and Mary talks openly about her belief that her mother gave up at the end because she wanted to be with her husband who had died a few years previously. Although not necessarily religious, she had beliefs about an afterlife and an appreciation about what was important to others and indeed to her. Mary states that she is unafraid of dying, believing that she will one day be with her mother, and sometimes craves this because of the sense of loneliness. When supporting anyone with an ID to come to terms with loss, carers must remain cognisant of spirituality as part of the holistic nature of support, since to ignore this may be ignoring a significant element of the person's grief journey.

When two people live closely together (albeit as partners or as mother and daughter), the familial ties may be deep rooted and significant. When one of the people becomes significantly ill, the other person usually takes on the major caring role, and in this case this major caring role fell to Mary who looked after her mother. When death eventually occurs in such a partnership, the void left in the life of the survivor can be huge. Coming to terms with this can be hard as so much time was previously taken up with supporting the dying person. Initially as her mother's health deteriorated and she became housebound, Mary would have been involved in the shopping, cleaning and general care for her mother. Mary's mother died in hospital, so regular hospital visits and bedside vigils, in addition to the household chores of the family home, would then be left to Mary. People with ID are rarely major caregivers, indeed they are usually recipients of care (continuously or at various key points depending on the nature of the ID) throughout their lives. When Mary's mother died, the overwhelming loss must have been significant, since her mother was her closest relative, her friend and her confidante, as Mary identifies that among all her previous losses 'Mum dying was the hardest thing'. The intimacy of such a relationship is unlikely ever to be replaced, and the losses associated with the loss of her mother are likely to be multiple and complex.

Apart from listening to (and hearing) Mary's pain and sadness, counsellors would help Mary to explore these issues, perhaps identifying resources and people who Mary might secure support and strength from in the months and years to come. Helping her to focus on what she can realistically build upon in the absence of her known source of support – her mother. Pets continue to play an important role in many people's lives, and again Mary is no different. Dogs and cats (to name the most popular pets) provide unconditional love and many intuitively know when their owners are sad and need companionship. Perhaps a focus for Mary would be looking after her dog in the future, keeping him/her safe and healthy.

The importance of storytelling

Grief is a journey, and as such has many tales. We live in stories not just statistics, and the importance of telling and sharing stories is well documented (e.g. Jennings 2005) particularly within loss and bereavement, as highlighted in Chapter 8. As Mary recognises 'It feels good to tell my story, easier somehow' and telling stories of loss can be healing in nature and cathartic (Read and Bowler 2007) as people seek to share their lived experiences to interested people. Telling the story often can help you to accept the reality of the loss, and it may become easier to recall and tell your particular story the more often you do so.

For bereaved people it's usually important to them that they tell their story as accurately and in as much detail as possible. Often the story begins with the way the bad news was broken; this can be news that death is imminent or (as in Mary's story) that death had occurred. Mary doesn't say whether she was prepared for her mother's death, but she does talk about how her mother had been ill for a long time. Bad news can stay with people for ever, and many bereaved people remember the intimate details around how they heard the news: where they were, who they were with, what happened next and so on. This was much the same in Mary's story, as she describes being with an advocate friend having a spot of lunch and then receiving the telephone call, going to the hospital and eventually going back to her friends at the advocacy organisation. One of the many advantages of going to see a counsellor is that a bereaved person gets to tell their story anew to someone they have never met before, as the counsellor seeks to explore what has happened in the grief journey. One must remember that this story is the bereaved person's story, how they saw what happened from their own perspective, and each family member may well tell their version of the story slightly differently.

Compassionate care

According to Priest (Chapter 6, p.93) 'Compassion, empathy, relationship building and making time underpinned the carers' approaches, and enhanced their skills of communication, assessment, and informational care', and Mary was fortunate enough to be able to access compassionate understanding from a range of people supporting her in her sadness: informal, compassionate, empathic support from other people with an ID, who were eager to hear her story and share their own stories of loss. More formal compassionate support from people trained to provide therapeutic interventions such as counselling and professional carers can provide much needed space and time to talk and work through grief work. Taking time out of busy schedules to listen to bereaved people's stories demonstrates a genuine interest in people and their wellbeing. It suggests that they have something valuable and worth listening to, to say and contribute. It also affirms the importance of the people who have died in the lives of those survivors left behind.

Conclusion

'People with ID have more similarities to the general population than they do differences, particularly where loss, death and dying are concerned' (Cartlidge and Read 2010, p.98) and this is well illustrated throughout Mary's story of loss and grief. Much of what Mary talked about is typical for many bereaved people, for example the uniqueness of grief, the loneliness, the isolation and the overwhelming sadness. Mary welcomed the opportunity to tell her story, and co-authoring this chapter has enabled her story to have permanence as a legacy in memory of her mother. The social context in which loss occurs is vital to how a person grieves and the opportunities they have to mourn their loss in ways they choose to do so. Having space, networks and a variety of people to talk to proved invaluable to Mary, providing her with many different levels of support (formal and informal). Mary knows that her mother is dead, but she believes that one day they will be reunited and this makes her unafraid of death. Reflecting on loss also provided an opportunity for Mary to recount the good times too, and she recollected the many happy memories she has from time spent with her mother going out and about. A key message from Mary's story is that help and support can take many different shapes and forms, as she says: 'Help and support can come from all different places and people'.

CHAPTER 3

Grief and mourning

Sue Read

SUMMARY

There are a considerable number of texts around loss, grief and bereavement, but few that focus specifically around this marginalised group, namely people with an intellectual disability (PWID). This chapter aims to clarify terms associated with grief, bereavement and mourning; provide an overview of contemporary grief theories; and integrate a range of models in relation to grief support for this population. It will introduce the concept of disenfranchised death and grief in relation to people with an intellectual disability (ID), and identify ways of addressing the impact of bereavement on their lives and of enfranchising this marginalised group at this sensitive time. There are no easy answers to supporting loss, since everyone is unique and different, but with sensitive support and compassion, many PWID can be helped to do the things they really need to do following the death of a loved one.

Introduction

Lewis describes the impact of loss so eloquently: 'No one ever told me that grief felt so like fear. I am not afraid, but the sensation is like being afraid. The same fluttering in the stomach, the same restlessness, the yawning. I keep on swallowing. At other times it feels like being mildly drunk, or concussed. There is a sort of invisible blanket between the world and me' (Lewis 1961, p.5). Although written in 1961, as C.S. Lewis tries to depict his overwhelming sense of loss following the death of his wife, many bereaved people today could easily relate to the simplistic yet vivid description he so poignantly pens. Death is usually perceived as the ultimate loss, perhaps because of its finality, irreversibility and how indiscriminate it appears to be. Death can occur at any age, often without warning, or at the end of an enduring condition (see Chapter 1) and often seemingly makes no sense at all to those left behind. Indeed for many years, I have referred to bereavement as one's attempt to 'make sense of nonsense,' because often there is no sense to be made as to why certain individuals die in the way that they do or at the time that they die. Many believe that to establish an understanding of grief, one needs to fully appreciate the complexities of loss, which is why the first chapter of this text focused on introducing loss and its potential impact.

The death of a loved one can evoke a plethora of reactions, which have been variably described and theorised over many years of bereavement research and grief literature. Worden categorises these responses to loss under four general headings: feelings, physical reactions, cognition and behaviours (Worden 2009, p.18), incorporating a range of responses (see Table 3.1).

Bereavement can be defined as the state of loss caused by death (Attig 2011); or 'the loss of something that is precious' (Ward 1989). Grief has been described as a response to loss or prompted by change and readjustment (Parkes 1996), although later Parkes contends that response to bereavement is much more than grief alone (Parkes 2006). Parkes recognises the wider, social implications of loss, incorporating perceived threats to one's sense of personal security; major changes in the person's life; and major changes in the lives of the associated surviving family members (Parkes 2006).

These responses can become a struggle in which release from the pain can be achieved either by evasion (avoiding talking about the loss) or confrontation (dealing with the impact of loss) (Machin 1998). Responses to loss can affect every part of the person, whether this be physical, behavioural, social and/or psychological (Machin 1998; Worden 2009).

Table 3.1 Overview of grief responses (Worden 2009)

Feelings	Physical sensations	Cognitions	Behaviours
Sadness	Hollowness in the stomach	Disbelief	Sleep disturbances
Guilt		Confusion	Appetite disturbances
Loneliness	Tightness in the chest	Preoccupation	Absentmindedness
Fatigue		Sense of presence	
Anxiety	Tightness in the throat	Hallucinations	Social withdrawal
Shock	Oversensitivity to noise		Dreams of the deceased
Yearning			Avoidance behaviours
Helplessness	Breathlessness		Searching and calling out
Relief	Muscle weakness		
Numbness	Lack of energy		Sighing
Emancipation	Dry mouth		Restless hyperactivity
			Crying
			Visiting old haunts
			Carrying objects that remind one of the deceased
			Treasuring objects that belonged to the deceased

Mourning

Mourning has been described as the process of accommodating the loss (Worden 2009), which has received much attention over the years. Mourning has been largely theorised as tasks, stages and phases, an overview of which is found in Table 3.2. In recent years, contrary to resolution being perceived as the end stage of grief work, the emphasis is now on maintaining links with the deceased and preserving memories, often described as continuing bonds (Klass, Silverman and Nickman 1996) which can be a healthy part of a survivor's ongoing life. For example, if a person's father died when they were young, when they celebrate their twenty-first birthday they still have a father; he just isn't around anymore to celebrate with them. It is difficult to define when mourning has been completed. Worden (2009) suggests that this is when a bereaved person can think about the deceased without pain; whilst some believe that grief does not have a definitive end, and that bonds tie us to our loved ones forever (Rosenblatt 1996), which others might consider as complicated grief (Worden 2009).

The dual process model of grieving was developed in recognition of the 'diversity of stressful experiences in bereavement' (Stroebe and Schut 1999, p.197), where grievers would oscillate between loss and restoration orientated dimensions. This model is applauded for not providing definitive time expectations around mourning rituals or customs, and for recognising the social context of death and bereavement as being fundamental to grief work.

Experiences of bereavement are very personal, and personal stories are indeed often perceived as the 'heart of the matter' in grief work (Attig 2011, p.xxiv). Stories have kept me grounded in my teaching, research and writing throughout my career, and will continue to do so. For these reasons, contributors to this text have been encouraged to incorporate stories of personal experiences or case examples to ground their thinking around bereavement and loss in the stark reality of practice. Whilst there is a sound evidence base underpinning the empirical foundations of previously identified grief theories, there is very little research that has translated such theoretical understanding into the world of ID.

Table 3.2 Overview of mourning as tasks, phases and stages

Lindemann (1944)	Kübler-Ross (1969)	Bowlby (1980)	Klass *et al.* (1996)	Parkes (1996)	Doka (1989 2002)	Worden (2009)
Stage Model	**Stage Model**	**Attachment Theory**	**Continuing Bonds**	**Phases Model**	**Disenfranchised grief**	**Transitional task model**
• Shock	• Denial	• Numbness	• Acknowledging the impact	• Shock and numbness	• Griever is disenfranchised	• Accept the reality of the loss
• Acute mourning	• Anger	• Yearning and searching	• Forging a new relationship	• Yearning and searching	• The relationship is disenfranchised	• Process the pain of grief
• Resolution	• Bargaining	• Disorganisation and despair	• Maintaining a relationship with the deceased	• Disorganisation and despair	• The loss is disenfranchised	• Adjust to a world without the deceased
• Acceptance	• Depression			• Reorganisation		• To find an enduring connection with the deceased in the midst of embarking on a new life
	• Acceptance					

Bereavement and people with intellectual disabilities

If we understand the different ways people react to loss,
we understand something about what it means to be
human…something about the way we experience life
and death, love and meaning, sadness and joy.

(Bonanno 2009, p.3)

People with ID do experience grief (Hollins and Esterhuyzen 1997; Oswin 2000), but the impact of grief is varied and often complex (Conboy-Hill 1992; Hollins and Esterhuyzen 1997; MacHale and Carey 2002). It is recognised that 'the response to bereavement by adults is similar in type, though not in expression, to that of the general population' (Bonell-Pascual *et al.* 1999, p.348), and PWID are prone to multiple and successive losses (Elliott 2003). As identified previously in Chapter 1, PWID are extremely vulnerable from a death and dying perspective for a host of different reasons:

- They are actively excluded from death and dying (Read and Elliott 2003).

- The more complex the needs, the less is the likelihood of being involved (Read and Elliott 2003).

- People usually experience sudden as opposed to anticipatory grief (O'Nians 1993).

- They have an external locus of control (meaning they are reliant on so many for so much).

This vulnerability means that PWID often don't get to do what they really need to do following a bereavement, and sometimes don't even know what they can do (e.g. visiting the Chapel of Rest). Loss always occurs in a social context (Read and Elliot 2007), and that social context is crucial in facilitating any grief work (or what Worden describes as 'mediators of mourning', Worden 2009, p.57).

When Todd and Read (2010) conducted a series of focus groups with PWID in Cardiff, Wales, and Staffordshire, England, to explore their understandings and experiences of loss, dying and bereavement, they were immediately struck by the number of loss and death experiences encountered by participants. Since loss and death appeared as a regular, fundamental feature of everyday life, they were perceived as normal, acceptable events in the lives of PWID. They also found that pets played an important role in many people's lives and even though participants found it sad and difficult to talk about their experiences they were eager to do so, recognising that many worry about friends and family members dying and about dying themselves. Whilst many people had experience of bereavement, and shared their (often) sad stories of loss, they had significantly less contact with dying people, which Todd and Read termed the hidden face of dying (Todd and Read 2010).

Challenges to appropriate support

The emotional needs of PWID continue to be neglected (Arthur 2003), and this is due to a plethora of reasons. Whilst behaviours can be observed, measured and evaluated, emotions are less quantifiable and difficult to accurately ascertain and measure. Cultural and societal taboos generally, and emphatically bad attitudes, around death and disability are still prevalent, directly influencing whether people are engaged in discussions about loss (Oswin 2000). Some carers may doubt an individual's ability to grieve (Elliot 1995; McLoughlin 1986; Read 1996) or feel inadequacy, fear and uncertainty in talking about such sensitive topics (Emerson 1977; Oswin 2000). Some parents and carers still tend to focus upon the symptoms of grief rather than addressing the cause (Crick 1988), but this of course doesn't make the sadness go away; it only temporarily masks it until it resurfaces at a later date.

The combination of varying levels of cognitive ability, limited attention span and emotional vocabulary (Conboy-Hill 1992), together with low expectations, stereotyping and stigma (Kitching 1987) combine to provide PWID with limited experience of grief and grief rituals (Cathcart 1995; Raji and Hollins 2003). Challenges to reciprocal communication remain one of the biggest barriers to effective support in grief work with PWID and these are as follows:

- The individual lacks an appropriate verbal repertoire.

- The support person may not know how to communicate effectively.

- There may be uncertainty around what has been absorbed/understood.

- Counselling and support is often reliant on 'talking therapies'.

- There may be lack of clarity about what the person wants.

- There may be lack of clarity about what the person knows about what has happened.

For a small percentage of people, there is the need for more specific professional help and support in the form of psychological support from psychotherapists or counsellors (Hawkins 2002). Some people may be described as having complicated or prolonged grief, where they struggle to (unsuccessfully) re-establish their lives without the dead person (see Chapter 4). Those who have not been able to grieve their loss in any appropriate or meaningful way are often described as experiencing disenfranchised grief, where responses to loss are not recognised, legitimised or socially supported (Corr 2002).

Disenfranchised grief

Disenfranchised grief can be described as the grief that people experience when they incur a loss that cannot be openly acknowledged, publicly mourned, or socially supported (Doka 2002). Disenfranchisement is seen amongst populations 'who are not recognised as having the status of persons who experience grief' (Corr 2002, p.44), where people are deemed not to have the right to grieve (Doka 2002). Particular populations likely to experience disenfranchised grief include people with mental health issues, children and young people, older people, prisoners and PWID (Doka 2002). When populations become doubly disadvantaged (e.g. PWID living in secure environments) the disenfranchising effects will be more so, as evidenced in Chapter 14. The typology of disenfranchised grief is identified by Doka (2002, pp.10–14) as when:

- The relationship is not recognised.

- The loss is not acknowledged.

- The griever is excluded.

- The support person may not be clear about what the person needs.

- The support person may not know what the individual has been told (or indeed understands) about the death.

Regardless of whether a parent has visited their son with an ID for a long time and professional carers question whether the son will notice if they ever visit again, if the parent dies, the son has a right to know this. The son has the right to know the truth, to be offered the opportunity to mourn their loss, and to decide whether to attend the funeral. Whatever well-meaning carers think, once the funeral is over, the son will never again get the opportunity to mourn their parent amongst other mourners who loved them. They will never be able to participate in the shared expressions of sadness and loss, and ultimately they will never learn about loss and how to cope with it if they are never exposed to the loss experience in a supportive manner.

More recently, Read argued that PWID are also at risk of disenfranchised dying, which she defined as 'death that is not openly acknowledged with the dying person…the dying person is socially excluded from the process of dying and deliberately excluded from the decision making process' (Read 2006, p.96). Characteristics of this incorporate a lack of recognition of the autonomy of the dying person with ID; when the pending death is not recognised or legitimised with the PWID; and when the person's 'rights to know' are overlooked. The sentiments behind the principles of disenfranchised dying are reflected well in Chapters 10 and 16.

Responding to disenfranchised grief

Supporting disenfranchised grievers involves initially acknowledging the loss and legitimising the emotional pain of the loss; active listening; showing empathic understanding; and seeking benefits (or meaning making) from the loss (Doka 2002). Doka also recognises the importance and constructive role of rituals in bereavement, seeing them as symbolic acts and powerful, therapeutic tools. Many PWID may not get to participate in the rituals surrounding death (e.g. visiting the Chapel of Rest, organising the funeral, selecting the hymns, organising funeral cars and flowers) and consequently may not feel part of the mourners. Some may not even attend the funeral. Of course attending to these early rituals also helps to affirm the reality of the death and is a social rite of passage. The different types of therapeutic rituals identified by Doka (2002) are:

- funerals (structure and social support)

- rituals of continuity (lighting candles on certain days)

- rituals of transition (marking the change or transition stage)

- rituals of reconciliation (allowing a person to offer or accept forgiveness or to complete some degree of unfinished business)

- rituals of affirmation (allow individuals to affirm the loss and recognise any good things that have come out of the loss experience).

Ways of helping bereaved PWID

Since 'people with learning disabilities [sic] are a part *of* us, rather than being apart *from* us' (Todd 2006, p.23), professionals need to explore ways of practically supporting PWID experiencing loss and bereavement, using existing theoretical models to help. The Continuum of Support Model (Read 2005b) provides a useful framework for health and social care practitioners to develop meaningful support strategies from different levels whilst integrating existing, generic approaches. Whether using stages, phases or tasks, many of these models work well together, but we lack a firm evidence base as to what works well with this population, and how such models translate into meaningful practice. Some of the methods presented in Chapter 8 fit well into the idea of continuing bonds, where life story and memory work, photographs, artwork or pictures are used to create and maintain tangible links to loved ones who have died.

The first steps in any loss and bereavement support begin with the anticipation, recognition and acceptance that PWID do experience loss and grief; the greater challenge is to become their 'exquisite witness' (Jeffreys 2011, p.3) – the person who steps in to help facilitate their grief. The following list provides a number of ways of helping for consideration (see Conboy-Hill 1992; Lavin 2002):

- Acknowledge that PWID do respond to loss and grief and do so in profound ways.

- Look out for changes in behaviour that might indicate distress.

- Be open and honest and treat people with full adult status.

- Actively listen to find out what the person makes of their situation.

- Repeat ideas to encourage the person to understand what is happening around them.

- Keep ideas simple and concrete.

- Use clear words and pictures in all information.

- Use a variety of resources to support individual needs.

- Be creative in approaches used (see Chapter 8).

- Teach an emotional vocabulary.

- Help people to accept the reality of the loss.

- Help people to recognise their feelings.

- Be an advocate (see Chapter 11).

- Refer on when appropriate.

- Use reactive and proactive opportunities to teach about loss and death.

Such approaches can help to enfranchise bereaved PWID, enabling individuals to behave in a certain way, to speak out about something, to give voice to feelings associated with the loss or participate in particular activities or rituals that are important to them (Corr 2002). People with ID are reliant on so many people for so much, and bereavement and loss support is one aspect of their lives in which they so often need the support and guidance of others.

Impact on helpers

Supporting people with loss and bereavement can be difficult but extremely rewarding and often humbling. Jeffreys (2011) describes such people as exquisite witnesses, symbolising anyone who steps in to help a grieving person (see Chapter 1). Worden (2009) identifies that working with bereavement and loss can impact on helpers in three distinct ways. First, it can remind us of our own previous losses; second, it makes us aware of our potential future losses; and third, it reminds us of our own pending mortality. Clearly this indicates the need for support for the helpers too, whether in the form of regular peer support, professional supervision or counselling. A healthy helper means healthy support, so this aspect shouldn't be overlooked or neglected.

Conclusion

Whilst death and dying remain sensitive issues for everyone, they can be more challenging for some people if they are not encouraged or enabled to participate in the grief rituals they need following the death of a loved one. Since 'grief is a social phenomenon' (Worden 2009, p.73), collaborative working may be the key to effective, compassionate support when supporting bereaved PWID. Working alongside PWID whether as bereaved people or as co-researchers has taught me so much about loss and humanity and particularly about what is important to them from a research perspective. Research can be a vehicle for active consultation and the engagement of PWID; it also promotes reciprocal learning for the co-researchers in so many meaningful ways (Read and Corcoran 2009).

There are no easy answers to supporting loss, since everyone is unique. No one dies the same death twice; similarly no one grieves the same way for the same death. This uniqueness makes for the mystery surrounding loss and grief, but also makes the teaching of grief work and support more challenging amongst the helping professions. There are different ways of conceptualising loss and grief responses, with various frameworks that provide ideas for helping others to understand loss at a practical, psychological and sociological level. Frameworks can provide a stimulus to thinking about how these conceptualisations might inform how we support people or indeed how grief is mediated (Worden 2009). However, few of these frameworks have been empirically tested with bereaved PWID, so there remains much work to be done around this.

People with ID have more similarities *to us* than differences *from us* (Cartlidge and Read 2010) particularly during times of loss and bereavement. Carers need to build on these similarities and not become constrained by the differences, when offering compassionate bereavement support.

Our major challenge is the acceptance of death as a natural part of life, by ourselves, by our patients, by families, and by our culture.

(Smith 1994, p.207)

CHAPTER 4

Complicated grief

Philip Dodd and Noelle Blackman

SUMMARY

For some, the experience of a bereavement can result in severe grief symptoms, coupled with a lack of ability to function, with negative implications for health and wellbeing. Sometimes people experience severe psychiatric and psychological symptoms requiring specialist input, including psychology, psychiatry and psychotherapy. This chapter will introduce the concept of complicated grief, identify the impact of this on individuals and explore how complicated grief can be addressed in effective and meaningful ways. Important research and practice with the general population will be highlighted and explored in relation to people with an intellectual disability (PWID).

Introduction

Although grief in response to bereavement is a normal, inevitable part of life, it is now well accepted that grief may, in certain instances, be acutely distressing, persistent and functionally impairing (Kristjanson *et al.* 2006). Complicated grief involves the experience of certain grief-related symptoms and emotions for a time, and severity, beyond which could be considered adaptive. These symptoms include separation distress-type symptoms, such as longing and searching for the deceased, loneliness and preoccupation with thoughts of the deceased, in addition to symptoms of traumatic distress, such as feelings of disbelief, mistrust, anger, shock, detachment from others, and experiencing somatic symptoms of the deceased (Prigerson *et al.* 1999). In addition, the death of a close attachment figure can be directly associated with the onset of more non-specific mental health difficulties such as depression, anxiety and self-blame, among others (Parkes 2006).

The study of complicated grief suffers from a lack of clarity concerning definitions of what could be considered to be 'normal' or 'abnormal', with numerous terms being adopted to describe pathological or traumatic bereavement responses, including absent (Deutsch 1937), distorted (Brown and Stoudemire 1983), and traumatic (Prigerson *et al.* 1999) to name but a few. This results in a lack of clarity with regard to research, clinical recognition and support.

Complicated grief reactions have been examined from a number of perspectives over the last century. The internalisation of lost objects and loss in general remain central in psychoanalytic theory. Freud, in his paper 'Mourning and Melancholia' (1917), noted similarities between mourning ('normal' grief) and melancholia ('pathological' grief), but also attempted to differentiate between them.

Deutsch (1937) examined 'absent grief', which she felt would ultimately be expressed in an alternative form, including repeated depressive episodes. According to Klein (1940), individuals who do not successfully negotiate the depressive position in infantile development are more likely to develop pathological grief later in life. Lindemann (1944) reinforced the Freudian concept of 'grief work', in which the expression of affect was seen to help weaken the bonds to the deceased; however attachment theory represents the most comprehensively explored theoretical framework within which grief can be understood.

Attachment theory

Grief is the emotional response to the loss of a significant relationship; it therefore seems important to understand something about relationships in order to gain some understanding of the impact of grief. The development of attachment theory (Bowlby 1960) focuses on the formation of the significant early relationships of human infants with their primary carer (usually, but not always, the mother), and how these patterns of relating build the 'internal working models' of the world within the child. These internalised models then become the blueprint for all relationships for each person throughout their lifetime.

Ainsworth applied Bowlby's theories, developing them further by making the important distinction between strength of attachment and security of attachment (Ainsworth 1963). Using systematic methods, she classified specific patterns of insecure attachment (Ainsworth, Bell and Stayton 1974), which were further developed by Main (Main and Goldwyn 1984). The three insecure patterns of attachment are: anxious/ambivalent, avoidant and disorganised.

Understanding attachment and the child with intellectual disabilities

Birth complications and possible parental neglect and abuse of disabled infants are both risk factors associated with the likely higher incidence of insecure attachment amongst PWID, when compared to the general population (Clayton 2010). The first few days of a baby's life are a crucial time for the parents and child to bond (Ainsworth *et al.* 1974; Bowlby 1979; Schaffer 1958). However birth complications can lead to parental anxiety and/or depression during the early weeks following the birth. The mental health and emotional robustness of parents at the time of birth will affect the attachment process, as will the surrounding environment. When a baby is born with an obvious disability, there are often many obstacles influencing the important process of child and parent bonding (Blackman 2003). Receiving news about their baby's disability in often stark or insensitive ways will be traumatic; this has been described as the trauma of disability (Sinason 1992), which can have a lifelong effect on the family and individuals within it.

Parents may need to grieve for the 'perfect' baby that they did not have (Bicknell 1983). They will have to cope with the responses of other family members, friends and professionals and the general social stigma that disability carries (Sooben 2010). With the advancement of neuroscience we now understand much more about the importance of a loving, dynamic relationship on the developing brain of an infant and of course the opposite of this also.

Understanding how attachment patterns affect bereavement and grief

In adulthood, it is at times of stress that deep-rooted maladaptive attachment behaviours can become more pronounced. The way in which we cope will to some extent be determined by the experiences and expectations which are set up within our primary relationships, in other words, our early attachments. Bereavement is one of the most stressful periods many people will experience and this is why it is important to understand attachment theory and its life-long impact. At a time of bereavement, the way in which we have learned to cope at times of stress is likely to determine how we grieve (Palletti 2008). We now know that complicated relationships such as those that are neglectful, incestuous or violent can also affect the distress and intensity of grief (Parkes 2006; Worden 1991).

Bowlby hypothesised that there were disordered forms of attachment in childhood that could increase vulnerability following bereavement. These ideas are very important to consider in light of PWID being vulnerable to disordered attachment (Minnis, Fleming and Cooper 2010). During grief work (grief related psychotherapy), people cognitively redefine themselves and their situation; this is a necessary process of realising and reshaping internal representations to align them with changes that have occurred.

A description of long-term bereavement psychotherapy with a woman with ID with a disorganised attachment (Blackman 2012) refers to the powerful transference felt by the therapist during the often silent sessions. The silence held by the client in sessions for many months can be understood as mirroring her early experience with a neglectful mother. Sinason (1992) has described how one way that infants learn to survive the daily experience of feeling frightened due to the absence of an emotionally available mother, is to 'give up all hope of communication and become quiet, sleep a lot, and become deeply depressed' (p.189).

In order to enable the client to move beyond the silence and support her to regulate her feelings, the therapist used music and relaxation. An infant who has developed a secure attachment will learn to regulate their emotions through the careful containment of the mother (Gerhardt 2004), done in a mainly non-verbal way. Gerhardt states that 'Caregivers who can't feel with their baby, because of their own difficulties in noticing and regulating their own feelings, tend to perpetuate this regulatory problem, passing it on to their own baby' (pp.23–24). The therapist in the case described helped the client to recognise when she was becoming stressed or feeling angry or sad. This was done by providing safe containment built up through the therapeutic relationship allowing her to begin to bear the feelings. The therapist helped the client to notice the tension held in her body that signified strong, negative feelings. Together they developed strategies she could use to relax.

The client gradually began to recognise different feeling states outside of the sessions before she became consumed with them. She began to use techniques she had learned in the therapy room to self-soothe instead of self-injure. It took some time for her to be able to implement this on her own. With the client's permission the therapist began to arrange more regular communication with the staff, enabling them to understand the cycle of destruction that the client was 'stuck' in. They were then able to work supportively to help her to break this pattern using the coping mechanisms that she had learned.

After eight years of bereavement psychotherapy with this very disturbed client, she was able to move from having lived for most of her adult life in secure settings – due to regular acts of self-injury and attempts on her own life – to moving into a flat of her own (with a few hours of weekly support). Several years later she has been able to remain stable and independent.

Resilience and predictors for risk

Recovery-orientated bereavement research has been focused on trying to understand the environmental and personal characteristics that affect the bereavement outcome for individuals, in order to identify what it is that increases vulnerability in some bereaved people (Stroebe *et al.* 2006). The findings from this research have significantly shaped the national framework of bereavement response (Department of Health 2008).

One significant study (Van Der Houwen *et al.* 2010) focused on multiple potential risk factors which were simultaneously examined, including the effects of attachment style and the development of depressive symptoms. Significantly the impact of social support on the expression of symptoms was highlighted, which seems particularly relevant to PWID, given the high probability of insecure attachment patterns combined with frequent lack of social support.

Specific complicated grief presentations: general population

In the general population prolonged grief disorder is the main complicated grief presentation described in the literature. Prolonged grief disorder is made up of symptoms of 'separation distress' and 'traumatic distress', coupled with evidence of poor social and occupational performance. It is generally agreed that symptoms of separation distress are at the core of prolonged grief disorder, relating to the idea that prolonged grief is a form of an attachment difficulty resulting from separation, as originally described by Bowlby

(1980). Traumatic distress symptoms represent bereavement specific manifestations of being traumatised by the death. The proposed traumatic distress symptoms included efforts to avoid reminders of the deceased, feelings of purposelessness about the future, a sense of numbness, feeling shocked and stunned, difficulty acknowledging the death, feeling life is empty without the deceased, an altered sense of trust and security, and anger over the death (Prigerson, Vanderwerker and Maciejewski 2008). Much work has been conducted to refine and validate these diagnostic criteria, reflected in the recent inclusion of prolonged grief as a distinct diagnostic entity in DSM-V (American Psychiatric Association 2012). Prolonged grief disorder has been shown to be a distinct clinical syndrome, with a prevalence rate of 10 per cent (Barry, Kasl and Prigerson 2002; Latham and Prigerson 2004). It has been shown to be distinct from bereavement related depression, post-traumatic stress disorder and anxiety (Boelan, van den Bout and de Keijser 2003), has shown a poor response to tri-cyclic antidepressants (Reynolds *et al.* 1999) and interpersonal psychotherapy (Shear *et al.* 2005); and it is also associated with a distinctive sleep electroencephalogram (McDermott, Prigerson and Reynolds 1997), and distinct MRI radiological changes (O'Connor 2012).

Prolonged grief disorder has been shown to be associated with a number of risk factors including dependent relationships (Cleiren 1992; Johnson *et al.* 2000) parental loss, abuse and neglect in childhood (Silverman, Johnson and Prigerson 2001), insecure attachment styles (Van Doorn *et al.* 1998), separation anxiety in childhood (Vanderwerker *et al.* 2006), preference for lifestyle regularity (Cleiren 1992) and lack of preparation for the death (Barry *et al.* 2001). Additionally people who experience prolonged grief disorder suffer significantly, especially if the condition goes unrecognised or treated. Suicidality (Latham and Prigerson 2004) and major depressive and anxiety disorders (Boelan *et al.* 2003) are significantly more likely to occur, especially if the prolonged grief is left untreated after six months post index loss.

Of course concerns have been raised about associating severe psychopathology – such as that proposed in prolonged grief disorder – with bereavement, a life event that is universal and is at the heart of the definition of life itself. It has been argued that people given a diagnosis of prolonged grief disorder will be stigmatised (Stroebe *et al.* 2001). However a recent study by Johnson *et al.* (2009) looked at the issue of stigma associated with significant grief morbidity. The vast majority of people in their sample who were found to have a prolonged grief disorder reported that they would be relieved to know that they had a recognisable psychiatric condition, and 100 per cent of those with prolonged grief disorder reported that they would be interested in receiving treatment for their severe grief symptoms. There was a significant association between the severity of grief symptoms and reported negative reactions from friends and family members.

Complicated grief in intellectual disabilities

Ability to grieve

It was long considered impossible for PWID to experience grief. A possible result of this is the fact that little empirical research work has been done to look specifically at the normal or complicated grief response in PWID. Much of the work describing PWID and their reaction to bereavement has been based on descriptive case reports (Lannen *et al.* 2008). Research has been previously conducted to explore individuals' understanding of the concept of death, assessing whether an individual has a cognitive understanding of grief and bereavement. Concept of death is made up of finality (death is final), non-functionality (functioning ends at the time of death), causality (death occurs for many reasons) and universality (death is a certainty) (Speece and Brent 1984). Research suggests that PWID have limited concept of death, and that this is related to the level of cognitive functioning (MacHale, McEvoy and Tierney 2009; McEvoy, Reid and Guerin 2002).

The impact of bereavement on emotion, behaviour and mental health in PWID

Psychiatric illness

The relationship between life events, such as parental bereavement, and the development of psychiatric illness continues to be of great interest (Brown and Harris 1989). This is an under-researched area in PWID (Nadarajah *et al.* 1995), however, it does seem reasonable to assume that PWID are at least as vulnerable as the rest of the population to the ill effects of life events (Ghaziuddin 1988). To date a comprehensive prospective grief study has not been carried out with PWID. Hence our understanding of the impact of bereavement is largely based on case studies, or small-scale case control studies (Blackman 2012b; Brickell and Munir 2008; Dodd *et al.* 2005b, Dodd and Guerin 2009).

Hollins and Esterhuyzen (1997) carried out a systematic study of the reaction of people with ID to bereavement. They recruited adult subjects (n=50) from day centres, who had lost a parent in the preceding two years, and compared them to a non-bereaved matched control group. The authors point out that although increased symptoms of psychopathology were found, this does not automatically indicate pathological grief, since many of these symptoms form part of what we understand to be 'normal grief'.

BEHAVIOUR AND EMOTION

Harper and Wadsworth (1993) carried out 43 structured direct interviews with adults with moderate to severe ID, using the Iowa Loss Instrument, designed by the authors. They found 25 of the individuals questioned reported that at least one death was very disruptive to their lives, complaining of symptoms of anger, anxiety, confusion and discomfort thinking about the death. Eighteen of the individuals for whom the loss had occurred at least a year previous to the interview reported continuing problems in their lives including feelings of loneliness, anxiety, sadness and behaviour problems.

In the study by Hollins and Esterhuyzen (1997), a significant increase in irritability, lethargy, inappropriate speech and hyperactivity was demonstrated in the bereaved group compared to the control group. At follow-up, general behaviour was found to have deteriorated between the initial assessment and the follow-up approximately five years post reference bereavement, suggesting continued difficulties, possibly related to the bereavement.

PATHOLOGICAL OR COMPLICATED GRIEF

As previously reported, prolonged grief disorder is now the most widely used term within the general population when describing complicated grief. However it has not been used to date in any research with PWID. The terms pathological or complicated grief are more common in this body of literature. In general little emphasis is made in the reporting of research with PWID emphasising the distinction between typical and pathological grief, in contrast to the research with the general population. There are many challenges that exist in trying to examine complicated grief in this population, including the fact that many of the screening questionnaires looking at prolonged grief disorder in the general population assess psychological responses that are often difficult to establish in PWID (Brickell and Munir 2008). However it is generally agreed that PWID are at a greater risk of developing pathological grief responses due to communication difficulties; secondary losses, such as loss of the family home/a move to live with paid carers; insecure attachment; and cognitive difficulties in achieving an understanding of the meaning of the loss, an important coping strategy used by many individuals in the general population. This can be made more difficult when PWID are not provided with appropriate grief and bereavement psycho-education, sometimes compounded then by being excluded from grief and bereavement rituals (Brickell and Munir 2008).

Given the need to identify PWID who are experiencing difficulties following a bereavement, some research has been conducted looking at complicated grief symptoms in PWID (Dodd *et al.* 2008). The study found that bereaved individuals experience complicated grief symptoms following the death of a parent, with one-third of the bereaved group experiencing ten or more clinically apparent symptoms. Separation distress symptoms (e.g. yearning, distrust of others) occurred more frequently than traumatic grief-type symptoms (e.g. disbelief, bitterness over the loss), in keeping with the view that attachment difficulties are at the centre of the PWID experience of loss, as highlighted in our case study. The authors also found evidence of a correlation between increased bereavement ritual involvement and the development of symptoms. The authors speculate that the individuals in the study may have taken part in bereavement rituals without appropriate preparation or previous experience of such rituals (e.g. with bereaved friends or more distant family). Therefore this lack of ritual context may contribute to the development of symptoms.

The research team has subsequently developed a self-report measure of complicated grief symptoms. Preliminary data analysis has identified differences in the frequency of symptoms as reported self and proxy reports, with some evidence that paid carers report internal symptoms such as experience of auditory and visual hallucinations less frequently. In addition people with ID may be more likely to experience criteria associated with separation distress rather than traumatic grief. Finally, approximately 20 per cent of participants appear to meet the draft diagnostic criteria for persistent complex bereavement-related disorder (American Psychiatric Association (DSM-V) 2012).

Therapeutic approaches

Given the fact that little specific research on complicated grief in PWID has been carried out, there are few reported evidence-based therapeutic interventions for complicated grief. For the general population specific psychotherapeutic approaches have been developed (Shear *et al.* 2005), in addition to biological treatments (Simon *et al.* 2007).

Staff training

Given the critical role of professional carers and staff in supporting PWID generally, a number of studies have considered the views, knowledge and needs of this group in relation to the issue of bereavement. Staff members have an important role in preparing PWID to respond to the challenges of bereavement and supporting them following a loss. However, professional carers are arguably not adequately prepared to identify a possible negative reaction to bereavement (Dowling *et al.* 2006) or to provide effective supports to PWID at the time of bereavement (Dodd *et al.* 2005b; MacHale *et al.* 2009; Murray, McKenzie and Quigley 2000). To date, no study has been published looking at therapeutic interventions for people with ID and complicated grief.

CASE STUDY: ANNE

Anne (pseudonym) was a woman with mild ID in her 40s, referred to a loss and bereavement group for a historic loss (the sudden death of her mother 12 years earlier) which had led to an unresolved complicated grief reaction. Up until the point of joining the group she had tried to avoid thinking or talking about her mother, remaining very anxious and withdrawn. The anxiety was becoming extreme and was beginning to impact on her quality of life.

Anne had an anxious pattern of attachment; this would be consistent to having experienced many separations in early childhood and also to a parental message that she would not survive without them. She had spent much of her early childhood in and out of hospital undergoing complicated medical procedures and had lived in the parental home until her mother's death. We could surmise that Anne's parents had been very protective of her after such a difficult early start in life. Children with this pattern of attachment can be difficult to please or placate and can grow up with low self-trust; they are also prone to severe protracted grief (Parkes 2006).

When Anne first joined the group she found it difficult to take part, spending each session sitting quietly with her head bowed, crying silently. However, she showed commitment to the process by independently attending punctually every week. The therapists facilitating the group encouraged curiosity amongst the group members about the thoughts and feelings others in the group might have. They supported individuals to consider and reflect on similarities and differences in each others' stories.

After a few weeks Anne began to listen attentively to the other group members as they spoke about their own losses and experiences. Her experience was becoming normalised; she was learning that other people had experienced similarly devastating losses but that they were finding ways to cope. She eventually cried less in the sessions but still found it hard to say very much. The group provided a container (Bion 1963) for Anne; she could see that her feelings could be tolerated by the therapists and other group members. The group began to tentatively explore how she may be feeling even without her participation to begin with, by 'wondering out loud' if she may be feeling one way or another. This seemed to lessen her experience of being overwhelmed and to dispel her sense of isolation. Gradually she began to recognise that the group really could support her and during one session she told the group about the day her mother died. This was the first time that she had ever told anyone the story from her perspective. Following this session she became more 'alive' and less passive in the group, commenting and reflecting on other people's experiences.

Anne learned that the group did not try to 'protect' her from emotional pain, which was what she had experienced in her family. Instead they showed her that they were willing to help her to bear it by sharing and listening. Through this experience she learnt that she was more able to cope with difficult experiences than she had realised. This was tested out when she had another very difficult bereavement during the course of the group. She had planned a trip to America to visit her brother and was very excited as she had not seen him for many years. Sadly, just one week before she was due to fly out, she received the tragic news that he had died unexpectedly. She was of course shocked and saddened by this, yet she coped with the news very well and was able to talk about her brother with the others in the group. She shared her feelings about his death and also memories that she had of him. It was really possible through this bereavement experience to see how much Anne had changed, and how much more resourceful she had become in coping with difficult experiences.

Conclusion

There is growing evidence that complicated grief is a significant cause of suffering for a minority of the general population who have been bereaved. For people with ID, the impact of grief is poorly understood in general, and our understanding of the impact of complicated grief is developing slowly.

The need for the availability of psychological, social and psychiatric interventions for individuals with ID who are experiencing complicated grief is clear, and work is needed to develop evidence-based interventions.

CHAPTER 5

Spirituality and faith
Beyond beliefs to practice
William Gaventa

SUMMARY
This chapter will first establish some core understandings of spirituality and faith, then move to ways to address spirituality and faith in supports and services, then to an example of one provider agency's first efforts to do so. Finally, creative ways and strategies that professionals can use will be presented, together with how they are responding to the spiritual needs and desires of the people we support in end-of-life experiences and those in their community of friends and family.

Introduction

End-of-life experiences, loss, and grief raise the core questions of life and what it means to be human, and perhaps even more so in the area of care giving for, with, and by people with an intellectual disability (PWID) as they move towards the end of their lives or grieve the loss of friends and families. Those questions are asked in many ways: What does it mean to be human, to live, to die? Who am I? Who have I been? Who will I be? What's the purpose of this? Why the suffering? Who will be with me? Where is God in the midst of this?

Those are questions of identity, purpose, and community. Adding to those the questions of what gives or maintains hope in the face of loss, how we love one another at this major life transition, and what we hold on to, in other words what faith, gives us a framework and context for understanding our own experience. If we are honest, those questions have surrounded people with intellectual disabilities most of their lives in their interaction with others, partly because others, like me, see and feel in them our own vulnerability, limitations, and finitude (Gaventa 2010a).

These experiences raise questions and feelings for both the individual and his or her friends and carers. Dealing with death, grief, and spirituality also means that professionals are dealing with two of the three hardest areas where the 'personal' intertwines with 'professional' (the third being sexuality). All are dimensions of care giving which involve deep feelings, vulnerability, our own stories and histories, and what we believe about them. One of the great ironies and paradoxes is that at least three areas of belief may get in the way of effective care giving (or practice):

- What we as professionals believe about spirituality and death may get in the way of effective care giving (or practice).

- Common beliefs about the capacity of people with intellectual disabilities to experience and/or understand spirituality and death may also be one of the biggest barriers.

- What we believe about what it means to be 'professional' may also get in the way, if it means not integrating our feelings and experience into our care. The question is not whether or not we do that integration, but how, and our clarity about doing so.

Moving beyond beliefs (i.e. what seem like rational understandings of death or spirituality/faith to practice) to the lived experience of spirituality, faith, grief, and loss is thus the focus of this chapter. In my experience, what is most helpful to individuals with intellectual disabilities is to have the opportunity and guidance to experience and practice the social, cultural, spiritual, and religious customs and rituals that surround end-of-life experiences and loss and which keep one connected to supporting and caring others. The challenge is how to honour what people want, need and understand as well as how to stand with them in doing so. It is an arena where there is no single answer, and one that invites us, as professionals and caregivers, to put the best of our values and affirmations about the people we serve and support into practice so all of us can learn, grow, and move through loss and end-of-life experiences.

Spirituality, faith, and people with intellectual disabilities

There are many ways to define spirituality, but for me the simplest and most comprehensive involves three dimensions with multiple connections between them:

- spirituality as one's experience of, and belief about, the sacred and holy

- spirituality as core meanings and values that one brings to experience and that come out of it

- spirituality as connection, with one's self, others, the divine however defined, place, symbols, and time.

Thus, one might define or express spirituality in mindfulness, community and culture, religious beliefs and communities, sacred places in one's life, symbols of spiritual experience, and time, both hope/dreams and past, and memories that shape and guide us.

The core values of services and supports in the last two decades have been independence, productivity, inclusion, self-determination, and cultural respect. The core questions at the heart of those values are universal spiritual questions: identity (Who am I?), purpose (Why am I?), community (Whose am I?), control (Why does suffering happen and what do I do in the face of it?), and respect (Who I am as an individual and cultural being?) (Gaventa 2006).

Cultural and spiritual traditions other than those we call 'western' may well have other ways of answering those questions such as those with core values of interdependence and community rather than independence and less focus on productivity and employment as a way of dealing with purpose – hence the importance of cultural respect and the capacity to work as professionals in cross-cultural settings. One cannot pay attention to (and respect) cultural diversity without dealing with spiritual and religious beliefs and practices that are often at the heart of different communities.

Therefore one can say that everyone has a spiritual dimension to their lives. Not everyone would call themselves persons of faith or religious, but billions of people do. Religions can be seen as systems of thought, experience, and practice that have guided individual and community journeys and explorations of those existential questions over centuries. The core component separating religion from spirituality is the belief in, and experience of, a Divine being, i.e. a sense of connection with God or 'the Gods' and God's people, however defined and practiced.

The same is true for PWID. Those questions of identity, purpose (worth), community, self-determination, etc. are ones that we believe are important to people with disabilities, based on evolving research, learning, and practice. Exploring what is most important to people with disabilities and honouring their preferences, wishes, and choices are two of the hallmarks of person-centred planning. Even if we assume that people are people, and hence spiritual beings, one cannot assume that others have believed or honoured the fact that spirituality is part of the lives of PWID nor that they have had the opportunity to be part of communities of faith and religious practice.

Even as recent decades demonstrate much progress in this area, a primary barrier has often been the beliefs and practices of both professionals and faith communities that have got in the way of supporting inclusive spiritual expression and participation. People and professionals in faith communities have often mirrored or blessed, with divine authority, stigma, and stereotypes. Professionals have wrongly believed that they cannot address spirituality as a professional because of stereotypical images of being 'professional', or that public funding streams do not allow addressing spiritual needs or concerns. However, PWID and their families continue to indicate that spirituality and faith communities are very important to them and wish that those needs and dreams would be honoured and addressed by both faith communities and human services (Carter 2012). In an age that seeks to help people find valued roles and identities in typical community settings, one cannot, and should not, ignore what may be the primary source of meaning and of community support in many different cultures.

Assessing and integrating spirituality into professional practice

Assessing the spiritual needs and gifts of people with intellectual disabilities in the past was often either ignored or summarily done (e.g. What religion are they? What are the burial plans?). That is changing as more and more professional disciplines (e.g. psychology, medicine, psychiatry, social work, and nursing) have expanded and deepened their research and understanding of the role of spirituality and religion in holistic supports. Professional chaplains have evolved from clergy who are seen as ministers doing religious practices in institutional settings (i.e. worship, prayer, healing rituals, etc.) to members of interdisciplinary teams who can address spirituality directly, help other professionals do so, and also build or strengthen connections between an individual and his or her preferred ways of practicing their spirituality and faith (Gaventa 1996; Roberts 2011).

One outcome has been the development of a variety of spiritual assessment tools and charting/note taking that can help a team of caregivers address spirituality and faith in person-centred ways. The assessment tools vary from relatively simple to very complex, and often are tailored to specific settings. I will introduce three, but make two fundamental observations.

First, the whole concept of 'assessment' frequently connotes for many a process of objectification or measurement, an over-against stance that has the paradoxical role of separating the assessor from the person being assessed while also serving as a tool to help other professionals connect with the individual and what is happening. The objectification and measurement, and/or diagnosis, is very hard to do in the arena of spirituality and faith. In fact, most people resist it, either because it feels like intrusion into very private, personal areas (Poston and Turnbull 2004) or because of the ways that religion has too often been used to judge. But the Latin root of the word 'assessment' means 'to sit next to', which can shift one's whole perspective on assessment that flows from trust and connection (Hilsman 1997).

Second, best practices in person-centred planning with people with intellectual disabilities can easily address spiritual needs and hopes and matters of faith and religion, assuming the facilitators are willing to do so. Hopes, dreams, and values are at the heart of person-centred planning, leading to maintaining or expressing what is of core importance to someone, often in the form of some desired community connection and inclusion. Having a vision of the ways that faith communities can and might help address many of those dreams and goals is an important skill for facilitators, even if someone's experiences in the past have been negative.

Assessment models

The FICA Spiritual History process (Puchalski 2013), has four areas of simple questions that, with good listening, can lead into broad arenas of need and hopes:

F   Faith and Belief: 'Do you consider yourself spiritual or religious?'
'Do you have spiritual beliefs that help you cope with stress?' 'What
gives your life meaning?'

I   Importance: 'What importance does your faith or belief have in our
life?' 'Have your beliefs influenced how you take care of yourself
in this illness?' 'What role do your beliefs play in regaining your
health?'

C   Community: 'Are you part of a spiritual or religious community?'
'Is this of good support to you and how?' 'Is there a group of people
you really love or who are important to you?'

A   Address in Care: 'How would you like me, your healthcare provider,
to address these issues in your healthcare?'

Those questions are easily adapted into a non-medical setting. In a
second, more comprehensive tool – the 'The Seven by Seven Model
for Spiritual Assessment' (Fitchett 2002) – spirituality is one of seven
dimensions of assessment that need to be explored in the holistic
process (see Table 5.1).

Table 5.1 Fitchett's 7x7 model (2002)

Holistic assessment	Spiritual assessment
Biological (medical) dimension	Belief and meaning
Psychological dimension	Vocation and obligations
Family systems dimension	Experience and emotion
Psycho-social dimension	Courage and growth
Ethnic/racial/cultural dimension	Ritual and practice
Social issues dimension	Community
Spiritual dimension	Authority and guidance

Other spiritual assessment processes explore all of these in dimensions
that involve the questions or feelings someone has, and how they
perceive God's role in their lives. For example, if someone facing death
is feeling or fearing judgment, what might that say about their image
of God, and how might a trained spiritual caregiver address that with
them? How does one address those who are angry at God, and possibly
also feel guilty for feeling that way (Gaventa 2006)?

A third form of assessment complements other chapters in this
volume. Kauffman (2005) specifically recommends doing a 'loss
assessment' when someone with intellectual disabilities comes into our

services and supports. Loss assessments address a person's experiences with death, loss, and grief. I have used one during workshops for professionals, because, like any good person-centred planning strategy, one should not do this for others without experiencing the process oneself. Questions can include 'What are early memories?'; 'What were my feelings?'; 'What are the family, cultural, and religious traditions that have been involved?'

Such conversations with individuals and families, perhaps as part of a spiritual assessment, can help discover incredibly valuable information that can be utilized when future losses happen as well as help to set the stage for outlining a provider agency's policies and recommendations. That is the place to begin the discussion with families about what will be important for their son or daughter when there is a death in the family in order to avoid the far too frequent exclusion of people with intellectual disabilities from communal rituals of mourning. The conversation can shift to help an individual and loved ones to think about and/or make plans for their own death as outlined in one or more of the new guidebooks to help people plan ahead (California Coalition for Compassionate Care 2007; Kingsbury 2010).

Beyond assessing to addressing

Assessments do little unless they guide actions, decisions, and supports. To give you a feel for how a process can be used, let me cite an example. During the academic year of 2011–2012, a relatively simple spiritual assessment process led by a clinical pastoral education intern at the Arc of Atlantic County in south Jersey, with the guided involvement of direct care staff through informal dialogue with the people they serve, led to an excellent return in the number of participant responses. The core of the assessment was trying to establish what was most important to the people served in the area of spirituality. The intern then took the responses and formatted them into a 'wordle' image, in which the higher the number of similar responses, the larger the letters. The result is found in Figure 5.1 (Manson 2012).

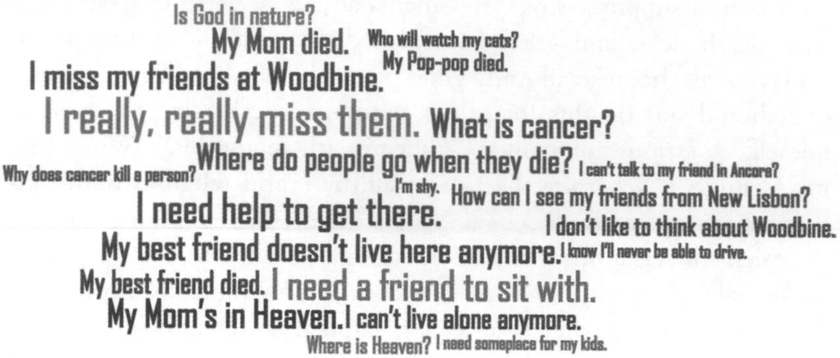

Is God in nature?
My Mom died. Who will watch my cats?
My Pop-pop died.
I miss my friends at Woodbine.
I really, really miss them. What is cancer?
Why does cancer kill a person? Where do people go when they die? I can't talk to my friend in Ancora?
I'm shy. How can I see my friends from New Lisbon?
I need help to get there. I don't like to think about Woodbine.
My best friend doesn't live here anymore. I know I'll never be able to drive.
My best friend died. I need a friend to sit with.
My Mom's in Heaven. I can't live alone anymore.
Where is Heaven? I need someplace for my kids.

Figure 5.1 Important aspects of spirituality

Source: Manson (2012)

The reader is invited to draw their own conclusions about spirituality and faith, but let me make some observations. Note the ways that a majority of the responses relate to loss of connections, friends, parents or places (Woodbine and New Lisbon are two state institutions.) Note questions and thoughts about cancer and death, as well as those about the unknown ('what will happen?') and 'if I am going to a faith community, I need a friend to sit with'. On an individual level, these led to new initiatives to connect people with old friends or new communities, like the man everyone assumed to be Christian but had in fact grown up as a conservative Jew, and who came alive at the opportunity to practice his family faith in new ways. It led to particular attention to several individuals with cancer, many conversations about God, faith and opportunities for people to make choices about what they wanted to do, and new ways of engaging community resources. It also involved a very creative memorial service in a Saturday afternoon respite program after one of its participants died earlier in the week. Staff and individuals put handprints and thoughts on a large, long sheet of paper, which then ended up being used and displayed at the young girl's community funeral as a way of honouring everyone's feelings. All of this also involved addressing caregiver feelings about spirituality, faith, loss, and grief as they worked together to facilitate new supports that expanded the kinds of connections around an individual being served.

Something old, something new: honouring and creating rituals of loss and grief

Thankfully, there are growing numbers of resources for professional and family caregivers on helping individuals with intellectual disabilities to deal with death, grief, and loss, or, one might say, to help the caregivers help and also support the care giving *by* people with intellectual disabilities. Resources to help caregivers to support the person with a disability include the pioneering 'Books Beyond Words' series from the UK (Gaventa 2013a).

The core to many of these resources, as well as tried and true religious and cultural rituals of grief and loss, is that their importance and impact is as much in the experiencing and participating as it is in the 'understanding.' Caregivers have seen the negative impact when an individual has not been told about the death of a family member nor allowed to participate in the family's cultural and religious practices of mourning. The reasons sometimes given are that they 'are not able to understand' or 'to handle it.' One might note that many do not 'understand' death and that there are often wide variations in the capacity of people in general to 'handle it.' In my experience, PWID generally have more capacity than others to do so because they are often not making judgments about their own thoughts or feelings and are much more open with them. Most of those rituals involve actions that are geared to help people with their thoughts and feelings (and also help where words fail), ones that can be done with the help of others: looking at pictures, going to a wake, seeing someone's body, taking food to a grieving family or friends, writing a card, lighting candles, saying prayers, sending flowers, going to a service, going to the graveside internment, visiting a grave, and other actions of acknowledging, honouring, and remembering.

Everything possible ought to be done to help individuals participate in the ways they wish to. That may involve assuring families of staff support with their son, daughter, brother or sister and helping clergy or others in charge of services prepare. The core principles are being honest and open, maximizing involvement in the spiritual and social experiences around death, keeping people connected to supporters they already know, and maximizing opportunity for the expression of grief and loss (Kauffman 2005). If one looks at 'disability' from the evolving threefold definition by the World Health Organisation (WHO and the World Bank 2011), the parallels to grief, loss, and death are obvious:

- We cannot do anything to reverse an impairment or genetic condition, nor can we prevent loss and ultimate death.

- We can do more about the resulting dis-abilities, finding creative ways to help people both feel and understand, in person-centred ways, what is happening to them.

- But we can certainly do a great deal about the ways that disability is magnified by lack of opportunity to participate, i.e. deal with the social contexts of both belief and practice that have inhibited participation.

The creative forms of participation continue to multiply; for example, some pastoral care interns working with community agencies in New Jersey developed 'Celebrations of Life' and other memorial services with and for friends and staff in addition to other family and community rituals. Several agencies have developed their own format and rituals, e.g., sending balloons aloft with prayers and wishes. Families at times have been stunned by the depth of care and feelings as well as the breadth of impact of their loved one on others. Staff and friends can be pulled into the planning so they are participating at all steps of the process (Gaventa 2013b). Agencies in New Jersey are slowly discovering their capacity to honour an individual's wishes to be in hospice care with them rather than to be sent to a nursing home or hospital. Even for people who do not seem to have many community connections, people are discovering that (1) someone's community may be broader than we think, and that (2) there are ways to in fact build community through the processes of helping someone prepare for their own death or helping people grieve and mourn the loss of a friend (Gaventa 2010b, 2012). More and more stories emerge about the power and 'sacredness' of those kinds of community experiences and celebrations for everyone involved.

In addition to honouring community and cultural rituals of addressing the spiritual dimensions of grief, loss, and death, care giving organizations are developing their policies and practices (i.e. rituals) of coping with grief, loss and end-of-life issues which honour the spirituality and faith of everyone concerned. Examples include:

- person-centred strategies for planning ahead and making new connections

- regular times for discussion or training about grief and loss

- customized practices (rituals) so that staff and others served know what will happen when someone is dying or dies and how they will be involved and can respond

- developing grief and loss teams that include community supports such as clergy and hospice

- recognizing the disconnect between needing time to grieve and mourn with the fiscal and social pressures to move on and fill a 'slot'

- developing, from the top down, agency wide policies and strategies that reinforce the practices that they find most helpful. (Gaventa 2013b)

By doing so, those organizations address some of the key factors that make grief, loss, and death even more difficult: fear, denial of feelings, pretence, and loneliness.

Ending on a note to professionals

Developing creative responses and practices by professional caregivers with children and adults with intellectual disabilities means, first of all, that professionals recognize the ways that loss, grief, and end-of-life experiences impact on them personally and their role. Professionals may say 'I am not family or a friend' because that is what they think is expected as a 'professional.' However, if you have known and worked with someone over time, they could very well consider you their friend or surrogate family member whether or not you see it that way. Professional honesty calls for us to recognize both our own feelings and the ways that the people we serve and support have impacted us. Professional understandings of vocation and calling in fact depend on the spiritual meaning and purpose that we find in our work and relationships. The very word 'profess-ional' comes from the professed commitments and values that are made in vocations of service. That recognition can lead in directions which are crucial to our capacity to help others journey with their grief, sense of loss, and feelings about death and dying, including the following:

- Be clear about your feelings and values. Professionals should not be 'value-free' but 'value clear.'

- Seek support from others at times you feel that your feelings are impacting on your relationships negatively. But also realize you may be more self-judgmental than needed.

- Realize that it is appropriate to mourn in the presence of others with intellectual disabilities and professional caregivers. Mourning with others is one of the things that defines community (McKnight 1985), but it is also a way of modeling for others the deeply human ways of expressing grief and seeking support.

- As people with intellectual disabilities age or move toward the end of their lives, one of the most professional and helpful things we can do is to share with individuals what they have meant to you and to find your own ways to say 'goodbye'. It is one of the crucial times in someone's life that they need to know if they have made a difference to others. Don't be left with an 'I wish I had told her…'

- Being professional means recognizing your limits, i.e. knowing what you don't know, and then being willing to ask others for help (e.g. hospice staff, clergy, colleagues) as early as possible so caring relationships and networks can grow both in scope and depth. A person important to you may also become so to others.

Seen another way, we as professionals need to recognize and utilize our own spirituality in our care. Individuals and families recognize a caring and committed professional when they see one and know them, over time. Caregiving systems need to learn more about how to utilize professional spirituality in ways that enhance commitment and care. Too often, we have no idea how to do that and rely instead upon compliance with rules and standards (Gaventa 2008). Professionals also know and feel something about the 'soul' of the organizations and systems in which they work. Developing the skills and strategies in our caregiving roles to embrace the spiritual dimensions of care, perhaps starting with the needs and issues around grief, loss, and end-of-life experiences, may open the door to a much more profound recognition of the importance of relationships, mutuality of support, and community where ultimately, labels and roles make very little difference in our call to be human together.

CHAPTER 6

Psychological support in healthcare

Helena Priest

SUMMARY

Taking a holistic approach to contemporary healthcare delivery implies that psychological care and support are fundamental in meeting patients' needs. This chapter aims first to introduce, define and describe psychological support within the general holistic caring context and with reference to contemporary policy. Second, a model is introduced outlining the prerequisites, skills, knowledge, personal qualities, and outcomes of psychological care. Finally, using illustrative case study material, it aims to integrate these ideas into approaches that might be used to support and care for people with intellectual disabilities, particularly within the context of loss.

Holism and holistic care

To set the exploration of psychological care and support in context, we need to look at the concept of *holism* and examine how it is relevant to healthcare. The word holism, from the Greek for 'whole', means that the parts that go to make up the whole of something, when properly put together and balanced, make the 'whole' work correctly. Two essential assumptions of holism are that the 'whole' is greater than the sum of its parts, and that any change to one part will affect the correct working of the whole. A good analogy is the many separate parts that go into making a clock; unless they are assembled in the correct places and in the correct order, the clock may look like a clock, but will not function correctly as one. Similarly, a human being is not just a collection of elements haphazardly put together, but a whole that includes and yet transcends these individual elements in order for a person to function effectively – that is, to be healthy.

So what are these 'parts' or 'elements' that make humans human? People are sometimes described as bio-psycho-social beings; that is, we all possess a biological or physical body that exists in a social world, but also, we are in a given psychological state at any point in time. Some writers would also add spirituality into the mix – the sense of being connected to something greater than oneself – and indeed, the inclusion of the previous chapter on spirituality (Chapter 5) endorses the importance of this element. If we wish to provide healthcare or support to any individual, therefore, we cannot simply 'extract' the physical element and address it individually; we must also take into account the person's social world (friends, family, work, home), psychological world (thoughts, feelings, behaviours), and spiritual concerns. Furthermore, we must recognise that all these elements interact and that a problem in any one area will have an effect on the others. For example, someone coping with a loved one being ill or possibly dying is likely to feel very anxious, and simultaneously, this feeling (or emotion) of anxiety is likely to be accompanied by the physical symptoms of nausea, dry mouth, and trembling. In turn, there will most likely be major changes to that person's day-to-day social activities, and a need to search for reasons or explanations for this loss and support, perhaps from a spiritual or religious source. There is thus a constant interplay between the biological, social, psychological and spiritual elements of humanity. In sum, to be whole is to be healthy, and in order to provide care and support to promote health and wellbeing, we must try to take into account all these elements of the whole person.

Defining psychological needs

The 'psycho' in the holistic 'bio-psycho-social-spiritual' model of human beings is the psychological element, made up of emotional (feeling), behavioural (doing), and cognitive (thinking) needs, which must be met if we are to remain happy and healthy. In fact, when we have our psychological needs fully met, we are said to achieve 'the fullest height' possible (Maslow 1973). Of course, life experiences often intervene and interfere with our achievement of this ideal state. We experiences losses of all kinds – of health, of money or material goods, of significant relationships, of security, of potential, and of opportunity (see Chapters 1–3). At these times, we may be particularly vulnerable and our need for psychological care and support is heightened.

Psychological needs and ill health: why psychological support is important

Taking loss due to physical illness as an example, it has long been known that hospital admission leads to psychological distress, often made worse by factors intrinsic to being in hospital, such as lack of information and being away from family (Wilson-Barnett 1976). Outside the hospital context, around a third of presentations to General Practitioners are thought to be for psychological reasons (Centre for Economic Performance's Mental Health Policy Group 2006). Common psychological reactions triggered by illness include shock, anger, distress, depression, anxiety, grief, loss of control, dependency, and damaged self-image (Nichols 2003). Failure to have these reactions recognised, acknowledged, and addressed can lead to uncertainty, anxiety, and loss of control (Priest 2012), and if prolonged, can contribute to delayed recovery, increased mortality rates, and the development of serious mental health problems, which can exacerbate the physical illness itself (Linden 1996; Nichols 1993, 2003). Long term, failure to address psychological needs can lead to more serious mental health problems which can in turn adversely affect a person's functioning such that activities of daily life and relationships are adversely affected.

In contrast, when effective psychological support is provided, this contributes to improved recovery from illness, shorter hospital stays, reduced pain and distress, and improved patient satisfaction (Devine 1992; Linden 1996). Di Blasi et al.'s (2001) literature review suggests that doctors who provide support, reassurance, and positive information (and are thus more humane and compassionate in their approach) are more effective in achieving positive health outcomes than those who adopt a more formal and factual style of interaction with their patients. In Priest's (2012) study, nurses felt that when patients received timely and effective psychological care, their wellbeing was maintained or improved and their anxiety reduced; they experienced a feeling of safety; and were empowered within the constraints of their illness. Despite this knowledge, the emotional and psychological aspects of care are often overlooked or inadequately addressed (Harrison 2001).

The nature of psychological care and support

A number of frameworks for understanding the essential elements of psychological care have been proposed. These include Nichols' (2003) three-level framework, in which Level One includes support activities that can reasonably be expected of all care staff, no matter how junior or inexperienced, such as awareness, listening, and communication skills. In Level Two, more skilled activities such as informational care and education, emotional care, counselling, support, advocacy, and referral are added to this foundation, while Level Three includes more specialist input, such as psychological therapy, likely only to be delivered by trained practitioners. Priest's (2012) model of psychological care (Figure 6.1) endorses these elements, and adds in the need for an underpinning relationship between carer and patient, together with a supportive clinical culture/environment, effective role models, and adequate time to deliver psychological support. However, the model also highlights that psychological care can actually take very little time, and may be delivered effectively through small and apparently insignificant acts.

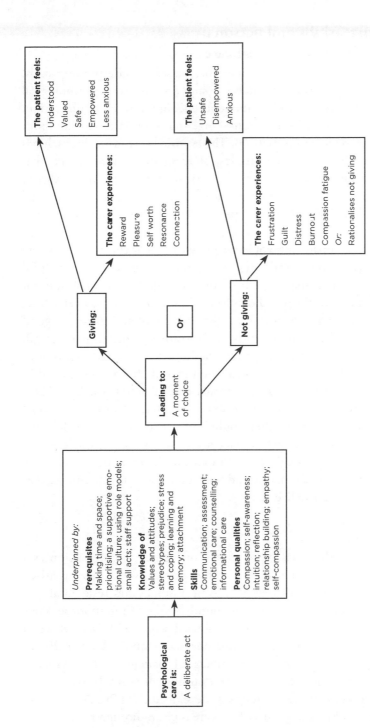

Figure 6.1 A model for psychological care

Source: Adapted and reproduced from H. Priest (2012) *An Introduction to Psychological Care in Nursing and the Health Professions*, p.57, with kind permission of Routledge/Taylor and Francis Group

Knowledge, skills and personal qualities for psychological care

As can be seen by the model (Figure 6.1), a set of underpinning skills, knowledge, and personal qualities support effective psychological care delivery. The skills component encompasses communication, assessment, emotional care, counselling, and informational care (both giving and receiving information). The knowledge component includes knowledge about values, attitudes, stereotypes, and prejudice that can impact on our perceptions of others, together with knowledge of human stress and coping, memory, learning, and attachment. Personal qualities of the carer that support psychological care include compassion and self-compassion, self-awareness, intuition, reflection, relationship building, and empathy. It would be a rare carer that could demonstrate possession of all these attributes at all times; nonetheless it is helpful to know the range and scope of knowledge, skills, and qualities that best underpin effective psychological support and care delivery. It is, however, important to note that even when in possession of good knowledge, well developed skills, and positive personal qualities, an individual carer can always choose whether or not to pay attention to another's psychological needs – the 'moment of choice' as depicted in the model (Figure 6.1). Reasons for that choice include the knowledge that attending to another's emotions can in turn place emotional demands on the carer that they might prefer to avoid. Nonetheless, the outcome of that choice will impact not only on the person receiving care but also on the caregiver. It is important therefore that carers have an understanding of the nature and role of compassion, self-compassion and self-care in care delivery.

Compassion

In recent years there has been a surge of interest in compassion as a central and essential element of effective care delivery. This has arisen in part due to well publicised failings in hospitals and residential care facilities within the UK, such as found by the Winterbourne View inquiry (DH 2012a), where staff had abused people with an intellectual disability (PWID), and the Stafford hospital enquiry (Francis 2013), where higher than expected numbers of patients had died after inadequate care and treatment over a number of years. In response, a 'Compassion in Practice' strategy was developed (DH 2012b, p.13), in which compassion is defined as 'how care is given through relationships based on empathy, respect, and dignity – it can also be described as intelligent kindness, and is central to how people perceive their care'. We now know that compassion is not only important for our own wellbeing and for having good relationships with other people, but also some of the reasons for this; namely that thinking about compassion and kindness to ourselves and others actually stimulates areas of our brain and body in ways that improve health and wellbeing (Gilbert 2009). It follows, then, that compassion is a necessary if perhaps somewhat invisible component of effective holistic care delivery. It is also an important element in preventing staff stress and burnout, as discussed below.

There is little specific focus in the compassion strategy (DH 2012b) on the needs of PWID, although it is stated that there will be 'work with learning disability nurses to reduce the health inequalities experienced by people with a learning disability' (p.17). Action area two of the strategy is concerned with ensuring that service users are treated with dignity, empathy, and respect, which requires professional carers to listen to feedback and act on it, and enable people to be involved in their care. Compassion is now clearly being taken seriously in measuring the effectiveness of holistic care.

Self-compassion

Providing effective psychological care can be experienced as a pleasurable activity, in which a connection with the patient is felt, and one that brings personal reward. However, when it is not possible for whatever reason to provide effective care, this can lead to guilt, frustration, a sense of failure, and personal distress, as shown in Priest's model (Figure 6.1). Many writers have identified burnout and compassion fatigue as the inevitable consequences of trying to deliver effective psychological support without adequate practical and emotional resources (Cropanzano, Weiss and Elias 2003). These are not entirely interchangeable terms; Maslach (1982) described burnout as a combination of emotional exhaustion, depersonalisation and sense of reduced personal accomplishment amongst workers following prolonged and excessive work stress, whereas compassion fatigue can be experienced even as a result of hearing about or witnessing another's trauma and of trying to help (Figley 1995). Self-compassion means extending compassion to one's self when feeling inadequate or generally suffering (Neff 2003). Both Nichols' (2003) and Priest's (2012) models highlight the need for those delivering psychological care to be cared for themselves, by, for example, observing and learning from effective role models and by accessing formal or informal staff support. Gilbert's (2009) important work on self-compassion also helps us to understand the costs and challenges of caring and provides practical strategies, such as compassionate mind training, to reduce the risks of compassion fatigue and burnout. These themes are explored further in this book in the chapters on carer fatigue (Chapter 9) and support for professional carers (Chapter 10).

Psychological support and intellectual disabilities

Having explored the nature and elements of holistic care, psychological needs and psychological care in general terms, we turn now to consider how these principles might apply in the context of people with intellectual disabilities whose healthcare needs are compounded by experiences of illness and loss. It is well recognised that the psychological and mental health needs of people with intellectual disabilities are sometimes neglected (Arthur 2003; Priest and Gibbs 2004). Reasons for such neglect include:

- over-protectiveness by carers

- carers' feelings of fear, inadequacy and uncertainty in how to deal with emotional distress (Read 2008)

- a belief that people with intellectual disabilities lack the ability to express meaningful emotion, compounded when there are reduced communication and linguistic abilities

- diagnostic overshadowing (Reiss, Levitan and Szyszko 1982), whereby behaviours which might be indicative of emotional problems are attributed instead to the symptoms of the person's intellectual disability

- lack of appropriate assessment tools and tailored therapeutic interventions

- lack of appropriate or integrated services

- poor staff knowledge.

However, in recent years there has been an equally widespread recognition that PWID can and do express the full range of human psychological responses and experience the full range of human mental health difficulties. Indeed, there is general consensus that they do so at a greater frequency than the general population (Cooper *et al.* 2007).

In response, there have been many enhancements in specialist service provision (Bouras and Holt 2010), together with the development of widely available assessment aids such as the PAS-ADD tools (Moss 2010) and specialist staff training such as the National Certificate in Supporting People with Learning Disabilities (Skills for Care 2013). Today there is little justification for carers not having psychological needs at the forefront of their mind when assessing the holistic support needs of people with intellectual disabilities. We will consider how such increased awareness, better knowledge, and resources have been used to good effect in John's story below.

CASE STUDY: JOHN'S STORY

John is 50 years old and has an intellectual disability and insulin-dependent diabetes. He lives with three other men who also have intellectual disabilities. Four months ago, Peter, one of the housemates, died suddenly. John did not go to the funeral because his father forbade it. John's mother had died ten years previously and it transpires that John has never been told that she had died, but that she had simply been admitted to hospital. His father said this was because he wanted John to be protected from the sadness of losing his mother. John has no photographs of his mother, and when he asks his father about her (which he frequently does) he is told that she is still in hospital having tests.

Since Peter's death, John's behaviour has deteriorated. He sits for long periods of time crying in Peter's bedroom, which is currently unoccupied but will shortly be allocated to someone else. Additionally, his diabetes is no longer under control and he needs frequent visits to the outpatient clinic for his insulin levels to be monitored and for John and his carers to have continuing advice about the management of his diabetes. John becomes very agitated when faced with the prospect of these hospital visits.

[Case study adapted and reproduced from Priest, H. (2012) *An Introduction to Psychological Care in Nursing and the Health Professions*, p.136, with kind permission of Routledge/Taylor and Francis Group].

Residential services such as the home in which John lives focus on helping residents to live a healthy and productive life within the limitations of their disability, and so care staff often have limited experience of dealing with physical ill health or psychological problems, and even less of facing the death of their residents (Todd 2006). However, as people with intellectual disabilities are living longer, it is important that carers are aware of residents' holistic healthcare needs and develop a repertoire of knowledge and skills with which to respond. As has been noted, in the past people with intellectual disabilities were often thought incapable of experiencing psychological difficulties. Such a misperception may have meant that John's psychological support needs around death and bereavement had not been fully considered or addressed. John had been excluded from information about the death of his mother and from the important rituals around death, because his family wanted to protect him. But John had been close to his mother and missed her deeply; he could not understand why she no longer came to see him.

It is likely that experiencing Peter's death reminded him of his earlier loss and triggered his unresolved grief, contributing to the changes in behaviour and deterioration in his physical health. John clearly had informational and emotional needs. It was only due to careful observation by his carers and recognition of his psychological support needs that were impacting on his physical health, that they were able to initiate appropriate interventions. They met with John's father (with the support of a bereavement counsellor) while remaining sensitive to the family's wish to protect John from further distress. Eventually, his father gave permission for staff to explain to John what had happened to his mother. A process of informational support and grief work was initiated, exposing John gradually and gently to the reality of his mother's death. This included going with John to visit his mother's burial place, helping him to choose flowers and dress for the occasion, and obtaining photographs of his mother for John to display in his room. Carers used some of these photographs and other personal items provided by his father to create a memory book for John to look at whenever he wished.

While these were small acts in themselves, taking relatively little time, collectively they had a huge impact on John's ability to understand events and process his emotional reactions to them. As John's physical health and diabetes status had also been affected by his changing psychological needs, it was important to progress very slowly to avoid further deterioration. Time was made during journeys to the hospital for John to talk about the impact of Peter's death, and later the new resident was introduced to John and his fellow housemates, who were encouraged to get to know him a little through shared social activities before he eventually moved in to the house. Over time, John became less anxious and more in control of his own life, and gradually his physical health improved.

In John's story, we have shown how elements of a psychological care model were used to support a person with intellectual disabilities experiencing major loss and change. Compassion, empathy, relationship building and making time underpinned the carers' approaches, and enhanced their skills of communication, assessment, and informational care. Their knowledge of attachment and perception helped them to understand some of John's reactions, and knowing the importance of preserving memory prompted them to help John to create a memory book. We note that it was sometimes only such small acts of care that made significant contributions to enhancing his psychological wellbeing. The carers were helped and supported themselves by the bereavement counsellor and their care managers, who recognised the time and investment required to help support John through his grief journey, and indeed the impact of loss on the staff themselves. With this support, and through witnessing and being reinforced by the positive changes in John's life, they were protected to some extent from experiencing compassion fatigue and burnout.

Conclusion

This chapter aimed to introduce psychological care and support and to consider its relevance in working with people with intellectual disabilities. In so doing, it presented a model of the contextual prerequisites, skills, knowledge, and personal qualities needed to provide effective psychological support. It also emphasised the need for self-compassion, support, and self-care in ameliorating the demands of providing psychological care. Applying such a model is not easy, as psychological needs and care are often hidden, especially when there are more obvious and competing priorities and demands on staff time and resources. Nonetheless, if we are to support people effectively, we should strive to hold the concept of holistic care at the forefront of our minds, especially when working with people with intellectual disabilities in the context of illness and loss.

PART II
CONTEMPORARY
PRACTICE ISSUES

Chapter 7

Loss and resilience

Linda Machin

SUMMARY

This chapter will use a framework for understanding diverse reactions and responses to loss, the Range of Response to Loss model (RRL) (Machin 2001; Machin 2014), and through an associated measure, the Adult Attitude to Grief scale (AAG) will explore the way in which one client seeking bereavement counselling was helped to understand her own grief reactions and supported in uncovering her inner strengths. The version of the AAG scale used here has been modified for use with people with an intellectual disability (PWID) and is used as the basis for a focus on resilience and the possibilities of growth through grief.

The challenge of loss

Loss and life

Life is full of losses. The journey from birth to death is punctuated by change and associated losses. Some change and loss may be woven into the fabric of experience so that it is hardly noticed, except perhaps in passing, while others signal a significant life event – birth, marriage, death. Erikson (1980) described the life-course journey of biologically and socially determined change as a series of developmental crises which have to be mastered in order for psychosocial competence to be acquired. Alongside these common developmental encounters with loss are more profound overt circumstances of loss which are not universally experienced – broken and damaged relationships, illness/disability, unrealised hopes which are central to a sense of fulfilment, for example childlessness in the face of a deep desire to be a parent, and unlike death in the normal sequence of life events, death which is untimely or traumatic. These two dimensions of loss, developmental and circumstantial, are set within a social, political and cultural context which will either sustain people at a time of loss or leave them isolated and without support (Machin 2014). The meeting of the adversity implicit in life's losses will promote a spectrum of coping responses from vulnerability to resilience.

Resilience

Traditional literature on grief and bereavement was particularly concerned with maladaptation to loss and its pathological variants (Bowlby 1980; Parkes and Weiss 1983). With the rise of positive psychology (Joseph and Linley 2006; Seligman and Csikszentmihalyi 2000) researchers and practitioners have recalibrated their understanding of grief to include resilience as both a natural capacity to emerge from loss and as a goal for therapy. Contemporary theoretical perspectives (Greene 2002) suggest that the key characteristics of resilience are:

- *personal resourcefulness* consisting of qualities of flexibility, courage and perseverance

- *a positive life perspective* consisting of optimism, hope, a capacity to make sense of experience and motivation in setting personal goals

- *social embeddedness* consisting of the availability of support and the capacity to access it and make use of it. (Machin 2007a; Machin 2014)

Resilience may be cultivated as a natural and integral part of maturation, through the development and refinement of skills and perspectives necessary to meet adversity effectively. In consequence a significant life-changing or traumatising loss may be faced by an intuitive capacity for resilience. For people who have not built up innate resilience a difficult loss experience may itself be the catalyst for the acquisition of new strategies and coping strengths. It is important to recognise, however, that resilience is not just an internal quality but is reinforced where there are favourable external conditions, for example an uncomplicated loss experience, the availability of support and other life demands which are manageable. Conversely, vulnerability is likely to occur where circumstantial factors produce demands which exceed the capacity to manage them (Folkman 2001), for instance a difficult last illness or death, taxing caring responsibilities or relationship/financial/housing problems. The challenge for practitioners is to address personal and circumstantial vulnerability whilst also seeking to harness innate resilience and facilitate new opportunities to cultivate it.

The nature of grief

The range of response to loss (RRL) model

In listening to accounts of grief heard in practice and research the author identified three contrasting modes of response to loss (Machin 2001):

- *overwhelmed* – a state of being deeply sunk in the despair of grief

- *controlled* – a state where emotion is avoided and there is a clear aspiration to retain a focus on day-to-day functioning

- *resilient* – a state in which a balance between facing/accepting the emotion impact of grief and functioning effectively at a cognitive/social/practical level, can be achieved.

In proposing this framework for defining grief it was important to explore whether there was a conceptual fit with other key theories in order to give some confirmatory justification for the model. While reflecting on the language brought to therapy by clients, this model parallels the concepts of both attachment theory (Ainsworth *et al.* 1978) – (anxious/ambivalent attachment and the overwhelmed response to loss, avoidant attachment and the controlled response, and the secure attachment and the balanced/resilient response) and the Dual Process Model (Stroebe and Schut 1999) – (loss orientation parallels the state of being overwhelmed, restoration orientation reflects the state of control and the capacity to oscillate between the two reflects the balanced/resilient state). Each of these theories in varied linguistic and conceptual ways identifies the same range of phenomena in the manifestations of grief as those proposed in the RRL.

The Adult Attitude to Grief Scale

A further test of the soundness of the RRL model and its conceptual propositions was to devise a scale to examine its validity. The Adult Attitude to Grief scale (AAG) was made up of nine self-report statements, three associated with each category in the model, on a five point Likert scale from strongly agree to strongly disagree. The notions embodied in the statements were:

Overwhelmed:

- the intrusion of thoughts and feelings

- a feeling that the pain of grief will persist

- a sense that life has less meaning as a result of the loss.

Controlled:

- a belief in the need to be brave and stoical

- a need to control the emotions of grief

- a need to get on with life.

Resilient:

- an ability to face the grief

- an awareness of inner strengths

- a sense of optimism.

Analysing the AAG alongside other psychometric tests (for depression, impact of events and detachment) the categories in the RRL model were statistically validated in a study of bereaved people seeking counselling help (Machin 2001). The research also showed that the AAG scale could provide a profile of individual participant's grief by charting the biases and blends in their responses to the three categorical statements. This prompted two further studies to test the practice usefulness of the AAG scale (Machin 2007b; Machin and Spall 2004). The studies demonstrated that the scale was effective for assessment, as an indicative guide for therapy, that is pointing to those aspects of grief most troubling to the client and providing a focus on resilience, and as a way of appraising the changes in grief tasking place over time. Following these studies the AAG scale has been adopted in many palliative and bereavement care settings (Agnew *et al.* 2009).

A conceptual development in the RRL model

A distinction can be made between *passive reactions* to loss which occur reflexively and instinctively, and *active responses* which involve coping with grief through engagement with its consequences (Attig 1996; 2011). Using these distinctions, the overwhelmed and controlled dimension of the model can be seen as a spectrum of grief *reactions* and resilience can be seen as a coping *response*. If resilience constitutes one end of a coping spectrum then its opposite, vulnerability, needs to be included. Using this rationale vulnerability has been integrated as the fourth component of the Range of Response to Loss (RRL) model (see Figure 7.1).

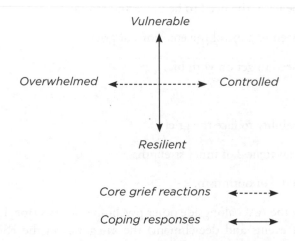

Figure 7.1 The interacting dimensions of the RRL Model

Although not included in the AAG scale as a separate category it became clear that vulnerability could be deduced where there is agreement with the core grief reactions (overwhelmed and controlled categories) and it is absent where there is agreement with the resilient responses. A formula for calculating vulnerability from the AAG scores reflects this reasoning: resilient scores are deducted from the combined overwhelmed and controlled scores to give an indication of vulnerability:

$$O + C - R = V$$

The proposition has been supported in a research project (Sim, Machin and Bartlam 2013) and incorporated into the practice use of the scale. The scoring system is demonstrated in the case study below. It should be noted that the direction of the scores is reversed for the resilient items in order for a simple addition to provide an indication of vulnerability (see Table 7.1).

Table 7.1 The modified AAG scale used with Mary showing her quantitative responses to each item, marked with a cross, and her qualitative comments below.
© Linda Machin 2001/2012

Adult Attitude to Grief Scale (Learning disability)	Strongly agree	Agree	Neither agree nor disagree	Disagree	Strongly disagree
Overwhelmed items					
2. I can't stop thinking about…Mum… since she died.	4 X	3	2	1	0
Photographs. Thoughts. Other people still have their Mum. Anniversaries. I'm always thinking of her.					
5. I think I will always be sad about…Mum…dying.	4 X	3	2	1	0
My Mum was the most important person. Without Mum I'm nothing. Memories aren't enough.					
7. Since…Mum…died, life has changed and become more difficult for me.	4 X	3	2	1	0
I don't want to do anything. I want to be with Mum. My Mum's friend said 'It is not your time yet'.					
Controlled items					
4. I think I should be brave about…Mum's…death.	4	3	2	1 X	0
I can't be brave. I need people with me. I am so alone.					

cont.

6. I don't want to show any sadness about…Mum…dying.	4	3	2	1 **X**	0
I am sad and sometimes cry. Sometimes I get angry.					

8. I think it's best not to keep thinking about…Mum…but to get on with the day-to-day things I always do.	4	3	2	1	0 **X**
Moving to the bungalow was hard. Mum promised me she would be with me until I settled down. She did not. I am angry.					

Resilient items

1. I feel OK about being sad because…Mum…has died.	0	1	2	3	4 **X**
No it's not OK. It's really difficult and lonely.					

3. I am sad but I can cope with the fact that…Mum…has died.	0	1	2	3	4 **X**
Mum gave up wanting to live when my step-dad died. I feel like giving up as well.					

9. Life has been difficult since…Mum…died but I think things will get better.	0	1	2	3 **X**	4
Everybody thinks it is easy. I know it is not.					

(The scale is clustered into the three subsets – overwhelmed items 2, 5, 7, controlled 4, 6, 8 and resilient 1, 3, 9. The numbers relate to the order of items in the AAG scale.)

Working with the AAG in practice

In using the AAG in practice a person-centred approach is crucial (Rogers 1961, 1980). It is likely to redress the ways in which clients with an intellectual disability may not have been valued, and the way in which their grief may have gone unrecognised/disenfranchised (Doka 2002). In the context of loss and bereavement having the opportunity to tell the story of loss is pivotal to a sense of being heard, accepted and understood (Howe 1993) and to learning to live with the consequences of the loss and finding new perspectives and meanings.

The goal for the counsellor, in collaboration with the client, is to facilitate a move from vulnerability to resilience. This comes from finding the inner resources and social support necessary to face grief and its consequences, from exploring realistic life options and from coming to a sense of meaning which can be sustaining for the bereaved person. This calls for an approach by the practitioner which is sensitive to the individual need of a client and which can flexibly use a range of therapeutic approaches (Machin 2014). The following case study demonstrates the starting point in the therapeutic journey.

CASE STUDY: MARY

Background

Mary is 46 years old. The cause of her intellectual disability (ID) is not known but its consequences have resulted in a limited capacity to read and write, a reduced understanding about money and managing, and health problems associated with not eating properly. In spite of these limitations Mary lives alone but gets support from the day centre she attends part-time. Mary's mother, who died five years ago, was very protective of her and kept her isolated from social contact. Contact with her father, who died recently, was spasmodic after he left the family home when she was a child and her siblings see Mary infrequently – 'when they want something'. She believes that she is an embarrassment to them.

Bereavement support

With the support of the day centre staff Mary sought help, following the death of her father, from a service with a specialist team offering bereavement care to people with a learning disability.

Assessment

The counsellor working with Mary used the modified AAG scale to assess her grief. What became clear from her responses was that Mary was not grieving for her father.

'Dad left a long time ago. I saw him sometimes. He never cared for me and sometimes hurt me. Mum always looked after me. I went to his funeral – my brother and sister said I had to. I want to forget about Dad. I never thought about him. His death has made me think more about Mum. I was just getting over losing Mum. I want her back.'

Mary's father's death triggered unresolved grief for her mother. The (modified) AAG was used again but this time with the focus on the death and loss of Mary's mother supplemented using an easy read pictorial scale (Figure 7.2).

Figure 7.2 Images used with clients who can more easily select their response to the statements on the AAG scale in a visual format (Read 2007)

Understanding Mary's grief – the counsellor's perspective

The pattern of Mary's grief can be seen through the quantitative scores and qualitative comments. She was predominantly *overwhelmed* by a new surge of grief for her mother. The hint in these responses that Mary might try to harm herself was sensitively explored but she was clear that she would not act on her wish to be with her mother.

While she had been trying to be 'OK about Mum's death' the current bereavement was undermining her previous instinctive *controlled* reaction which had helped protect her from her grief. Letting other people see her tears was not easy but she was less inhibited in showing anger. Some of this anger was related to feeling let down by her mother's reassurance that Mary would get married and have children before she died.

The AAG responses also point to a lack of *resilience*. The inability to deal with her sadness, the immense sense of loneliness and temptation to 'give up' all convey the difficulty Mary was having in coping with her loss. Using the AAG scores to calculate vulnerability, Mary had a score of 25 (out of a possible maximum score of 36), a severe level of vulnerability. This contrasted with a score of 13, a low level of vulnerability, related to her father's death.

Intervention

The assessment process, using the AAG scale, opened a window into Mary's grief and shifted the focus from her father to her mother. It provided a structure within which she could tell her background family story and describe her varied grief reactions. It was also the catalyst for Mary to give expression to her grief; she cried and showed a high level of distress. This provided her with the opportunity to convey to her counsellor how profound were her feelings of loss. He was witness to the reality of her grief. The tearful connection with this re-emerging grief initiated for Mary an important new phase in gaining the support she needed. This breakthrough in communications may often be missing for bereaved people with an intellectual disability.

Later session

The AAG was used again as the structure within which Mary could develop her story of loss. The level of agreement with the overwhelmed items was reduced (scores changed from 12 to 8) and of particular note was her disagreement with the statement – 'I can't stop thinking of (Mum) since she died'. There was an increased agreement in Mary's responses to the controlled items (scores changed from two to six). She especially agreed with the need not to keep thinking about her Mum but to get on with the day-to-day things she always did (item eight). Mary was ambivalent about the resilient items although able to feel more comfortable with her sadness about her mother's death (item 1). When the overall responses were calculated for vulnerability the score was 19, a reduction from 25 and a move into the low level of vulnerability.

The quantitative picture of Mary's grief told through the AAG was matched by the changes in her story of loss. The counsellor observed that the opening of her pain in the earlier session had both helped dissipate the pent-up emotion and cleared the way to explore part of her story that had previously been untold.

Mary began to talk of a mother who was not perfect and who had let her down as she was growing up. Mary had been treated badly by her father and talked of her paternal grandfather 'doing things to me which he shouldn't'. She had little schooling and was eventually sent to a residential special school which she hated and ran away from when she was 16. Her mother didn't want her back as she had found a new partner since her husband had left. For a while Mary lived with her maternal grandparents. When her grandparents died her mother moved back into the family home with her new partner.

Against this background Mary felt let down and she craved a different kind of mother. This was achieved in the later years when the two women were in a very dependent, symbiotic relationship but the earlier hurt persists in the form of disappointment and a reflection on 'what if life had been different'.

The remarkable shift from a highly emotionally charged session to a calm reflection on parts of her history which previously had not been disclosed, demonstrated a clear move from reacting to coping, and from vulnerability to resilience. Mary was able to put the pain and the possibilities into perspective and see that she wants to move on, recognising the people who are there to help in this. This is a promising foundation for the ongoing work to consolidate Mary's capacity for resilience.

Conclusion

The RRL model is a framework for identifying the reactions and responses made to grief. For clients with a greater degree of cognitive disability than was the case with Mary, this might be used as a template for the counsellor to explore the relative presence of overwhelmed and controlling reactions, and the personal and circumstantial factors contributing to vulnerability. With clients like Mary, the Adult Attitude to Grief scale enables the concepts in the model to be applied to practice and used to reveal the highly varied manifestations of grief seen in bereaved people. In its modified form the AAG scale was used with Mary and helped uncover her grief and her exploration of life beyond loss: a case study of emerging resilience.

Acknowledgement

The author wishes to express appreciation to Mary for willingly sharing her grief story and to the Dove Service, North Staffordshire, for giving access to their counselling work.

CHAPTER 8

Working creatively
to facilitate loss

Sue Read

SUMMARY

Many people with an intellectual disability (PWID) have variable communication impairments, subsequently many people may feel uncomfortable using the written or spoken word as their main vehicle or channel for reciprocal communication. The aim of this chapter is to explore a range of creative approaches that can help carers to engage with PWID in tangible, meaningful ways when supporting loss. It introduces different ways of working with people (such as life story work, memory boxes and books, using photographs, art, poetry and storytelling) that can help individuals to explore loss in constructive ways and which can be often captured in mediums that can be stored and kept over time. Such approaches contribute well in establishing and maintaining continuing bonds with deceased loved ones.

Introduction

> *Communication is the essence of human life.*
>
> *(Light 1997, p.61)*

Communication is a fundamental feature of everyone's lives, and part of what it means to be human. We all communicate for a whole host of reasons: to socialise, to learn, to get what we want and need and to show people how we feel, to name but a few. Communication has been defined in many different ways, but a simplistic definition by Mencap (a UK charity) portrays the very essence of what communication effectively means: 'Perhaps the simplest way of thinking about communication is that it is the passing on of information from one person to another using any means possible' (Mencap 2013b).

Some people with an intellectual disability (ID) are very articulate and can communicate thoughts and feelings in a very profound and meaningful way. However, others may struggle to find the words to communicate without the use of communication tools or alternative communication systems. Communication is not simply about the ability of the person with an ID to communicate to another person; it's the ability of the other person to interpret, respond and ensure the response has been heard and understood that is also important (Read and Morris 2008). Ker, Fraser and Felce (1996) estimated that more than 50 per cent of people with an ID had some form of communication impairment, which can involve impairments of cognition, hearing, language, comprehension, speaking, reading, social interaction or writing (Ambalu 1997). Try to imagine:

- not being able to read this page

- not being able to tell someone else about it

- not being able to find the words you wanted to say

- opening your mouth and no sound coming out

- words coming out jumbled up

- not getting the sounds right

- words getting stuck, someone jumping in, saying words for you

- people assuming what you want, without checking with you

- not hearing the questions

- not being able to see, or understand, the signs and symbols around you

- not understanding the words, phrases or expressions

- not being able to write down your ideas

- being unable to join a conversation

- not being able to describe how you feel

- not being able to say what you want or need

- feeling sad and not understanding why

- missing someone but not understanding the feelings of loss

- people ignoring what you are trying to say, feeling embarrassed and moving away

- people not waiting long enough for you to respond in some way, assuming you have nothing to say and moving away.[1]

Not being able to communicate your needs and wants can be extremely frustrating, particularly at sensitive times such as loss and bereavement, as a person may be desperate to tell someone just how sad they really feel, but lack the emotional and practical apparatus (skills) to do this.

Supportive communication

Much of the art of counselling and support lies in the craft of communicating. However, many years ago, Strohmer and Prout recognised that 'the less articulate client with mental retardation [sic] may feel uncomfortable in verbally orientated session' (Strohmer and Prout 1994, p.7), and hence carers (and indeed counsellors) cannot solely rely on verbal communication when supporting people who have an ID. Strohmer and Prout go on to describe four strategies to enhance communication with this population:

- providing the client with a *language or way to communicate* thoughts, feelings and concerns

- providing avenues and activities to encourage *expression*

- directly *altering existing techniques* that would be used with clients without a disability of the same age

- using child and adolescent focused approaches whilst attempting to deliver them in an *age appropriate* way.
(Strohmer and Prout 1994, pp.9–10)

---

1   Adapted from Mencap, and from material on the Communication Forum website at: www.communicationsforum.org.uk

In addition to these helpful ideas, building upon *how* the person already communicates and *what* they enjoy communicating about may also provide initial ideas for therapeutic dialogues as a 'way in' to talking with the person. Carers may need to use a range of different and creative ways to enable them to connect with a person with an ID, and to maximise their opportunities for meaningful support at times of loss. However, a fundamental skill to effectively communicating with a person with an ID may be the ability to *listen well* to what the person is trying to say, paying attention to any verbal and non-verbal cues, and also to what the person actually doesn't say as a means to extrapolating true understanding and meaning. Adopting different, creative ways of working can help carers to communicate better with the person, particularly in the loss context.

Creative approaches to listening well

'Art, music, drama and storytelling offer rich possibilities for stimulating the imagination and extending experience' (Grove and Park 2008, p.1) and there is a developing trickle of literature supporting the creative arts and other approaches with people with an ID (e.g. Read 1999), even for people living in restricted or forensic environments (Cocking and Astill 2004). However, generally, many professional carers may not fully appreciate or have a good working understanding of these approaches in this particular context (Gilrane-McGarry and Taggart 2007). What follows briefly is an introduction to some of the more popular approaches and suggestions as to their usefulness in the loss, dying and bereavement context.

Artwork

Artwork, incorporating drawing and painting however simplistic, can promote self-expression, encourage tension release and help carers to understand latent emotion. Whilst trained art therapists remain the experts in facilitating therapeutic artistic work, all carers can encourage drawing and painting as a means of self-expression, which can be fun to do and can produce good outcomes, even to the untrained eye.

Family trees

These can be personally drawn outlines of trees, or existing pictures, used to help the person to identify who comprises their family unit.

This helps the person to reflect on exactly who is involved in their family now, and who has died within their family circle. Completing a family tree can provide the carer with factual information about a person's family members. Including those who have died on a family tree is useful in both reminding individuals and their carers who has died and the deceased can be distinguished from the living by using a different coloured ink or crayon (such as black) to write the name or by simply encircling or underlining the person's name.

Creating a family tree can be useful in establishing a therapeutic relationship and is a concrete exercise that promotes cathartic responses. Often, whilst a person is writing or sticking a picture or drawing of their family member on the tree they talk about the person, sharing stories and reflecting back on a relationship that was once strong, ambivalent, traumatic or problematic. Even for those people with a small family, tracing the family can be rewarding and satisfying and helps to promote an identity recorded in a concrete medium.

Life story work

People with an ID often lack heritage or history, and life story work is an excellent way to establish a history of the person giving them a sense of place, space and heritage. Within the life story itself, stories often unfold involving difficult and challenging lived experiences such as abuse (Roberts and Hamilton 2010). Hence the life story can be a really powerful route to exploration of sensitive topics as well as a celebration of a life already lived. Developing life stories can be a continuous process, helping to capture hidden memories in a concrete way, and affirming and promoting the unique identity of each person. Life stories have been successfully used within the research process itself (Koenig 2012), and within specific loss and bereavement (Read and Bowler 2007) and social care contexts (Ellem and Wilson 2010). Developing a life story can also be great fun for anyone who is helping as well as for the person with an ID themselves.

Approaches to life story making come in a variety of different formats, and they can incorporate many different ways of compiling the story. In addition to the usual ways of adopting and developing a favourite scrap book or box, including photographs (of friends, the self, family or places); drawings, ticket stubs or programmes (from a favourite play, concert or restaurant); rail tickets or flight tickets (from a favoured journey or holiday); a pressed flower (from a wedding or funeral wreath) can all form part of a person's life story. Storage of the contents on a computer can preserve the life story work (with consent to do so from the person), protecting it in case parts become lost or damaged.

From a loss and bereavement perspective, life stories can provide important factual information about the background of the bereaved person. Developing the life story can enhance the therapeutic relationship with the helper, and ultimately promote the concept of continuing bonds (Klass *et al.* 1996), forging new, or maintaining existing, links with the deceased as they become an interwoven part of their life story.

A note of caution. Life story work is precious, personal and highly sensitive, and therefore should ideally be kept by the person who owns the life story wherever feasibly possible. It should never be treated lightly, and only shown to others with the person who owns it present, and with their full consent.

Memory books and boxes

The process of developing a memory book or box is similar to the development of a life story book or box; the biggest difference is its explicit focus. A memory book or box is usually focused upon an individual who is not around anymore, either due to death or transition (i.e. the person has moved away). The book can take the format of pictures (of people, places, favourite haunts or houses), stories, audio tapes, ornaments, clothing, drawings or poetry.

CASE STUDY: CAROLINE

For Caroline, following the death of her beloved father (and her only remaining living relative), the memory book became a treasured and important possession. Caroline had Down syndrome, and did not communicate verbally. Developing the book was painstakingly slow at first, but she quickly got the hang of it and began to bring along photographs of her father's house, his favourite chair and the car he drove to collect her from her community home each week. Whilst Caroline could not talk or write, she was good at drawing around her hands and colouring them in, a legacy from spending many previous years in a long-stay institution. Consequently, the cover of her memory book was really unique; it was numerous overlapping outlines of her left hand all coloured in a neat and somewhat abstract fashion. Even though it didn't carry her name, Caroline's book was truly distinguishable by the hands drawn and delicately coloured on the front (as illustrated in Figure 8.1).

Figure 8.1 Caroline's memory book cover

Whilst Caroline couldn't say the words 'I feel sad today' or 'I miss my dad today', she would simply fetch her book from her room and take it to a preferred carer who would then sit down and look at the book with her. The memory book became an important trigger for carers to appreciate when Caroline felt sad and needed that bit of extra support, illustrating well the cathartic nature of a memory book.

Similar to life story books and boxes, memory work is personal and sensitive and can be incredibly powerful when used in this focused, constructive way.

Storytelling

> *Clinically and therapeutically, stories and narratives*
> *are integral to the provision of care.*
>
> *(Gunaratnam and Oliviere 2009, p.1)*

Everyone has a story to tell and for many sharing the story is an important part of connecting with others and others connecting to the storyteller. Storytelling remains a unique human activity that can have tremendous impact, influence and importance in the lives of PWID (Jennings 2005). Talking and sharing grief experiences has been shown to significantly lower depression (Stoddart, Burke and Temple 2002), but for some PWID being able to articulate their sadness in a meaningful way may prove difficult if they lack the repertoire of verbal skills to articulate the story in a traditional way, struggle with the written word or simply cannot easily access a safe space to share their story (Read *et al.* 2013). Sharing stories can also be cathartic, and can help others to learn about the nature of loss and its profound and potential impact on individuals (Read and Corcoran 2009), particularly for marginalised groups in restrained environments (see Chapter 14).

Jennings reminds us of the importance of storytelling, as she recognises that they can:

- be cathartic

- have a healing nature (listening well)

- be concrete

- have a sense of permanence

- be creative

- be fun

- contribute to life story/memory work.

(After Jennings 2005)

In addition to the cathartic nature of telling a story of loss and grief, sharing it with others can help others to learn about loss and how people cope and validate the loss experience because people value the story and want to hear it. However, different spaces are conducive to different storytelling opportunities (Jennings 2005). Sharing stories in (for example) a doctor's waiting room, may be significantly different from sharing a story at a bereavement counsellor's appointment, hence the context is important.

In a developing culture where social media is becoming a natural communication system for many, digital storytelling/histories are becoming increasingly important to this population (Manning 2010), and provide a wealth of potential. From a loss, dying and bereavement perspective, telling, sharing and capturing the story may reinforce the reality of what is about to happen (or has happened), and preserve the memories in a very concrete way. A story can be captured on various sized paper using words; on paper using pictures and/or drawings and on a computer using a combination of words, picture and photographs. A story can be dictated orally, potentially transcribed if need be, or videotaped. To prompt the telling of a story, Jennings' (2005) book is a useful tool, as are the storytelling cue cards developed by Read *et al.* (2013).[2]

This set of cue cards was purposely designed to encourage individuals with an ID to tell their story of ill health, loss and bereavement, and are colour coded for ease of access. They can be downloaded and used on a variety of laptops and other computers and devices and hence have a flexibility that traditional paper will never have. Similarly, for people with profound and multiple ID, *Odyssey Now* (Grove and Park 2008) is a delightful handbook from which to explore traditional stories using an accessible, multi-sensory approach.

Pictorial books and films

There is a developing literature and resource base incorporating pictorial books explicitly for PWID, such as the range of small picture books from the Books Beyond Words series specifically designed for PWID.[3] Similarly there are resources for other populations that can be easily adapted. Pictorial books are multi-functional, promoting the expression and acknowledgement of feelings in a very profound way. They simplistically portray sensitive situations and often captivate the reader in ways that words alone can never do. Using such books can help to enhance the caring relationship and are educational and informative.

Similarly, films and DVDs are powerful mediums that, if sensitively produced, are multifunctional (they can be used as educational tools in anticipation of loss or in response to loss). Such concrete mediums often captivate the audience, particularly if PWID are involved in the film itself.

---

2   These are freely available on the following web link based at the University of Keele, Staffordshire, UK: www.keele.ac.uk/nursingandmidwifery/research/picttalk.

3   www.rcpsych.ac.uk/publications/booksbeyondwords.

Photographs

Most people now have access to a digital camera, and photographs are very powerful and personal and have huge flexibility and potential, particularly in supporting loss and grief work. Apart from capturing memories in a very immediate and concrete way, photographs can be used in conjunction with various other approaches. They can make an important contribution to memory work, helping the person to recall important people or places. They can encourage the person with an ID to talk about people they care about, and help the carer to appreciate who their family members actually were or indeed still are. Digital photographs can be stored on a computer (with consent from the owner of the photographs) and can easily be downloaded and replaced if lost or damaged.

Reminiscence work

Reminiscence work involves 'making sense of the past, to understand the present and act in the future' (Stuart 1997, p.6) and has been used successfully with PWID in a range of different contexts such as exploring its use in ageing (Van Puyenbroeck and Maes 2005), raising life satisfaction and mood (Van Puyenbroeck and Maes 2009) and bereavement (Gilrane-McGarry and Taggart 2007). Stuart suggests that reminiscence can be successfully used in advocacy, assertiveness training, therapy (such as counselling) and for pleasure (Stuart 1997). Reminiscence can constructively help in the loss and bereavement context by helping the bereaved person to identify previous coping strategies and to establish a therapeutic relationship and as an enabling tool (Stuart 1997). However, more evaluation and research is required to establish its clinical and therapeutic effectiveness specifically with PWID (Van Puyenbroeck and Maes 2008).

Poetry

Killick and Schneider suggest that 'everyone has people, events, thoughts, feelings "buried inside" and that there are ways of bringing these to the surface so that they can be examined, shaped and perhaps offered to others' (Killick and Schneider 2010, p.2), and poetry is one way of facilitating these latent experiences. Poetry has been used successfully with PWID (e.g. Read 1999, 2001; Westgate Pesola 2008), but may need to be introduced in a slightly different format to encourage successful engagement. Using lead-in sentences to encourage free flowing poetry and prose may be helpful, and outcomes can be cathartic and extremely powerful, as evidenced on the following page, where Stephen writes about his experiences of accessing services.

> *Vulnerable Person,*
> *A poem by Stephen Heath*
>
> Where the vulnerable have no voice,
> with the current system they have no choice
> because the illness is their only voice.
> Cut backs, set-backs, no lifeline
> in between services they have no choice
> because in between services they have no voice.
> Got no choice.
> Self referrals gone down the drain
> just like the rain pouring down my face again.
> Community out there that are in between are vulnerable.
> After four in the week got to cope or give up hope.
> Crying out, reach out for help from them
> and being turned away as if they are
> from some kind of different planet.
> Have no choice got no voice
> because in between services they got no choice.
> When I'm down, I think I'm better dead.
> Got no voice.

Conclusion

People with ID have more similarities to us than differences from us (Cartlidge and Read 2010; Read 2005), particularly from a loss, dying and bereavement perspective. For those who struggle to use the spoken word as a main communication medium, those around them need to adopt different methods in order to enhance that communication process. Creative approaches can help carers to reduce communication barriers and help them to access the inner, dynamic world of the person with an ID. Using creative approaches can help to develop a therapeutic, compassionate relationship by:

- helping to reduce the client's uncomfortable-ness

- developing concrete, visual aids that provide identity, history and heritage

- promoting understanding of personal state (including loss and ill health)

- enhancing holistic care

- being enjoyable.

However, whilst carers may use a variety of methods to access the inner dynamic world of the person with an ID and to promote communication, they often accompany all of this activity with talking. Dialogue is a natural and indicative part of any therapeutic relationship; it is educative and can promote reciprocal understanding. Accompanying any of the techniques described in this chapter with dialogue is a natural response, and shouldn't distract the person with an ID from the task in hand. Often, the task itself can become a distracter, and provide a freedom for the individual to talk about pain, loss and sadness whilst attending to the activity, whether it is artwork, or contributing to their family tree.

Chapter 9

The teeter/totter of caring fatigue and caring satisfaction

Ted Bowman

SUMMARY

In this chapter, what some refer to as the costs of caring will be discussed, alongside some of the gains. Attention will be given to satisfaction and distress, especially for carers in the inner circle of the life of someone with intellectual disabilities. In addition, perspectives often overlooked or under-acknowledged in discussions of carer compassion fatigue and caregiver burnout will be addressed. While the stresses are many and real (see Solomon 2012), they are only a part of what contributes to carer fatigue. Topics addressed in this chapter include:

- identifying how burnout might have more to do with loss than with distress

- exploring normalizing ambiguity and ambivalence

- integrating chronic sorrow and honest joy as a both/and, not either/or

- recognizing one's team as a crucial element of social support.

Introduction

What do you say to someone who is suffering? This seemingly universal question appears to be as old as time yet is still current. The thirteenth century poet Rumi wrote that being human is a guest house: 'Every morning a new arrival /A joy, a depression, a meanness,/some momentary awareness comes as an unexpected visitor./ Welcome and entertain them all!' (Rumi 2007, p.12). Even among contemporary grief and bereavement practitioners, Rumi's admonition seems counter-cultural. Repeatedly, persons assert that they didn't know what to say to, or do with, a grieving or bereft person. It is important to acknowledge that this involves more than social awkwardness. In some cultures today, to say the word dying or death is seen as facilitating its occurrence. For many, avoidance is the first choice. A bereft woman, aged 25, wrote that most of those that sent her condolence cards after the death of her father tried to talk her out of her grief. 'My grief is profound: I am mourning the past, present and future. I resent the condolence cards that hurry me through my grief, as if it were a dangerous street at night' (Hinds 2007, online).

Sandra Gilbert poignantly described her sense of being wounded by bereavement. 'I was wounded, yes, by my loss, and grieving because I was wounded, but at the same time I had a strange and strangely muffled sense of wrongness – of being an embarrassment.' Her experience mirrored, she found, C.S. Lewis's, who wrote: 'An odd by product of my loss is that I'm aware of being an embarrassment to everyone I meet' (Gilbert 2006, pp.xix–xxi).

Consider then, what it must be like to live with (or try to interact with) someone living with intellectual disabilities when loss is a dominant part of personal and family narratives. The chasm described above becomes a deeper and wider trench, often resulting in isolation, misunderstandings, even more embarrassment, and fatigue. Sue Read, editor of this volume, asserts, rightly I believe, that persons with intellectual and other disability conditions often get seen only through the filter of their condition and that protection from things upsetting can cause family members and carers to disallow disabled persons participation in grief and bereavement rituals and support (Read 2007). Let's explore the continuum of carer responses regarding their situations.

Carer fatigue/carer satisfaction: the continuum

Organizational consultant David Cooperrider (Cooperrider *et al.* 2000) is credited with being one of the birthparents of an approach called 'appreciative inquiry'. This approach was developed in part as a reaction to traditional problem-solving methods and ways of working. Cooperrider asserted that even if you do problem-solving well, it still starts out with a problem; it is a reactive way of seeing and addressing something. Much of what has been written about appreciative inquiry has been in the arena of organizational development; still its strengths/resources/assets approach easily informs those addressing loss, bereavement and people with an intellectual disability (PWID).

Compassion fatigue, especially in the United States, has become almost a cliché because of its overuse. It is presumed in many quarters that carers – professional and family – must be experiencing compassion fatigue. If not, something is wrong or they are in denial. Caregiver stress is also a presumed topic at meetings and conferences for family members caring for children, partners, or parents; and if not caregiver stress, the meeting must emphasize self-care. Since there is a presumed problem, problem-solving will include caring for self. Self-care can simply be positive spin on a problem…caregiver stress.

Clearly I am not suggesting the absence of fatigue for carers of persons with intellectual disabilities. The daily demands are often sufficient causes of fatigue, exacerbated by altered expectations, shattered dreams about family life, and the failure of systems to respond well to those with special needs. But many carers speak as much (and as loudly) about satisfaction and gains as they do about fatigue. One parent voiced it this way: 'I have capabilities I didn't know I had. I've been able to be a full-time mom and hold down a job. I think, 'What if she (her daughter) hadn't been handicapped? Where would I be now?' I probably wouldn't be at this job or this committed to doing both things well' (Simons 1987, p.7). Beth Stamm describes compassion satisfaction as the pleasure you derive from being able to do your work well (Stamm 2012, p.25). The father of a child with Down syndrome, Michael Berube, wrote: 'I caught myself thinking about Jamie's nasal tube as if it were a chore on a par with filling out requisition forms in triplicate, and I stopped cold. Where did I get the capacity to deal with *this* as if were part of my daily life?' (Berube 1996, pp.90–91).

Recent studies about resilience and bereavement conducted by George Bonanno and others, revealed, to Bonanno's surprise, much more innate or natural resiliency than he expected (Bonanno 2009). There is an old saying that the direction in which you look will determine what you see. Caregiver distress is not to be overlooked or undermined, nor is caregiver satisfaction. Professional carers, if not careful, will assess only for distress, fatigue, and depression, thereby overlooking perspectives relative to strengths, assets and resiliency. In contrast, The British Association for Counselling and Psychotherapy describes their work in this way: 'Counselling and psychotherapy…are delivered by trained practitioners who work with people over a short or long term to help them bring about effective change or enhance their wellbeing' (BACP 2014). Words have power; one hopes these words inform practices of the members.

Burnout may have more to do with loss than with distress

Here is another counterpoint to much of the caregiver stress literature:

> The expectation that we can be immersed in suffering and loss daily and not be touched by it is as unrealistic as expecting to be able to walk through water without getting wet. This sort of denial is no small matter. The way we deal with loss shapes our capacity to be present to life more than anything else. The way we protect ourselves from loss may be the way in which we distance ourselves from life. We burn out not because we don't care but because we don't grieve. We burn out because we've allowed our hearts to become so filled with loss that we have no room left to care. (Remen 1996, p.52)

Let me underscore one of her assertions: 'The way we deal with loss shapes our capacity to be present to life more than anything else.' Similarly, in this volume (Chapter 17), a parent discusses shattered dreams or what some call the loss of the future. Read her personal account. Gay Becker, a medical sociologist, wrote: 'When expectations about the course of life are not met, people experience inner chaos and disruption. Such disruptions represent a loss of the future. Restoring order to life necessitates reworking understandings of the self and the world, redefining the disruption and life itself' (Becker 1997, p.4). Note the last sentence and its resonance with Remen's work previously noted. Unless and until carers grieve their shattered dreams and expectations, they may have trouble dreaming new dreams because they are overshadowed by the dreams not yet mourned. Care fatigue and stress may occur. One parent wrote: 'Once we let go of the child we wanted, it freed us up to give all that love to Peter!' (Simons 1987, p.7). Andrew Solomon cites the widespread use of 'Welcome to Holland', calling it a modern fable. Written in 1987 by Emily Perl Kingsley, a parent of a child with Down syndrome, it drew on the metaphor of expectant parents traveling to Italy only to arrive in Holland instead. Solomon reports that hundreds of parents of children with disabilities told him that the essay gave them hope and the strength to be good parents. Here is a key line from 'Welcome to Holland' related to grief and loss: 'if you spend the rest of your life mourning the fact that you didn't get to Italy, you may never be free to enjoy the very special, the very lovely things…about Holland' (Solomon 2012, pp.169–170).

Particularly for carers of persons requiring extensive care, the daily demands for provision of that care can camouflage or inhibit grief and grieving. Further, most carers, whether family members, strangers, professional carers or the empathic volunteer, want to do or say something that lightens the load, eases the burden, acknowledges the distress, or shows caring to a suffering person. Hence, daily care needs take precedent. Solomon places this yearning in historical context. It was in 1866 that John Langdon Down first described Down syndrome. From then until the middle of the last century, most of the descriptions and services ranged from recommendations to euthanize, to put in an institution, or were associated with little expectation. Even famed psychologist Erik Erikson sent his newborn son to an institution in 1944, within days of his birth. One of the first reports of support for parents appeared in 1949 when a mother posted an advertisement in the New York Post seeking to meet with other parents. Early Intervention (EI) programs in the United States began as late as the 1960s. Most of these and subsequent efforts have been initiated, requested, and demanded by parents who began to see the untapped potential and gifts of their children that had been hidden for too long. Now three-quarters of children with an intellectual disability in the United States live with their parents. Solomon describes pioneering parents and professionals who have altered patterns of care over this time span as changing ideas about humanity (Solomon 2012, pp.169–219). It is telling, however, that loss itself is not overtly addressed in his otherwise impressive discussion of Down syndrome. While Solomon's historical overview is about Down syndrome, it is also apt for other intellectual disabilities. Given this significant change in services, families and other significant carers of those with intellectual disabilities must pay attention both to losses and provisions of quality care.

Normalizing ambiguity and ambivalence

Another stressful dimension of disabling conditions is that they frequently contain aspects of ambiguity. A person can look well, but may be in some ways unwell. A child on the autism continuum may appear to be present but may be absent emotionally. A person with

Down syndrome may be intellectually challenged and empathically astute. Brain injuries or conditions often affect moods and their swings.

Ambiguity means a lack of clarity, and while all families contain degrees of ambiguity, the yearning for predictability and continuity (the so-called stable family) can exacerbate and compromise caring in families that include someone with a challenging condition, especially one that ebbs and flows.

Consider the ripples of ambiguity and its impact. I've heard parents speak about relief to discover that their child had cerebral palsy, not relief with the condition but relief to finally have a diagnosis: from the ambiguity of not knowing. The conceptual basis for the ambiguous loss model lies in family stress theory. Ambiguous loss is an extraordinary stressor – a producer of uncanny anxiety and unending stress that can block coping and understanding (Boss 2006, p.11). One mother described a case review process for her child as one in which 'others had talked about her disease; I had asked about her life' (Chaisson 1996, pp.157–159). Boss describes experiences like this as the absurdity of not being certain about a person's absence or presence. Her shorthand for this confusion is physical presence and psychological absence or psychological presence and physical absence (Boss 1999). Medical and psychological carers too often focus on the assessment, diagnosis or condition while parents and other carers focus on the person with the condition. Imagine the distress when one moves from intellectual normalcy to compromised cognitive functioning or looks well but is limited in cognitive or affective tools. 'Have they told you that you might not be able to speak?/Walk. Lie Down. Decide/Make a will, sign directives,/name a proxy/wake up for the children…' These are lines from a haunting poem by Patricia Kirkpatrick describing her experience of a brain tumour and her ambiguous assessments and prognosis (Kirkpatrick 2013, p.37).

The presence of ambiguity and ambivalence will have an impact on caregiving and the carer. One giant step toward relief is for the ambiguity and ambivalence to be named, understood, and validated. Otherwise, carers can believe that they are crazy or something is wrong with them. Caregivers deserve understanding that there are situations, days, and times that they wish this too will pass. Caregivers sometimes wonder if their efforts amount to anything, make a difference, even 'who cares but me?' Responses to such thoughts and feelings must include exploration of changed perceptions over time.

Changing perceptions – embracing paradoxes

Dialectical thinking is easier said than done. As stated earlier, most humans prefer clarity and certainty to ambiguity and paradox. Dialectical thinking involves holding two or more ideas at the same time. It involves living with contradictions. The English poet, Elizabeth Jennings, wrote about her changing perceptions of a granddaughter this way:

> *Perceptions of a granddaughter*
>
> We are shallow if we say that you
> Need our pity since you have a lack.
> There are many things that you can do
> Much as we can. You can read and make
> Pretty things. You show
> Skill though it is hard for you to learn.
> You teach us patience, yes, but so much more,
> …Today I met you and tonight I can't
> Forget what you are teaching

> (Jennings 1996, p.18)

Nancy Mairs described living with multiple sclerosis as: 'My life is a lesson in losses…Thanks to multiple sclerosis, one thing after another has been wrenched from my life – dancing, driving, walking, working – and I have learned neither to yearn after them nor to dread further deprivation but to attend to what I have' (Mairs 1997, p.1014). Bereavement scholars call this a dual process. Loss is present and deserves attention; resources toward resiliency are also present and deserve attention (Stroebe and Schut 1999).

Static conditions also require changed perspectives. Robert Naseef described some autistic conditions as mirroring the movie *Groundhog Day*. In that film the lead character wakes up repeatedly to the same weather and day as the day before (he was a weather forecaster). Naseef asserts that perceiving in only one way can bind carers to the stories of the past, cloud the present, and limit their sense of the possible (Naseef 2013, pp.83–84). To lower stress, Boss urges both, to change perceptions for both the static and the ever-changing condition or situation:

she is both gone and still here
I take care of both him and myself
I am both a caregiver and a person with my own needs
I both wish it was over and wish that
  my loved one keeps on living
I am both sad about my lost hopes and dreams
  and happy about some new hopes
and dreams
someone died and is gone but still lives in my heart

           (Boss 2011, p.14).

This model is consistent with earlier parts of this chapter when it was noted that both compassion fatigue *and* compassion satisfaction deserve attention, that rewards and challenges are often present, and that few situations are only of one form.

Whether static or unpredictable, chronic conditions can prompt chronic sorrow and distress. It is one thing to address and cope with an acute situation; it is very different when the condition continues…and continues. If the only direction one looks is at the chronicity and its inherent challenges, daily life can be dominated by sorrow and stress. If, on the other hand, even while honestly facing the chronic realities one also seizes humanity, life, and living, perspective can be altered and distress relieved. Both/and rather than either/or thinking can be liberating.

One's team: a crucial element of social support

It's a routine story. Someone comes to visit or offer support to a household that includes someone intellectually challenged. The guest is greeted warmly at the door by the parent, sibling or another 'carer'. The guest asks: 'And how is _____today?' It is rare, too rare, for that guest to begin or to follow up that initial question with, 'And how are you doing?'

Caregiver isolation is often cited as one of the key factors in compassion fatigue and burnout. Less attention has been given to the importance of a caregiver team. A team is necessary because no one of us has the full range of perspectives, skills, and time to provide care to another. Legal help may be warranted; care coordination of a range of services is often necessary; respite when taken requires someone to step forward to accompany or care for the care receiver; and the list goes on. But, asking for help is difficult for many. Hence, caregiver fatigue occurs and keeps occurring. Carers need to be reminded that help-seeking is not self-centred; rather it can be other-centred. In order to bring one's best to someone needing care, the caregiver needs to do what needs to be done for that to occur. Respite – relief when someone else performs a task that is difficult for the caregiver – and even shared tasks can be beneficial for the whole household or family unit. Allowing others to provide some services at home or in a facility can free family members to be family members. Specifically related to grief and bereavement, intellectual disabilities may complicate the experiences of loss and require attention by sensitive carers. Oswin's principles toward normalization of bereavement for persons with a learning disability apply (Oswin 1981 in Read 2007, p.4):

- Just because people have a learning disability doesn't mean that they don't grieve.

- Such people have the right to grieve.

- Each person is an individual, and there is no reason to expect them to behave in a certain way because they have a disability.

- Because of the nature of the disability, some people may require special help or consideration.

If grief support is warranted it may be that family members put such support as the priority, allowing others to perform more mundane tasks. For example, in the midst of care for her dying husband, in response to my inquiry 'How can I be helpful?' his wife asked that I clean her house. Willing to do so but surprised at the request, I asked that she tell me more about the request. She then taught me about stress and grief: 'It's so hard to be here in the place of death and dying, I just don't have the energy to clean anymore.' I cleaned her house. Team members are those who are there for you when you need them to be there. Carers are less likely to be overwhelmed with distress when they activate or allow a team to support them.

Conclusion
Thich Nhat Hanh has provided a brief summary that is congruent with this chapter. Hahn asserted that if carers are unhappy, they cannot

help many people (Hanh 1987). Caregiver fatigue deserves caring attention that includes its counterpoint, caregiver satisfaction. Such a dual process orientation can bring balance. In so doing, the renewed caregiver can bring their better selves to acts of care rather than being depleted and worn down. Such actions are a win/win for all involved. Rumi would be pleased; all the guests are welcomed!

CHAPTER 10

Exploring key issues for professional carers offering end-of-life care in the community

Michele Wiese

SUMMARY

Professional carers have important roles to play when loss permeates the lives of people with an intellectual disability (PWID), particularly at the end of life. The overarching aim of this chapter is to critically explore end-of-life care from the professional carer perspective and community context. The literature informing the chapter is drawn mainly from the United Kingdom (UK), the United States of America (USA) and Australia. The literature does not limit itself to the intellectual disability (ID) sector, and where relevant, information is also drawn from the general community. A progressive case study has been woven throughout to illustrate salient points as they develop from diagnosis onwards.

Introduction

With increased life expectancy, for the first time in history people with ID are expected to outlive their parents, previously the predominant providers of care. Remaining family have varying capacity to offer required care, and as a result the community living services sector is increasingly relied upon to care for people with ID for the remainder of their life (Bigby 2010; Braddock *et al.* 2001). The term 'remainder' implies that staff of these services care for people with ID not only as they age, but also as the end-of-life approaches. The capacity of these staff to provide compassionate end-of-life care[1], and the issues they face, is the focus of this chapter.

Four key issues are proposed for this chapter that reflect the capacity of community living service staff to provide end-of-life care:

- policy direction

- clarity on service delivery model

- staff training

- collaborative communication skills.

Policy direction

Government-led policy direction on end-of-life care of people with ID is inconsistent and sometimes non-existent. For example, in the USA Botsford and King (2010) noted the across-state inconsistencies in provision of information to people with ID who are dying, availability of in-home nursing care and access to hospice. Meanwhile in the UK, the recent Confidential Inquiry Report into Premature Deaths of People with Learning Disabilities (CIPOLD) (Heslop *et al.* 2013) made particular reference to the inequitable access to specialist palliative care service[2] by people with ID, as well as the need for community living services to offer end-of-life care. Lack of policy direction from government translates to fragmented and localised service delivery initiatives, ultimately affecting community living services' capacity to ensure quality care of people with ID. Consider the scenario in the case study, John, Part 1.

---

1   This chapter adopts the end-of-life care definition offered by Froggatt *et al.* (2006): 'the care provided to support individuals at any time in the final period of their life where issues (physical, social, emotional and spiritual) arising from an individual's death and mortality are being addressed' (p.46).

2   This refers to service by individuals whose training and job description is to provide only palliative care. This service might include a community nurse, palliative care physician, chaplain and social worker. The service augments the care provided by the usual carers: in this chapter, community living services staff.

CASE STUDY: JOHN, PART 1

John's mum died last year. They had lived together his whole life. He subsequently moved to Carawah Community Living Service and shares a house with two other people with ID. Yesterday the service was informed that John's long-term coronary disease has significantly worsened.

Reflective question:
If you were a staff member in the community living service what would be your principles to guide John's care?

A review of the literature suggests three principles, each familiar to the ID sector, which together could guide community living services' policy on end-of-life care to people with ID: human rights, self-determination and supported decision making.

Human rights

Most developed countries have signed, and many ratified, the United Nations Convention on the Rights of Persons with Disabilities (the UN Convention) (United Nations Enable n.d.; United Nations General Assembly 2006). At the service level, this means that people with disability have equal rights to education, healthcare, work, relationships and everyday life (Caruso and Osburn 2011). By implication, adherence to the UN Convention means that John should be accorded access to end-of-life care in the same way as other members of the community.

Self-determination

This principle reflects the right to self-governance and control over one's life (Wehmeyer and Bolding 2001). The exercise of self-determination is predicated upon having a) sufficient information, and b) capacity to understand the information. Despite its individual focus, most would agree that self-determination is rarely experienced in a truly autonomous fashion, and it is increasingly acknowledged that human beings function in interdependent relationships (Reindal 1999). Arguably, interdependence is even more apparent as the end-of-life approaches, a period during which the individual becomes increasingly reliant on others. For the community living service supporting John, a care approach reflective of the principle of self-determination would be to ensure that he is given all the information about his dying and death in a way that he can understand, throughout the end-of-life care period.

Supported decision making

Acknowledging that the learning difficulties experienced by people with ID may mean decision making about end-of-life care is fraught; this does not abrogate the sector's responsibility to address the inherent principle. In line with the principles of the UN Convention and self-determination, the legal world is currently grappling with how the prevailing substitute decision-making model could be subsumed by an approach where people with disability would retain their legal decision-making power, but receive support to make decisions (Bekkema *et al.* 2013; Carney 2013). For John, this could mean support from trusted others to help him make decisions about things like the course of his care, will-making and funeral planning. The community living service's responsibility would be to assist with the gathering of trusted others, and then to act according to John's decisions.

Clarity on service delivery model
CASE STUDY: JOHN, PART 2

John has now been living in the community living service for two years. He has been happy there, and is very well liked. His activities have included part-time work at the local pet shelter, going out with friends and attendance at church. His heart disease now causes regular and significant pain, though medication relieves the symptoms. Many activities are tiring, and John is increasingly home-bound.

Reflective question:
As the house manager, what might you and your service management need to consider in planning for John's future care?

Acknowledging that there are many considerations in designing an end-of-life care service delivery model, this section of the chapter focuses on the key issues.

Agreed realistic assessment of capacity

From commencement, the team's capacity to commit to end-of-life care requires careful consideration. Research in Australia suggests that community living services do not consider all care dimensions, and have variously interpreted the extent of their care responsibility on a continuum from 'care to a point' to 'care at all costs' (Webber, Bowers and McKenzie-Green 2010). For John's community living services team, the issues to consider might include:

- the preferences of the dying person

- the needs and wishes of the other people sharing the home

- availability and flexibility of staffing

- staff willingness, knowledge and competence

- staff understanding of loss

- relationship with family

- what decisions need to be made

- how the dying person will be supported to make decisions

- access to required equipment

- accessibility of external services, for example medical, spiritual and palliative care specialists.

A careful assessment of capacity to care can be helpful in navigating the course of end-of-life care. Research has shown that without clarity about the extent to which care can viably be offered by the community living service, staff can be negatively affected as care unfolds. To illustrate this, for some people, complex medical care requirements in the final stages of life may require transfer to hospital, which, if not clearly understood by all involved, can leave staff with feelings of guilt and confusion (Wiese *et al.* 2012). An alternative goal, which honours the relationship between staff and dying person, might instead be to maintain familiar relationships, at home to the maximum extent possible, but then in the hospital space if that is necessitated (Tuffrey-Wijne 2009).

Balanced focus on pre- and post-death care

The bulk of research on end-of-life care by community care staff has focused on care after death, including issues such as grief and bereavement care for those left behind (McEvoy *et al.* 2010; Read 2010). While acknowledging that post-death care is important, so too is care during the dying phase (Wiese *et al.* 2012). Offering quality care during the dying phase sends two important messages. First, it communicates to the dying person that he or she matters, and is valued and honoured. Second, it gives those others with ID around the dying person an experience of dying care and an understanding of what it potentially will be like when they themselves enter that life phase. For John and his care team, the physical, psychosocial and spiritual components comprising the World Health Organisation definition of palliative care (Sepúlveda *et al.* 2002) may provide helpful direction for service delivery.

Shared understanding of what dying means

Perhaps not surprisingly, people have variable understanding of dying, and this complex phenomenon is not just particular to the ID sector (Wadensten *et al.* 2007). Knowing about dying and death is arguably the most critical aspect of the end-of-life care service delivery model, as without it the principles of self-determination and supported decision making are nullified. In the ID sector the research suggests that care staff have variable understanding of what dying means (Read and Elliott 2003; Wiese *et al.* 2012), tend towards an idealised view of the care role (Todd 2004), and then when engaged in it, have been overwhelmed by its complexity (Ryan *et al.* 2011a).

Many people with ID have at least some understanding of dying (McEvoy, MacHale and Tierney 2012; Ryan *et al.* 2011b), however, despite this staff tend to avoid the topic. Staff have expressed concern that people with ID may not be able to cope, and that they themselves did not have the skills to approach the topic (MacHale, McEvoy, and Tierney 2009; Wiese *et al.* 2013).

For John's care team, the service delivery model should reflect a commitment to ensuring that the individuals with ID (both the dying person and others who share his home), care staff and family have an understanding of dying and death. The learning difficulties associated with ID suggest a start-early approach (Maes 2012). Ideally, open discussion with John and his peers about dying and death could be approached by family, care staff and church leaders well prior to life-limiting illness, therefore reserving the end-of-life as a time for affirmation of wishes, rather than learning about the concept.

Quality of life until death

Recent research, both in the general community and ID sector, has focused on a return to age-old social and community aspects of end-of-life care. Care approaches have included the dignity-conserving model (Lutfiyya and Schwartz 2010), health promoting palliative care (Kellehear 2012), and person-centred end-of-life care (Kingsbury 2009, 2010). Taken together these models share key attributes reflective of a quality of life approach to care. A focus on quality of life until death suggests that every aspect of care focuses on the maintenance of the person's desired condition of living (Schalock 1997).

For some, dying can mean increased marginalisation and isolation from the community, waning social interaction and ultimately loss of social identity (Walter *et al.* 2012). For John, the maintenance of quality of life may serve to ameliorate the possibility of social death. Staff could focus their efforts on supporting John to maintain his previously enjoyed lifestyle, as far as practicable and with adaptations in response to deteriorating health. Efforts could include adapted activities like regular visits from friends, home prayer services with a church volunteer, or even video recording the animals at the pet shelter where he formerly worked.

Staff training

CASE STUDY: JOHN, PART 3

Nadia, a staff member at John's home, has worked in accommodation settings for eight years, but has never been involved in end-of-life care. Her main role has been to assist people to access recreation opportunities and maintain their households. She has had no personal experience with death, and despite a commitment to self-determination, has no idea how to realise that principle in the context of John's care.

The shift from living well to dying well may be a paradox that many staff find hard to reconcile. Independence, inclusion and participation in daily life have been key drivers of staff development and training efforts in the ID sector for more than thirty years. Translating this language to care practices when the client's body is deteriorating may be a mind shift that many staff find challenging (Todd 2009; Watchman 2005). Despite this challenge, the research overwhelmingly suggests staff's total commitment to providing end-of-life care (Brown, Burns and Flynn 2003; Ryan *et al.* 2011a; Wiese *et al.* 2012). This commitment can be harnessed, but the importance of preparing a competent, confident and compassionate staff cohort cannot be overstated.

The resources to support staff skills in end-of-life care are small but growing, and include a range of planning tools (Kingsbury 2009), communication aids (Hollins and Tuffrey-Wijne 2009; Read 2010) and guidelines (Blackman and Todd 2005; Read and Morris 2008). In addition, a range of professional development programmes are available, designed for the general community, but readily translatable to the ID service environment (e.g. Palliative Care Australia, undated; The Marie Curie Palliative Care Institute Liverpool, undated).

The following competencies are suggested as a minimum standard to prepare Nadia for end-of-life care with John:

- recognising the end-of-life

- valuing partnership with families

- understanding the ethical issues in care

- talking about dying and death with others

- looking after self

- planning for the end-of-life

- knowing the available external services

- developing a care plan

- managing physical symptoms

- providing physical comfort care

- providing spiritual comfort care

- providing post-death care.

Collaborative communication skills

CASE STUDY: JOHN, PART FOUR

A few months ago John's brother, Brendan, was appointed his formal guardian. This was necessitated by John's increasing agitation and memory loss over the preceding year. John is now in hospital again. Brendan broached the subject of Not-for-Resuscitation (NFR) with the manager of the community living service. The staff at the house are very upset.

Reflective question:
As the manager of the community living service, what approach would you have taken?

Open communication and working collaboratively may be no more important, and no more challenging, than during the end-of-life care period. For the policy principles of the UN Convention, self-determination and supported decision making to work, community living staff need sophisticated communication skills to work together with others. These others might include an array of individuals, including the dying person, family, other clients sharing the home, fellow staff, external health services (including specialist palliative care) and post-death coronial personnel (Wiese *et al.* 2012). Sometimes these individuals may come to end-of-life care with different prior experiences and viewpoints, underlining the importance of careful and sensitive communication.

The principles of collaborative communication provide a vehicle to enable successful partnerships between all individuals involved in end-of-life care. Key collaborative communication skills include: working towards a shared goal; commitment to resolving differences of opinion; recognition of individual knowledge; and respect attributed to each individual perspective (Alquraini 2012). One pivotal characteristic of collaborative communication between multiple partners is the appointment of a lead person, or case manager, able to coordinate communication between individuals and manage the implementation of agreed goals (Trivedi *et al.* 2013).

A useful mantra to guide collaborative communication might be, 'It doesn't have to be either/or. It can be both/and' (McGinn *et al.* 2005, p.562). With this in mind, the approach of the community living services manager in John's latest situation might be to a) encourage

John and his supported decision-making team to conduct advance care planning (Martin, Emanuel and Singer 2000) at the beginning of the end-of-life care period, so that everyone is clear on his personal values and the flavour of his wishes; b) assist Brendan to build a supported decision-making team, so that the decision he ultimately makes considers all dimensions, guided by John's values arising from advance care planning; and c) ensure the staff are aware of the challenges of the legal role of formal guardian, and continue to affirm their valued care role in John's life.

Conclusion

People with ID have a right to care that is equitable to other members of the community. With increasing reliance on community living services to provide care to the end-of-life, the understanding of how best to provide this care is embryonic. This chapter has provided a summary of the current research and practice issues. Professional carers in community settings are committed to, and capable of offering, compassionate and quality end-of-life care. The challenges, however, are many and require careful attention to policy guidance, service delivery design, staff training and collaborative communication.

CHAPTER 11

Advocacy, communication and empowerment

Patsy Corcoran

SUMMARY

This chapter explores the potential for advocacy to empower individuals with intellectual disabilities (IDs) during times of loss and bereavement. The purpose of advocacy is explained, and challenges and responses to disempowerment are explored. Examples of case-focused and cause-focused advocacy are provided to give an overview of independent advocacy, the process and the skill set of the advocate and advocacy facilitator. This chapter centres around loss with five individuals with IDs (three individuals and a married couple) who have been involved in advocacy partnerships with Asist Advocacy Service and have worked with Reach Group Advocacy for more than ten years.

Theories of conflict resolution, co-production and social capital are explored in relation to advocacy practice. The case studies within this chapter each focus on a different aspect of empowerment for individuals during times of loss and bereavement, namely: choice and control; exchanges and actions; understanding and learning; and resolving and remembering. The conclusion reflects on how advocacy support can facilitate positive impact and outcomes for individuals with an ID during times of loss.

Advocacy, communication and empowerment

Advocacy is the process of supporting someone to speak up and be active citizens. The act of speaking up to share one's views, raise issues and questions, participate in the development of future plans and agree or disagree with decisions are all essential features of active citizenship. 'Citizenship is the word we use to describe what it is to be recognised by other people as an individual who is a full member of the community' (Duffy 2003, p.2). Independent advocacy involves supporting individuals to represent their own views and also act as representative for those views when the individual is unable to represent themselves. Group advocacy is based on the principles and practices of independent advocacy, but involves individuals with ID being supported to discuss and raise issues together. Within group advocacy individuals are speaking up for themselves and also representing others with similar issues.

Challenges to empowerment

Individuals may face internal barriers or intrapersonal challenges (particularly related to experience and confidence) regarding making choices and decisions. These factors can be further exacerbated due to disability, mental ill health or mental capacity. Some people may be unaware of their right to an autonomous existence as a result of institutionalisation and prolonged absence of opportunities to exert rights and make everyday choices. This lack of awareness about rights and lack of confidence to exert rights can lead to confusion, frustration and feelings of disempowerment.

Communication is a vital aspect of decision making. Where there is a lack of shared communication (due to an individual's cognitive and/or physical ability) this can pose intrapersonal challenges to speaking up as the individual is unable to express their views and wishes in a way that is formally recognised by others. Failure to recognise an individual's expressed views or feelings can also lead to frustration and disempowerment for the individual and can be expressed through behaviour that challenges other people. Individuals may feel inhibited and may be influenced by previous experiences of not being listened to. Their motivation to speak up, challenge decisions and make their choices known may be impeded by a lack of trust and an established perception (or fear) of being ignored.

External, structural factors and interpersonal challenges may inhibit the individual's ability to voice their views and wishes. Individuals who are 'cared for' or deemed 'vulnerable' may be supported by professionals who have a legal responsibility to ensure their 'best interest' is served according to health and social care legislation. Where the best interest decision of the professional differs from an individual's views and wishes, this may cause conflict between the professional's duty of care and the individual. The individual therefore may face interpersonal challenges regarding speaking up, making choices and pursuing self-determined action.

The advocacy response

The primary role of advocacy is to facilitate effective communication regarding rights and choices. Based on the premise that 'information is power', independent advocacy is designed to build confidence, raise awareness and empower the advocacy partner by informing them about their options and rights and by representing their views. Communication between the advocate and advocacy partner is a core part of this process and is facilitated using a range of person-centred approaches and creative methods (see Chapter 8).

Independent Mental Capacity Advocates (IMCAs) and Independent Mental Health Advocates (IMHAs) are specialist advocacy roles enshrined in law (Mental Capacity Act 2005; Mental Health Act 2009). These laws ensure the right to independent advocacy support for individuals affected by mental ill health and for individuals deemed by decision makers to lack capacity regarding specific decisions. The specialist advocate informs decision makers of the person with ID's (advocacy partner's) views and wishes whilst legitimately representing their advocacy partner's rights within the decision-making process. If a person with ID experiences the loss of family members/others, independent advocacy can help to ensure their voice and their rights remain at the centre of decision-making processes.

Where an advocacy partner is able to express their views and choices the advocate represents these with instruction from the advocacy partner (instructed advocacy). When it is difficult to determine the views and choices of the advocacy partner due to ill health, disability, capacity and communication, the advocate can represent the rights of the advocacy partner without instruction. This non-instructed advocacy works by asking questions about decisions regarding the advocacy partner's rights. This approach was developed by Asist in 1998 as a direct response to the challenges within independent advocacy, where instruction is ambiguous or does not take place within the advocacy partnership due to communication or capacity issues.

Case-focused advocacy

Case-focused advocacy is a one-to-one process based on equality, rights, respect and empowerment, where an independent advocate supports an individual to be involved in the decisions that affect their lives. With roots in the USA, Canada and Australia, this type of advocacy started to become more formalised in the UK post 1950s. 'Advocacy can be described as the process of identifying with and representing a person's views and concerns, in order to ensure enhanced rights and entitlements undertaken by someone who has little or no conflict of interest' (Henderson and Pochin 2001, p.1). Employing problem-solving approaches and conflict resolution techniques (Burton 1993) the advocate supports the advocacy partner to explore an identified issue, providing clear information on a range of options available in order to ascertain the wishes of the advocacy partner. 'Collaborative co-production requires users to be experts in their own circumstances and capable of making decisions, while professionals must move from being fixers to facilitators' (Realpe and Wallace 2010, p.3). Self-determination (according to co-production theorists) relies on opportunities to create solutions rather than being identified as part of the problem. The advocate supports and represents their advocacy partner in meetings with professionals to enable their contribution to solutions within decision-making processes. The independent advocate is free to fully represent the views and wishes of the individual in an impartial and non-judgemental capacity. According to Lord and Hutchison the principles of empowerment in community practice include the sharing of power between decision makers and people who use services, the building of capacity and strength of people who use services and finally the 'citizens must be the ones to identify the problems and solutions' (Lord and Hutchison 1993, p.21).

Cause-focused advocacy

Cause-focused advocacy has evolved from a tradition where people who share a label, an experience or a common cause meet regularly to raise issues that potentially affect the group. Reach is a Group Advocacy Project established in 2000 and is part of the charity Asist (Advocacy Services in Staffordshire). Reach works with adults with ID in Staffordshire and Stoke-on-Trent to speak up about issues that commonly affect people who carry the label of intellectual disability. Reach members are people with IDs who raise personal issues, exploring these within a group context to identify similarities in experiences and pursue group actions and outcomes. The work of Reach and Asist are based on equality, rights, respect and empowerment: the core principles of independent advocacy. The Reach model of advocacy is similar to user-led approaches described by Wilks (2012, p.29):

> Self-advocacy, peer advocacy and group advocacy [are] interlinked; peer advocacy is often seen as a mechanism which enables service users to speak for themselves and group advocacy enables individuals to express views collectively. There is the potential for these three approaches to act in concert, each supporting the other, with those who have developed skills in self-advocacy passing these on to others through peer advocacy.

Garbutt (2011, p.127) explores how 'advocacy is one way in which people with disabilities can stand up for their rights, assert their choices and challenge the structures and systems of which they find themselves a part'. Sutcliffe and Simons (1993) identify the support for people with ID to develop social and communication skills and facilitating group discussion as key factors of the advocacy facilitator's role, enabling people with ID to speak up for themselves and represent the voice of others. The requisite skills for advocacy (e.g. communication, listening, interviewing, assertiveness and negation) are described by Garbutt (2011, pp.124–127) and are shared by people with ID, independent advocates and advocacy facilitators. Asist believes that advocacy is a right of all citizens, a right that is founded on respect, empathy and compassion towards all citizens.

> *In group advocacy you've got your friends you can talk to and having friends who've been through the same thing as you can lean on each other through hard times through the times of loss and bereavement.*
> *Carl*

Co-production and advocacy

Co-production is internationally recognised as an empowering approach within statutory and other sectors and is fundamental to person-centred advocacy. From the start in early 2000 people with ID have worked with me to co-design an advocacy project for people with ID using a cause-focused approach which combines self, peer and group advocacy. People with ID work with Reach to:

- form speaking up parliaments in their locality to raise issues on behalf of people

- take part in strategic planning reviewing policies and work practice (Asist and Reach)

- represent people with ID within local, regional and national discussions

- take part in designing and developing best practice tools for professionals.

Reach supports people with ID to work alongside professionals from a variety of disciplines in order to co-produce policies, models and tools for best practice in health and social care. We work alongside researchers to explore the issue of loss and bereavement in order to develop tools for people with ID, for carers and for professionals. Reach worked alongside people with ID from Wrexham to co-produce a booklet entitled 'When someone you know has died' which enables people with ID to explore loss and to support each other during times of loss and bereavement. During 2009–11, seven people with ID also worked as co-researchers to develop an electronic image based tool to facilitate conversations about loss and bereavement. During this time, as a direct result of the thoughts and ideas of people with ID, the direction of the research changed (Read and Corcoran 2009) resulting in a communication tool based on storytelling for people with ID (Read *et al.* 2013).

Support for people with ID in many areas of their life over a long period of time when facing loss and bereavement can be vital.

> *Losing somebody is not just about what you are feeling at the time of losing that person but it affects your whole health it affects your own life...*
> *Carl*

Gotto *et al.* (2010, p.1) argue that social capital describes our relationships and social ties with individuals and groups based on reciprocity and is linked to self-determination. The individual gains more power through social ties, wider friendship groups and by joining advocacy groups as 'individuals not only gain personal social capital in this process but also accrue the benefits of these groups' larger pools of social capital'. Reciprocity and trust are integral to developing social capital resulting in greater citizen power and stronger community connections for people with ID (Bates and Davis 2004). People with ID co-produced this chapter by sharing their experiences of loss and holding discussions on advocacy support during times of loss and bereavement. With each person's agreement (using a consent form designed with clear words and pictures) we recorded discussions and took photographs of the sessions. Fictitious names are used for some people in the case studies, as they requested anonymity. The four main aspects of empowerment focused on in the introduction to this chapter emerged directly from these discussions.

The impact of advocacy

According to Lord and Hutchison (1993), empowerment indicates a process of change, of power-sharing, of supportive peer relationships and includes a growing political consciousness. People experience increasing control in their daily life, often motivated by strong feelings of frustration and anger alongside a determined, supported effort to exert influence through individual or group participation. People with ID who shared their stories of loss and bereavement remind us of how particularly important advocacy is and identified how advocacy support:

- contributed to increased feelings of empowerment

- nurtured confidence to express thoughts, feelings and wishes

- provided support to communicate and express needs and wishes

- increased the development of knowledge and understanding

- helped them work through emotions and conflict surrounding death.

CASE STUDY: CHOICE AND CONTROL - JOANNE'S STORY

> *You've had the experience, [advocacy is a] good thing 'cos you've got like if you were upset you've got the support there...you know that you've got the choice.*
> *Joanne*

Joanne is a woman with ID who has worked with Reach for more than ten years, speaking up about a wide range of issues; participating in strategic planning; reviewing services; and sharing her experiences of living with an ID. Using these personal experiences, Joanne has worked with Reach and a range of professionals to research and develop a variety of best practice tools. What is striking about Joanne's story is how important choice and control was to her at the time of her father's death and remains so. Joanne explains that she found her dad dead at home on returning from a shopping trip. Having worked together to co-produce tools to facilitate conversations about loss Joanne has built trusted connections with people involved in the work and Joanne contacted Professor Sue Read to discuss her decision not to go and see her dad at the chapel of rest. Later Joanne felt confident to take an active role in the funeral planning.

> *What me dad liked and how he was and different photographs 'cos I chose the music...we choose his favourite song...and every funeral I've been to they play that and that's what gets me upset but not as much now but sometimes it just brings the feelings back...*
> *Joanne*

When asked why she wanted to continue with the advocacy work of developing communication tools during the time her father died, Joanne explained that though the work was difficult and at times upsetting, it was helpful to her.

During our work together we watched a home movie of a family wedding 30 years ago. Whilst watching the film Joanne shared memories of the wedding, of her relationship with her father and explained that she wanted me to see for myself who he really was. Joanne explained how funny her dad was and proudly shared a glimpse of her family life with me. This is part of the process of advocacy, listening and sharing her story. Storytelling is used as a therapeutic tool for children and adults with ID with a focus on 'the story the [adult] needs to tell as well as the story [they] need to hear' (Jennings 2013, p.18).

Joanne used her memory box (Figure 11.1) to help her reflect on how advocacy has supported her through loss and bereavement (see Chapter 8) and used our meeting to explore this in anticipation of the anniversary of her dad's death. 'Continuing bonds are well represented in popular culture, through music [and] memorium[s]' (Valentine 2008, p.4).

Figure 11.1 Joanne's memory box

> It's given me more it's given me more confidence and like if me friends were having it...if they [to] wanted talk to me they know how I was going through as well.
> Joanne

CASE STUDY: EXCHANGES AND ACTIONS – TOMMY'S STORY

Tommy is a man with ID who communicates with some speech and signs (Makaton, British Sign Language, body language and gestures) along with the written word. Tommy has worked with Reach for more than ten years. Medina (2006) identifies reciprocal reliance as key to constructive communication. During our advocacy partnership Tommy and I have developed strategies to communicate using visual cues and non-verbal and verbal exchanges based on trust and reciprocal reliance. Though Tommy had previously explained that he lost his family when he was young he had not previously expressed that he does not know where his family are buried. During our advocacy work we discussed choosing a place of remembrance. Tommy asked if I could phone his keyworker at home and tell them about our conversation. Tommy was interested in exploring this further with his keyworker, to find a place to put some flowers in memory of his family. Following our advocacy work I spoke to a member of support staff at Tommy's home, explaining about our work and how Tommy wanted to continue talking about his family and visiting a place of remembrance. Tommy worked with Reach and Keele University to research and develop the bereavement assessment tool (Read and Corcoran 2009). Following on from the research work Reach designed pictogram cards which Tommy now uses to express his thoughts and feelings about loss and bereavement (see Figure 11.2).

Figure 11.2 Tommy working with pictogram cards

Using the pictogram cards we reflected on our advocacy work. The following is an extract of a recorded discussion between Tommy and me.

> Me – And there was a picture of two people with some flowers near a gravestone
>
> Tommy – Mmm
>
> Me – And that's when you said you didn't know where your family were
>
> Tommy – No cos...[?] I was a little toddler
>
> (Here I did not understand Tommy's words so I asked Tommy to repeat this to me.)
>
> Me – When you were a little toddler, I got that last bit Tommy I didn't get the first bit, sorry, could you tell me that bit again?
>
> Tommy – I lost all my family when I was three months old

Me – And you were saying that when we were doing that work together you were saying you don't know where they're buried

CASE STUDY: UNDERSTANDING AND LEARNING – JOHN AND LYN

John and Lyn are married and both have IDs. Whilst Lyn has recently started working with Reach, John has done so for more than ten years. John and Lyn regularly take part in strategic work with Reach and share their experiences of living with an ID for the purposes of training and raising awareness. Both have experienced family loss and bereavement during this time. John supported his sister through her illness up to her death and has (together with his wife) spoken up about loss and bereavement.

Figure 11.3 Talking together

> *Well it's helped us a lot through working with Reach and with Sue (Read)…[we] find out what else other people think as well as us, we can do it…*
> *John*

> *Well it helped me the work what we did really did help me to understand you know what sort of cancers could come up or and that and when well when I were beginning lose me sister I ended up knowing, you know finding out more about it.*
> *John*

In 2010 John worked with Reach to check NHS leaflets about different types of cancer for accessibility. A small group of people with ID read through the leaflets and discussed the information about different types of screening and symptoms of cancer. At this time John was eager to be involved in the work as his sister had been recently diagnosed with cancer and John wanted to talk about his experience, ask questions and find out more information about cancer. Though this was a very difficult time and for John a sensitive topic, he was insistent that he wanted to be involved in this work. More recently, in 2012 John and Lyn took part In a meeting alongside people with ID to review a local bereavement service that they have both accessed for support. Both John and Lyn shared their own experiences of loss and bereavement during the meeting and reflected on support from a range of sources including advocacy. I invited John and Lyn to meet and talk about advocacy support during times of loss and bereavement for this chapter. During our meeting John recalled how he supported his sister during the last weeks of her life.

> *'Cos she could hardly talk then, you know it had really grabbed hold of her throat...and I said come on tell me what you want and I looked at her straight in her eye and I said what do you want...I knew exactly what she wanted... she was using sign language to me...*
> *John*

John used his own experience to help produce a peer support leaflet (Read 2012). John and Lyn both explained how working together with Reach helps them to manage their feelings, to have confidence to support others and to access support from Reach, from professionals involved in our work and from local support services. John feels it would be more difficult to support Lyn during emotional times without this support network.

> *But that's one of the things what people like to get off their chest where they can talk freely and there's not many [places] about...*
> *John*

CASE STUDY: RESOLVING AND REMEMBERING – CARL

Carl is a man with ID who has spoken up about people's rights with Reach for more than ten years. Carl delivers presentations and training to health and social care professionals and has helped to develop numerous training tools about dignity and respect. When Carl's dad became seriously ill and later died, Carl gained support through Reach and our wider networks. Carl explained that involvement in this work helped him resolve feelings of anger about his bereavement. Carl drew on his experiences to help develop a peer support booklet for people with ID. The booklet is a tool to facilitate conversation and reflection to help people with ID work through bereavement (see Figure 11.4). The booklet includes examples of questions people may have and how people may want to be involved in the process of bereavement.

Figure 11.4 Carl contributing to the peer support booklet

Carl talked about how independent advocacy support helped him through his bereavement:

> *I didn't think I'd be able to do this actually come in and talk about the death of me father but advocacy over the last two years has helped me because I've had people that I can turn round and talk to rather than talk to me sister and me brother who are going through the same thing.*
> *Carl*

When exploring how advocacy can support people through loss and bereavement Carl explains:

> *The group advocacy especially gives me something to look forward to and actually want to do, I want to turn up for meetings on time, I want to be able to talk about things that people might not be able to talk about like loss and death and bereavement. It was a big loss when he died but I'm glad that I had the group advocacy and the support from the group advocacy and the one-to-one advocacy that I received.*
> *Carl*

During our discussion Carl reflected on his friendships with other Reach members and explained that he supported his friend Joanne (see her case study earlier). That support was reciprocated by Joanne at the time of Carl's bereavement through advocacy networks, social media and mobile communications.

Reflections

Advocacy support can facilitate positive impact and outcomes for individuals with ID during times of loss where it is person-centred, timely and co-produced. Initially professionals may feel uncertain when approaching a person with ID regarding working in co-production when the person is or has recently experienced a significant loss. There may be a tendency to protect the feelings of the person with ID and to exclude them from this type of advocacy work. However, people with ID tell Reach that working in a constructive way to share their experiences and to produce resources to support people can help with their own feelings of loss and bereavement:

> *There is support when we do this work and we can take breaks from it if we need to we can go somewhere that is quieter and have time out. It does help especially when you've got friends that have gone through the same thing...you are doing it with somebody who has gone through the same thing and I think that helps being able to talk in front of people who have gone through bereavement and loss...so you are not on your own.*
> *Carl*

Reflection and feedback from people with ID are an essential part of co-production in advocacy. Asist has been at the forefront of developing accessible monitoring systems that enable advocacy partners to reflect and feedback on the outcomes of their advocacy experience.

> Within the advocacy movement it is widely recognised that this is the most important measure of success of the service... qualitative data...strikes at the heart of the relationship; do the people using the service really control it and has it been satisfactory? (Stefanelli 2006, p.20)

Asist monitoring via advocacy partner feedback indicates that 90 per cent of people are satisfied with the process and feel they benefit from the involvement of advocates and advocacy facilitators.

The impact of advocacy

Though there is some quantitative data about the impact of advocacy in general and a wealth of qualitative anecdotal evidence about the positive impact of advocacy on the lives of people with ID, there is still very little evidence-based research showing the potential impact of advocacy for people with ID during times of loss and bereavement. The case studies in this chapter indicate that people with ID are ready and willing to share their thoughts and experiences. Read (2011, p.537) explains how 'loss can be disempowering for anyone; but for people with [an ID] loss can be totally disempowering and often overwhelming'. Dennison and Mee (2011) demonstrate how people with ID are empowered by telling their own story. Advocacy can play a huge role within this particular context, promoting opportunities for empowering conversations and self-determined solutions by people with ID. More research working in co-production with people with ID is needed to fully explore the potential positive impact of advocacy during times of loss and bereavement and to ensure the voices of people with ID remain at the centre of empowering, person-centred research.

Conclusion

People with ID featured within this chapter represent the voices of many people who have experienced loss and bereavement and share common fundamental principles with everyone. According to Read (2011) people with ID have more similarities to us than differences from us. Throughout the bereavement process, with support we all have capacity to:

- embrace opportunities for choice, control and co-production

- utilise our social networks to promote active citizenship

- experience challenges leading to understanding and learning

- engage with conflict within bereavement leading to resolution and remembering.

Advocacy can play a pivotal role in supporting individuals with an ID throughout the continuum of loss and bereavement.

PART III
SPECIALIST CONTEXTS
AND CONSIDERATIONS

CHAPTER 12

Loss, the family and caring

Mike Gibbs

SUMMARY

Since the majority of people with an intellectual disability (PWID) live at home and not in professional care settings, the family will play a pivotal role in support generally but particularly through loss and change experiences. The family is often portrayed as the cornerstone of life: the central hub around which work, life and play evolve. Sometimes, when the equilibrium of the family is changed, the impact of this can be multifaceted and longstanding. Loss and change, particularly transitional loss, can affect the family equilibrium in many different ways.

This chapter begins by exploring the changing definitions and constitution of the family, identifying the changing shape of contemporary family life, and critically exploring the nature of transition (such as moving out of the family home, leaving school and going to work for the first time) and its prevailing impact on family members. When the family has a member who happens to have an intellectual disability (ID), such transitional losses may be similar or profoundly different, but will inevitably impact and influence all members of the family, but perhaps in differing ways.

Introduction: the changing face of the family

Loss never occurs in a vacuum but within a social context, and this context can often shape how survivors can accommodate their loss (Read 2008). Since the majority of PWID live at home and not in professional care settings, the role of the family will be crucial for ongoing, consistent support, not least maintaining a heritage and history. Much has been written about who and what the family is. Many of us talk of the traditional family as consisting of a married couple of the opposite sex with two children. This ideal may well have existed many years ago, however, it does not take into account the myriad of relationships frequented in contemporary cultures. Single sex relationships, step families, adopted children, children born through in-vitro systems, multi-generations living in the same household, cohabitation, widowed and divorced can all be described as being indicative of the family.

Many see the family as having close geographical connections, but with current social networking technology (including video calling, email, Skype and mobile phones) family members can be in different parts of the world, yet able to communicate effectively and maintain and develop their relationships. Today people are enjoying increased longevity and changing their value base ideas about marriage; some people are marrying several times during their life. Sexual behaviour is more widely tolerated outside the confines of marriage, but many adults still seem to uphold the sanctity of marriage and the concept of the family as being important. Should you be one of the many sole-livers, those that choose to live alone, then you are seen as not part of a family. There is no set definition of the family, yet there have been many attempts to develop one.

One of the problems in trying to define the family is that it is constantly changing. For example, Murdock examined a total of 250 differing societies across the world in order to help him identify the functions and structure of the family and eventually described the family as:

> A social group characterized by common residence, economic cooperation and reproduction. It contains adults of both sexes, at least two of whom maintain a socially approved sexual relationship, and one or more children, own or adopted, of the sexually cohabiting adults. (Murdock 1949, p.1)

In the 1950s this may have been an acceptable definition that reflected traditional practices. Today a number of facets of Murdock's definition need to be questioned. Why is there a need for children? Why does it have to have a heterosexual relationship? More recently, for research purposes, Farrell, Vande Vusse and Ocobock (2012) presented two very broad, relatively simplistic, terms to identify families: the *traditional family*, being one with married heterosexual people with their biological children, and the *non-traditional family* making up all the other combinations of family. Thereby, it is often difficult to encapsulate what we mean by the family.

For different people the family still means different things; but what the family does bring together is the idea of 'sharedness': shared values, beliefs and attitudes, no matter who constitutes the family. These shared attributes are based on the individual's role within the family, their life experiences and their experiences of family. Farrell *et al.* (2012) demonstrated very clearly that the family structure is dynamic and has changed significantly over the past four decades. In their study they attempted to discover if sociological theory and analysis methods have kept pace with the changing facets of the family. By reviewing four academic journals over a 17-year period they concluded that non-traditional families are not significantly represented in sociological journals and that the constant changing of family structures is significantly under represented. This demonstrates the complexities and transitional nature of the family. They recommended that clearer discussions of definitions of families should be utilised in family based studies.

The contemporary family

Viewing the family from a statistical perspective we can see a pattern to the changes taking place in family structures. According to the UK Office for National Statistics (ONS 2013) the number of live births outside marriage is increasing. In 2012, 47.5 per cent of children were born outside of marriage compared to 8.3 per cent in 1970. This is a clear indication that people's attitude to parenting and family construction is changing. The ONS also shows that marriage in a religious place is declining and so too are the number of marriages in civil places. This suggests that people's view of marriage is changing and thus has an effect of the constitution of the family. Cohabitation (where two people are not legally married) has doubled since 1996 and this makes cohabitation the fastest growing family type in the UK. The numbers of people choosing to live alone has also increased significantly. The redevelopment of multi-generational families, whilst not a new phenomenon, has reportedly increased by 30 per cent in the last decade. Clearly the literature demonstrates the changing shape and structure of the family, but the basic tenets remain, where shared values and support remain fundamentally important.

Families and people with an intellectual disability

In relation to families with a member with ID, it is very difficult to gain precise data and statistics which relate to these experiences. In England, the Learning Disabilities Observatory (LDO) published a report that compiled all publicly available information published by the government to give a concise summary. In the UK approximately 60per cent of people with ID live in the parental home (DH 2001b), although there are no definitive, accurate registers of PWID so we cannot verify the accuracy of these figures. However, the LDO estimate that there are 286,000 children and 905,000 adults with an ID living in England.

Even when the person with an ID lives away from the family in a professional care home environment, families continue to provide an important function, providing love, support, continuity and a sense of prevailing normality.

Loss and change

The concept of loss has been defined and introduced earlier in this book, however, in relation to the family it is worth considering what it means in this particular context. A key issue in the lives of PWID is that of transition, which can be seen as movement from one place or phase to another. In any structure of family life, transition is anticipated and expected, and usually accompanied by gains and losses. For example, the birth of children into a family sees changes in the way the parents face the new challenges of becoming a parent: how priorities shift and financial adjustments made. Adult children leaving home, going to work and developing relationships are all aspects of movement and transitions within the family. Growing older, retirement and eventual death are all part of the shifting fluidity of the family and most families are able to manage the challenges faced during these transitional times with support from each other.

Most of these transitions are seen as the norm, as anticipated positive aspects of family life as individuals mature and personal circumstances change and evolve. However, for the family who have a member with an ID, transition may require long term planning, adjustments and continuous support. Transitional loss can be seen as a significant change that can either (and sometimes include a combination of both) negatively or positively impact on individuals. Later in this chapter, this will be discussed in relation to parents and siblings. Transitional loss can involve external and internal factors. External factors include moving out of the family home, getting a job, starting a new relationship or relationship changes. In educational arenas the transition period when growing from a child to an adult is also parallel to moving from children's services to adult services and much has been reported in the literature about the complexities and anxieties of this. Internal factors include the person's self-worth and skill acquisition as (for example) moving from the family home to live independently can be fraught with new challenges, not least the range of skills needed.

As a parent, watching their child or young adult move out of the family home can bring conflicting thoughts and emotions as they question their child's ability, independence and the potential for crisis. For the parents it may stimulate thoughts about their own future life: what they might do with their time; the new freedom to organise holidays of their choice, being no longer constrained by their children as they were when they were still at home. Inherent to any transitional process, a person is likely to shape their own identity as they learn to adapt to new experiences. The sense of loss that may be felt may be similarly experienced by the individual and family members themselves. These experiences can be seen as a journey but sometimes anticipated journeys inadvertently change course, perhaps due to unexpected ill health or even death.

Anticipated loss itself may be difficult enough, but when transitions don't happen as expected or happen at differing stages in the family cycle, such difficulties can be compounded and the impact multifaceted. Take for example the following true family case study.

CASE STUDY: MRS JONES

In 1955, Mrs Jones was training to become a pharmacist, had been married to Bill for two years and during her final year of training had Andrew, who had Down syndrome. Mrs Jones stayed at home to look after Andrew and never did complete her training. Two years later she had another son. Over the forthcoming years Andrew was diagnosed with autism and in his late 20s he developed depression and anxiety. Having no speech as such made it difficult to communicate with Andrew but Mr and Mrs Jones were able to read his body language and day to day they managed to cope with the trials and tribulations of bringing up an adult son with severe intellectual disabilities. Their younger son left home at 18 to go to university and never came back to live in the family home but lived close by with his own growing family, offering help to his parents whenever he could. Family holidays were a thing of the past as Andrew could not cope with any change in routine; this also prevented any form of respite care. Sadly, Bill developed Alzheimer's disease and after several years of caring for him Mrs Jones reluctantly agreed for him to go in to a nursing home until he eventually died. Simultaneously, it was becoming increasingly difficult for her to cope with Andrew and so a plan was devised to help Andrew move to his own home at the age of 38. Today, Mrs Jones lives at home on her own, but has a new circle of friends, does voluntary work and spends her time visiting Andrew.

This true, typical case study demonstrates well how families learn to adapt to transition, the losses involved and their impact on everyone, the frequency and complexity of loss a family may experience and the impact that the losses have on individual members within the family. For a more detailed account of such experiences, see Chapter 17, which is written from a parent's perspective.

Effects of transitional loss

Most parents see having children as a positive, life-changing experience. They look forward to the birth of the child, making plans that include decisions about the decoration of the spare room to agreement over names and later projected lifestyles, what career their child might have and what sort of person they will be: all exciting dreams and flourishing plans. Yet for some these dreams and plans are shattered irrevocably when they are told of the news that their child has an ID. They lose those plans and have to make new and often challenging decisions that will affect their whole family for the rest of their lives. James (2011) suggests that parents can go through a range of transitional periods, the first being the diagnosis of an ID, which can take considerable time.

According to Boström, Broberg and Hwang (2009), receiving a diagnosis of an ID can be considered a loss or trauma by parents, but in their study they concluded that although parents experienced negative emotions in relation to the child and disability, mostly they described positive emotions which seemed to outweigh any negativity. Therefore it seems possible that although parents may grieve for the loss of their planned child, they do have other experiences that compensate for this.

A second period of transition identified by James is the school age of their child, either going to a special school, or moving between schools. For many parents, the start of the school career brings about many changes as new friendships develop, routines change and the parents' own careers maybe put on hold or rekindled. When children start to attend school these are anticipated transitional movements within the family cycle. For the family of the child with an ID, the transition from child to adult life and from children's services to adult services can be equally traumatic where parents experience loss. Where children will be moving from close knit circles of support, services and friends into a different world, many families may feel lost and forgotten during this period.

Bhaumik *et al.* (2011) identified the need for services to provide long-term support and to work in a multidisciplinary approach for the benefit of families during the transition period between education and adult services. Although the legal age of adulthood in the UK is 18, many services do not provide support until 19, and those school leavers aged 16 to 18 often fall outside services. The loss of educational support can have a major impact on families. James (2011) also highlights the transition process when the person with ID moves away from the family home, potentially causing a range of anxieties. The final two transitional periods that a family experiences are of health-related problems (and the challenges faced when entering healthcare services) and finally death.

It is natural for a parent to believe that their children will outlive them, however, it is well recognised that PWID die at a younger age than the general population (Emerson *et al.* 2013). Therefore, parents could experience the loss of their children and Part I of this book explores the sensitive nature of grief work and its impact.

Many parents will take the bold (but practical) step to imagine future plans. When a plan for the future is developed it helps to anticipate transition much better, appeasing any loss created by the future transition. Transition planning should be based on multi agency care which is delivered in a timely fashion to support both the person with ID and their family. Bhaumik *et al.* (2011) identified many unmet needs for both health and social care which led to exacerbating the loss during transition for carers. Taggart *et al.* (2012) examined ageing carers' preferences for future care and support systems, suggesting that the majority of older carers preferred the person to stay in their own home with either family and/or paid staff to support their care. This form of future planning helps to avoid or reduce any loss experienced by the remaining family members. Taggart *et al.* (2012) concluded that services needed to be prepared to support parents and sibling carers to proactively plan for the future.

The relationship that parents have with their sibling is often one of the longest relationships they will ever have. In a typical sibling relationship there is continuous activity around closeness, frequency of contact, rivalry and companionship; all of these are affected by age, gender and birth order. There is a wealth of literature that discusses the quality of this sibling relationship yet there is limited research on the loss or perceived loss that siblings experience when they have a brother or sister with an ID. Although siblings recognise their life could be different if their brother or sister wasn't disabled, their perceptions are not of loss but more of differentness. Indeed, studies of siblings of people with ID are not new, and Cleveland and Miller (1977) demonstrated that the experience of having a brother or sister with an ID can indeed be positive. This study focused on adults, and although some siblings acknowledge that they missed out occasionally they did not see this as a major impact on their life. In a more recent study Doody *et al.* (2010) explored the adult sibling relationship and found that adults who have siblings with an ID tended to live physically closer and saw their siblings more frequently. However, they concluded that the adult sibling relationship is not significantly different whether there is a person with intellectual disability in the relationship or not. In contrast to this Petalas *et al.* (2012) suggest that siblings of children with autism may find it difficult to adjust to stress at home.

In their review of 23 papers spanning 40 years, Heller and Arnold (2010) concluded that there is a wide range of effects of ID on siblings. Some of these research papers reported that having a brother or sister with ID was seen as a positive experience whereas others concluded the opposite and identified depressive type symptoms in the non-disabled sibling. Further studies in the review clearly identified that some non-disabled siblings expected to become the main carer at some time in their life. More recently, in relation to children, Moyson and Roeyers (2012) identified that often, young siblings refer to a discrepancy between what they *can* do as a sibling with the brother or sister with intellectual disabilities and what they would *like* to do. These children were seen to make adjustments to their expectations. If this were to be an interpretation of transitional loss then it is clear that in Moyson and Roeyers' (2012) study the children were discussing loss: loss of a relationship and loss of having to make adjustments to something that might have been different if their sibling had not got ID. However, no studies in Hellar and Arnold's review discussed the concept of loss, which may reflect how the review was conducted or the way experiences of the sibling relationship and consequences were described.

When older parents die siblings are usually seen as the next of kin. Many parents assume that the non-disabled sibling will continue the caring role after the parent dies. Davys, Mitchell and Haigh (2011) show that many factors appear to affect the sibling's experience and uptake of future role of carer, including gender, life stage, circumstances and level of disability of their sibling, and relationships between family members. However Benderix and Sivberg (2007) report that older siblings often reported feelings of sorrow that they were unlikely to experience an ordinary life. Siblings also experience a sense of responsibility and often become a main carer to their sibling. Siblings of PWID often experience problems at school by being teased because of their disabled brother or sister and some siblings often feel vulnerable because of aggression from the disabled sibling.

Overall the literature does suggest that having a disabled sibling does affect the life course of the non-disabled sibling, for example Taylor *et al.* (2008) suggests that some non-disabled siblings are less emotionally attached to their disabled sibling. The array of evidence does strongly imply that siblings at any age do experience transitional loss, but it is how they interpret their own circumstances that dictates whether or not it is conceptualised as a loss.

Conclusion

In conversation, we often refer to our family and make assumptions that whoever we are talking to understands the concept of the family. Yet we only have to peel back the layers of our own family to appreciate the complexity of the family system – that each family is dynamic and different – and it is this difference which enables them to deal with the losses and changes in myriad of ways. Help and support are often found within the family but outside sources from a range of levels can ease the experience of loss. Within the limitations of this text, we can see that the literature can help to unpack the complexities of dealing with loss and change in the family. However, it is still the individual members of the family that have to create their own strategies to deal with the loss and changes that having a family member with intellectual disability brings to them.

CHAPTER 13

Loss and people with autism

Rachel Forrester-Jones

*Dedicated to those people who have an Autistic
Spectrum Condition (ASC)*

SUMMARY

People within the autistic spectrum have a range of differing needs and
complex communication challenges. The aims of this chapter are to
define what constitutes as the autistic spectrum, describe associated
key characteristics of such conditions and explore how loss can be
sensitively supported when individuals have specific communication
and cognitive impairments and are diagnosed with an autistic spectrum
condition (ASC).

What is autism?

Autism is commonly regarded as a lifelong developmental condition
that affects how a person makes sense of the world around them
and how they socially interact with other people. Whilst all people
with autism may share certain social difficulties, each individual
will experience autism in different ways, which is why it is termed a
'spectrum' condition (the National Autistic Society UK (NAS) 2013).
Some people with an ASC are highly intelligent (and classified as
having Asperger's Syndrome; Asperger 1944). They may be able to
live independently while others may have accompanying intellectual
disabilities and need lifelong specialist support. People with an ASC
may also experience over- (or under-) sensitivity to sounds, tastes,
smells, light, colours or textures (NAS 2013).

Prevalence

Worldwide prevalence of ASC is estimated to be about 6 per 1000 children (Centers for Disease Control and Prevention 2012). A systematic review of prevalence studies from 1966 to 2004 (Williams, Higgins and Brayne 2006) has estimated that the global figure of ASC has increased over time and varies markedly with geographic location, probably due to variations in diagnostic criteria and age of individuals diagnosed. It is thought that around 1.1 per cent of the population (about 695,000 people) in the UK may have an ASC (NAS 2013). Prevalence of ASCs has been found to be higher in males than females (ratio of 4:1) hence the condition being labelled as a 'male brain' phenomena (Baron-Cohen 2008).

Diagnosis

An ASC is generally classified and diagnosed in terms of 'deficits' or 'impaired' behaviour traits, first defined as the 'Triad of Impairments' (Wing 1981; Wing and Gould 1979; Wing, Gould and Gillberg 2011) which included the following:

- **impaired social interaction** or deficits in non-verbal signs of interest in (and pleasure from) being with another person (e.g. making eye-contact; responding to smiles or affectionate physical contact such as hugging)

- **impaired communication** or an inability to 'converse' verbally (Lord and Bailey 2002) or non-verbally with another person, e.g. sharing ideas and interests in a meaningful way; individuals may also interpret language literally

- **impaired social imagination** or an inability to consider the consequences of one's own actions for oneself and for other people. Also known as 'mind blindness theory' (Baron-Cohen 2008), the person is unable to 'mind read' or see/pick up on other people's possible thoughts and feelings, for example to understand that the other person, whose facial expression is sad, might be upset. An associated deficit is in understanding a situation from another person's point of view sometimes known as false belief, or inflexibility of thought (Baron-Cohen 2008; Hill 2004).

The Diagnostic Interview for Social and Communication Disorders (DISCO) (Wing *et al.* 2002) is regularly used to assess impaired behaviours. Recent controversy has surrounded the International Classification of Disorders (IDC-10) (WHO 2010) and updated Diagnostic and Statistical Manual of Mental Disorders (DSM-5) (APA 2012) classification of ASCs since they limit ASCs to two criteria of symptoms: social communication/interaction and restricted and repetitive behaviours. Lord and Jones (2012) suggest that communication as a main diagnostic symptom is unreliable since not all people with an ASC have difficulties with communication. Furthermore, arguably, tendencies to repetitive behaviour patterns such as: adoption of ritualistic and rigid regimes (e.g. always frequenting a particular café at a particular time or putting on clothes in a particular order); compulsive behaviours (e.g. washing of hands or pacing up and down); and obsessive interests (e.g. in topics such as food, trains, or particular animals) are actually coping mechanisms used by people with an ASC to relieve underlying anxieties of their impairments (such as inflexibility of thought) rather than actual impairments in themselves (Forrester-Jones and Broadhurst 2007).

What causes ASCs?

The question of what causes ASCs also continues to court controversy and confusion. Theories from bad parenting (Tinbergen and Tinbergen 1986) to environmental factors such as chemicals (Landrigan 2010) and infant vaccines (Wakefield *et al.* 1998, later retracted by The Editors in *The Lancet*, 2010) have been found to be lacking in scientific rigour (Burgess, Burgess and Leask 2006). Rather, it is generally thought that ASCs may be the consequence of: a hereditary brain disorder, for example, damage to the frontal lobe, particularly the pre-frontal cortex in the brain (Baron-Cohen 2008); or/and a failed network connection in the brain (Leslie and Roth 1993; Baron-Cohen 2008); an 'autism gene' (Abrahams and Geschwind 2008); birth trauma, or disease (Frith 2001).

Whilst no one theory of the aetiology of ASCs has been proven conclusively (Muhle, Trentacoste and Rapin 2004), the central idea is that the brain of someone with an ASC functions differently from that of a neuro-typical (NT) person (i.e. someone without an ASC) to the extent that a person with an ASC receives and processes information differently, and so thinks in an alternative way to an NT person. This explains why a person with an ASC may naturally communicate, act and react in ways which appear altogether different (and odd) from an NT person (Forrester-Jones and Broadhurst 2007). Whilst it is useful to have a diagnosis of an ASC (for gaining appropriate social and financial support as much as anything else), we must be careful not to negatively socially construct ASCs in such a way as to ignore the additional abilities, gifts and levels of intelligence which are usually present in each individual with an ASC.

Experiencing an ASC

The following case study illustrates how someone with an ASC experiences their social interactions with others. I met John whilst I was researching the social support networks of adults who had been moved from institutions to community care residences under the National Health Service Act (2006). He gave his written consent for this case study to be used to illustrate some of the problems people 'like him' can have in negotiating social situations. I also talked to a member of staff who had known John for about 25 years, and I read his case history file. To maintain confidentiality, John is a pseudonym.

CASE STUDY: JOHN

John is 58 years old and has lived in a community care home for about 20 years. He previously lived in an intellectual disability hospital. About ten years ago he was diagnosed with having an IQ of just above 70 and an ASC. It is believed that his dependency on staff for support with daily living skills is a result of institutionalisation rather than anything else. Although John lives with three other people in a supported living environment, he does not generally get on with them (or the staff). This may be because John is poorly matched in terms of his living arrangements (since the other residents have severe intellectual disabilities and one resident is physically disabled in addition) but mostly, difficulties arise due to John's behaviour associated with his ASC.

John has an interest in trains and death (but more about 'death' later). His interest presents itself as more than a hobby; rather the topic of trains pervades his conversations to the extent that he presents as being 'locked into' the subject. Other people say he is 'obsessed' with trains. Apart from a few pictures of trains in his bedroom and some train timetables, John does not have a wide knowledge base about trains –

his obsession is more about 'going to visit the train station'. John seems unaware that his obsession with 'train stations' is boring to others. He does not easily pick up on other people rolling their eyes or grimacing when he is talking about trains. An inability to 'read' other people's body language and facial expressions can be disastrous, especially for first encounter meetings when it is important to show interest in the other person. Consequently, although staff have done some work to facilitate the development of John's social networks by taking him to local pubs and other social gatherings, John has few friends.

John also struggles to focus on more than one thing, or process more than one piece of information at a time, so that the speed of processing a lot of information may be slow. Because of this difficulty, John can miss information, or not gain the full picture of what is going on in a social situation. For example, during meal times, John is only able to focus on the words one person is saying to him about (for example) choices of food, and seemingly disregards any other conversation happening in the room or directed at him. He also has a tendency to engage in echolalia, that is, he repeats words or phrases (without seemingly fully understanding them). So, in response to the question 'do you want mushy peas with your fish and chips?' John will repeat 'mushy peas'. John also engages in pronoun reversal, referring to himself in the third person, saying 'he/it/John' rather than 'I' and 'me', for example, 'John has mushy peas'. This can lead to confusions within conversations (Bradshaw 2013a) and conversational break down, especially if there is a need to delve deeper into the phrase or the phrase has a double entendre. John often fails to understand or 'get' jokes (Attwood 2006; Bogdashina 2005).

Finally, John has a tendency to literal understanding: interpreting language at 'face value'. At one particular social occasion, John sat all evening with his coat on, refusing to take it off. This was because the host had asked him 'can I take your coat?' John had interpreted this as the host wanting to keep his coat for ever. When other people are around John, they can feel uncomfortable and find him tiring to be with.

Loss

Previous conceived wisdom that a lack of expressed emotion and pain exhibited by people with an ASC reflected an absence of felt loss or care and compassion, has recently been rejected. Rather, it is now recognised that people with an ASC experience loss in similar ways to people without an ASC (Long 2005), expressing a mixture of sadness, anger, anxiety, confusion and pain (Harper and Wadsworth 1993), synonymous with Kübler-Ross's (1970) five stages of grief. Nevertheless, there has been a general deficit in the way in which people with ASC have been caringly supported through loss. In *Autism and Loss* (2007), Forrester-Jones and Broadhurst provide exercises to help people with ASCs resolve particular losses, including social relationships, home and possessions, role and identity, health and wellbeing and death. Below, in revisiting the case study of John again, I outline ways in which people with ASCs may be supported following loss through death, though it should be remembered that support for each person with an ASC who is experiencing loss needs to be individualised according to their specific difficulties.

CASE STUDY: JOHN, CONTINUED

Experiencing loss

John (like many people with an ASC), finds it difficult to develop and maintain social relationships, largely because of his communication/social interaction difficulties outlined previously. Often, his behaviour is not understood or is interpreted negatively by prospective friends so he is quickly ruled out of social networks (Bauminger and Shulman 2003). Although John says he wants friendships, he is generally very lonely, trapped in his small, high density social network in which everyone is connected in some way, offering little privacy or dignity (Forrester-Jones and Broadhurst 2007). Since social relationships are a main component to the quality of our lives (Cummins and Lau 2003) the loss of a particular network member (through relationship breakdown, the person moving away or death) can therefore be catastrophic for someone who only has a few relationships.

John lost both of his elderly parents in quick succession during his early 30s. He attended their funerals, and was later taken to their double grave on one occasion. Religious and cultural rituals such as birthdays, weddings and funerals provide legitimate outlets for the outward expression of emotion as well as investing 'life milestones' such as death with meaning when it is difficult to verbalise (Blackman 2003; Forrester-Jones and Broadhurst 2007; Martison, Deck and Adams 1992). Accessibility to these rituals and explanations of them can help reduce fear and anxiety in the person with an ASC (Forrester-Jones 2013; Todd and Read 2011). Whilst John was taken to his parents' funerals, I was told that he had only a limited understanding of the meaning of the funeral rituals. This may account for why John has a tendency to talk incessantly about 'coffins going into the ground'.

John's parents used to visit him each week in hospital and their deaths meant that he no longer had any visitors; his two brothers never visited him. In effect, John therefore suffered a 'double loss'. Unsupported and unresolved grief can lead to clinical depression and associated behaviours such as phobias, obsessions and increased resistance to change. John reacted to his loss by talking continuously about graves as well as how much he 'hates' his family/brothers. This has carried on for over 20 years and is his other obsessional topic of conversation. Unfortunately, instead of being shown compassion for his loss, he was told by one of the male hospital nurses that 'big boys don't cry'.

Staff try to enthuse happiness in John by jollying him along. However, such so called 'support' should be avoided. Checking on a person's desire for knowledge about what has happened to the person and using open-ended questions such as 'How do you feel?' rather than 'Do you feel ok?' will provide the person with an ASC with more conversational power (and possibly avoid 'perseveration' or repeated phrases or topics of conversation that might seem at odds with the situation) as well as enabling the supporter to continuously gauge the appropriateness of talking about the situation (Forrester-Jones and Broadhurst 2007). Unfortunately, John's fixation on graves has been falsely interpreted by some members of staff as inappropriate and even callous (Howlin 2004). Since his grief response has been elongated in time, it may be that those around him find it difficult to understand what is really bothering him.

Helping John to resolve his losses

Acknowledging the lost relationship and associated difficulties is very important. If the person with an ASC is verbally able, like John, then talking about the 'lost' person and the gap they have left in the individual's social world can help. The 'lost' person may have provided more than companionship or support. For John, they enabled him to fulfil a particular role such as 'son'. If the person is ill and death is likely, involving and preparing the person with an ASC by explaining what is occurring (e.g. why the person or pet is having medical/veterinary treatment; why they look different) will help dampen anxiety and subsequent behaviour that may be of a challenging nature. Unfortunately for John, although his parents both died of cancer, this disease was not explained to him, and he was very shocked by their deaths. Since John has difficulties with literal understanding of words, then specific terms (e.g. 'fatally ill', 'dying' as opposed to 'poorly', 'unwell' or 'sick') should have been used whilst terms such as 'gone to sleep' (instead of 'died') should have been avoided. At the time I was visiting John, staff were still using such euphemisms. Usual terms for the dying or dead person should also be used (e.g. 'Mummy', in John's case, since this is how he referred to his mother). Unfortunately for John, few (if any) of the above caring considerations were offered which may explain some of his behaviours.

For those people with ASC who, unlike John, do not use language, augmentative and alternative communication (AAC) approaches (e.g. objects, gestures, symbols, voice output communication devices and signs) may be useful, so long as they are used consistently. For example, different faces showing various emotions may be used to ascertain fluctuating feelings of someone with a verbal communication difficulty (Forrester-Jones and Broadhurst 2007). Unfortunately, sometimes caregivers do not fully understand the benefits of AAC to the person with an ASC (Bradshaw 2013b; Lewer and Harding 2013) leading to all kinds of additional issues which are preventable. In order to maximise autonomy of people with limited verbal communication skills, carers should start from the premise that everyone can communicate and make their own decisions given sufficient and appropriate support (Mental Capacity Act 2005). Adequate time for processing responses to information, communicating at a pace and rhythm appropriate to the person's abilities, and a distraction-free environment in which interruptions and power differentials are minimised are crucial when communicating about loss with someone with an ASC (Forrester-Jones and Broadhurst 2007; Hegge 2012). Responding immediately to questions with honest, straightforward answers in terms that the person is most likely to understand is also crucial.

Commemorating events such as anniversary days by developing a ritual (e.g. putting flowers on a grave or writing down someone's birthday in a diary) can provide the person with an ASC with a specific time to remember the person and help manage obsessive behaviours. Emotions such as anger should not be repressed but understood as natural. Gathering information to produce a 'life story' (Forrester-Jones and Broadhurst 2007) of the person who has gone away – using photographs, videos, pictures of things that the 'lost' person liked, songs they enjoyed listening to or songs that are reminders of them, as well as other mementoes – and placing them in a box file or book (Allison 2001) creates something to be used to remember the individual in a structured way and at a particular time. The Social Network Guide (SNG) which enables an individual to chart their social support network (i.e. the people they know and what support each person provides) (Forrester-Jones and Broadhurst 2007) can be used positively to help the person with an ASC think about developing further relationships (and the SNG can be repeated to chart network changes).

Conclusion

Whilst the case study of John may have made for difficult reading, I hope that the sharing of his lived experience of both ASC and loss may help to prevent similar situations for other people with ASCs. Overwhelmingly, my feelings about John were that although staff who had been in his life had been caring, they simply did not understand him and his behaviour, and what had been missing from his life were compassionate responses to his ongoing loss.

Chapter 14

Loss in the secure environment

Ben Hobson, Sue Read and Helena Priest

SUMMARY

The losses that are associated with living in restricted environments are likely to be diverse and vast, yet there is limited research that explores the broad loss experience of people with an intellectual disability (PWID) living in secure environments. This chapter aims to describe the nature of the secure service; to detail the grounded theory that emerged from the lived experiences of people with an intellectual disability (ID) living in a low secure service; to discuss the theoretical implications and identify how service users and carers can be supported and empowered to explore loss.

Introduction: the nature of the secure environment

Secure environments have the dual purpose of providing treatment to patients while protecting the public, or the patient themselves, from their own damaging behaviour (DH 2010). In the United Kingdom (UK), patients are detained under the Mental Health Act (1983) at secure hospitals provided according to three levels of security: high security, which confines patients who pose a serious and immediate danger or have absconded in lower levels of security; medium security, for patients who present a serious but less immediate danger to others; and low security, for patients who pose a less serious danger to others with security measures to impede rather than completely prevent absconding (Crichton 2009). However, in reality low secure settings are generally poorly researched and defined (Yacoub 2010), particularly for people with an ID.

People with an ID may often be over-represented in the criminal justice system (Holland, Clare and Mukhopudhyay 2002). Those admitted to low secure settings are likely to have mild or moderate intellectual disabilities and another diagnosis (such as autism or schizophrenia), are likely to be referred from acute services and are likely to be detained under the Mental Health Act (1983) or to have 'stepped down' from medium security (Yacoub 2010).

In low secure environments, patients are required to have leave (under Section 17 of the Mental Health Act 1983) in order to access the community based on their current risk, as decided by a multidisciplinary team and signed by the Responsible Clinician. Patients' routines will consist of psychological, occupational and speech and language therapy as well as recreational time when the patient can choose within the confines of the environment. Patients' families are allowed to visit; however, for patients to visit their families they require Section 17 leave and appropriate funding or availability of staff. There is little research on the length of stay or outcomes for people with ID in low secure environments.

Loss in the secure environment: a vicious circle

Loss is widely acknowledged as a potential explanation for behavioural and mental health problems for people with intellectual disabilities (Hollins and Esterhuyzen 1997; O'Hara and Sperlinger 1997; Dodd *et al.* 2005), and having an ID itself is recognised as a significant predictor of mental health problems following bereavement (Bonell-Pascual *et al.* 1999). People with IDs who live in secure environments are more likely to have mental health problems than those who do not (Gore and Dawson 2009; Hobson and Rose 2008), and this is compounded by the fact that they often experience diverse losses throughout their lives (Gore and Dawson 2009; Isherwood *et al.* 2007). When losses go unacknowledged and unsupported, self-harm and challenging behaviour can sometimes result (Blackman 2003; Brown and Beail 2009). This can in turn lead to detention in secure settings, creating a vicious cycle of dependency and disenfranchisement.

Losses experienced by people with ID in secure settings

Machin's (2009) broad definition of loss includes losses due to broken relationships, illness, disability, disappointment and death which are all are relevant to this population. While loss due to bereavement is an important issue, there are likely to be additional losses experienced in the secure context, often perceived as multiple and successive (Elliott 2005). These might include loss of freedom from being detained, being separated from important relationships (Schuengel and van Ijzendoorn 2001), emotional trauma and loss of the ideal self (Isherwood *et al.* 2007). It seems important, then, to consider the broader concept of loss as it is experienced by people with ID who live in secure environments; how loss may have affected them throughout their life course; and how it might continue to affect their day-to-day experience. To this end, we designed and conducted a grounded theory study (Hobson 2012) to generate a framework about the loss experiences of PWID in a low secure environment. The ultimate aim of undertaking this study was to understand the nature and impact of these losses so that we could identify recommendations for future practice in secure settings.

Exploring the lived experience of loss

Consultation with PWID in the research process can help them to feel more empowered and valued (Read and Corcoran 2009; Read *et al.* 2013). To develop interview questions, check the accessibility of information and add to the credibility of the information produced (Chiovitti and Piran 2003), a focus group was conducted with in-patients at a low secure hospital in England. Participants suggested adding questions about having the opportunity to talk about loss and what people had learnt from loss. They also recommended using scenarios to make questions clear, using different coloured paper and using pictures to support understanding. These suggestions were adopted and an interview schedule devised. Questions included asking participants to describe their experiences of loss, if loss was related to offending and what had been learnt from loss. Further questions were developed as the grounded theory emerged in accordance with the methodology.

Eight individual interviews were then conducted, with participants encouraged to bring along any items that had personal meaning regarding loss. As grounded theory is concerned with 'lived experiences' (Charmaz 2006), individual vignettes which briefly describe some of the participants' experiences are presented below, to situate the data in the context of participants' lives (all names are pseudonyms and some details have been changed to protect anonymity).

CASE STUDY: PARTICIPANTS' EXPERIENCES OF LOSS

Tom, in his 30s, had previously lived in a medium secure service. He described not being able to see his family and pet dogs as losses for him.

Jim, in his 30s, said that he found losing his respect for himself and other people hard and that this had contributed to being put in prison. He said that he had recently experienced some gains, including respect for himself and other people.

Julie, in her 20s, described being locked up as a teenager in children's homes and secure units. She said that she had been abused as a child and had 'lost her childhood'.

Beth, in her 40s, said her biggest loss was her child who had been removed from her care. Following the adoption of her child by another family, she committed her index offence. She still thinks of her child often, especially on important anniversaries.

Carol, in her 30s, was removed from her family as a child and has lived most of her life in a secure environment. She talked about the loss of her step-father and not being able to attend his funeral.

Chris, in his 20s, talked about the loss of his mother and how attempting to deal with his grief led to increased alcohol and substance misuse. He was keen to do some bereavement work, but did not wish to do so while living in a secure environment.

Amy, in her 20s, had been in secure environments and children's homes since her teens. She said she had been experiencing flashbacks and hearing voices from a previous trauma which led to her getting into trouble. She said going to prison meant she had lost 'everything', but the low secure hospital was better as she had more freedom.

Robert, in his 20s, had been in a medium secure hospital and community homes both as an adult and a child. He said that he had been raped a number of times throughout his life and felt like taking his own life. He missed his mum but was able to talk to her on the telephone.

Data analysis revealed a series of critical interactions, primarily between the key categories of loss, being heard and identity, with the process of making sense interacting between each category, as illustrated in Figure 14.1. From this diagram, 'making sense' was a key process. How individuals made sense of their loss was influenced by how they constructed the meaning of loss based on who they were (their identity). In turn, their identity was affected by how they made sense of the loss and also by whether or not they felt 'heard'. The benefits of being heard changed how they constructed loss. The other processes (storytelling, getting help, control and dealing with loss) were active throughout; for example, making sense was part of dealing with loss and changed both the meaning of loss and identity. Each of these elements of the theory are now considered and illustrated below.

Figure 14.1 The grounded theory of loss in a low secure environment

Experiencing loss

Loss was experienced in a range of different ways. It was described as something that profoundly affected participants' lives, shaping who they were, their identity and how they thought of the future. Loss included not only bereavement, but also losing out on everyday experiences from being in a secure environment as well as the effects of abuse and trauma in early life. Loss was an everyday occurrence as well as an historical fact from the past; participants continued to experience loss from being in a secure environment and from attempting to deal with previous losses. Loss had a great impact on how people viewed themselves and the world around them. Chris said that what he had learnt from bereavement was that: 'Um, life's too short…like my dad could be alive today, tonight, could be dead tomorrow. That's how quick life can change.' Loss, bereavement and being abused had an impact on the individual's identity and caused them distress, which sometimes resulted in challenging or offending behaviour.

Being heard

The impact of loss was such that being heard was an important process for participants. Being heard by someone else, being able to 'get things off one's chest' was seen as helpful. Participants appeared to value the opportunity and the experience of talking about loss, especially to a person not employed in the organisation, who would keep the information confidential and not use the information for any other purpose, as Chris explained: 'It's…about losing family members or friends…I'm not really open talking about it, um, I want to get it out but I need to talk to someone like yourself or someone who doesn't know me.' However, participants found being heard a difficult process. Not only was it emotionally upsetting to talk about loss but also the participants themselves felt they weren't being heard by others. Staff were sometimes unable to recognise or acknowledge losses, may have felt ill-prepared or uncomfortable talking about such issues, may not have had the time to talk about them or may not have felt it was part of their job role.

Coping with loss

Not being heard often led to participants trying to deal with loss on their own in inappropriate ways or in ways that were helpful only in the short term, such as self-harming, using drugs or alcohol or becoming physically aggressive. However, they were able to recognise this and wished to learn alternative ways of coping, despite the difficulties of dealing with loss in a setting which may have emphasised behaviour rather than dealing with distress.

Control

Participants described having little control over many things, and talked about experiencing loss of previously-held controls. Beth spoke of losing her access to the kitchen to make herself a drink: 'I made myself a hot drink and then the work top was a bit wet...and then [member of staff] said that night for me not to go in after then...and staff made me my drink then.' Participants talked about controlling their own feelings and behaviour, and using strategies to get control in an environment where they had limited control. Some participants tried to regain a sense of control through self-harm or aggressive behaviour, although this often resulted in them having less control as staff sought to manage their behaviour. Being controlled by others or losing control due to loss or bereavement had a disempowering, and ultimately disenfranchising, effect.

Getting help

Participants felt that getting help from staff was sometimes difficult due to the professional nature of the relationship. As Robert stated: 'But they're [staff] here to do a job and clients are here as friends. And staff can't be friends, they're here for the job.' As patients were routinely told not to discuss their offences, they found it difficult to talk to other patients as they could not trust them fully or recognise that they had their own difficulties. Getting help appeared to be problematic before entering the secure environment and led to some participants' offences. They saw being in secure care as part of being helped, and this was especially true of the female participants. As Carol commented, 'the judge said I don't want this young person in prison anymore, I want her in a hospital because she's not a psychopath, she's gone through trauma, they said I was traumatised.' In contrast, male participants seemed to take a more matter-of-fact approach to getting help, typically seeing it as more about solving a problem and less about dealing with emotional distress, as Chris noted 'Er, I don't really feel anything about myself, I don't feel ill or nothing. I don't feel like mentally ill. I just think I've had problems in the past and I'm dealing with them now.'

Storytelling

Telling the story of loss was an important part of the process of being heard. Participants told stories of their losses, re-living their experiences. Carol described her step-father's death in detail: 'the ambulance crew came and started resuscitating him but there was no response and [they] started shocking him...and he didn't comply to the shock so they said they're going to stop now, so they said time of death.' Storytelling was not simply about telling the story; it was about being heard and having a witness to their loss and pain.

Making sense

One function of being heard was to try to make sense of experiences. Participants sometimes struggled to understand the circumstances surrounding their losses and this made it difficult to deal with them, as Carol described: 'I don't understand why people die and how they die, I don't understand. I keep asking and asking and asking why people pass away, how people, you know...like [member of staff] says people have different illnesses.' Making sense of the loss was often dependent on other people giving an explanation, and when this happened it increased the trust between participants and members of staff. However, when explanations were not given or information was withheld due to the disempowering nature of the secure environment, patients felt 'left in the dark' and the relationship between patient and staff suffered. Some participants blamed themselves in order to make sense of their experiences and lacked the knowledge to understand the nature of loss and its potential prevailing impact.

Coping styles

How participants dealt with loss and the ways in which they sought to gain control was mediated by individual coping styles and gender, as Carol concurred: 'They [men]...fight more than women don't they... So you get more self-harmers as women than self-harmers as men.' Differences in ways of coping were more apparent when individuals attempted to deal with their loss on their own. The experience of talking about loss was helpful for all participants, irrespective of what they had done or how well they had previously coped.

Discussion and implications

Participants reported finding being able to talk about loss in the research as beneficial so further clinical work regarding loss may also be beneficial. Participants had suffered a range of losses, such as broken/damaged relationships, missing out on experiences and bereavement, which suggests a broad perspective on loss needs to be taken (Machin 2009). 'Being heard' was the main task for participants in the context of disempowerment and loss of control, and helped them make sense of their loss. Loss had an impact on, and was influenced by, how participants viewed themselves, others and the world. Worden (2010) highlights a number of mediators of mourning, including social variables, which may interfere with completing the grief tasks. Dealing with loss is a social process and it can be helpful for people to support and reinforce each others' reactions (Worden 2009). It may be that the participants' need to be heard was in contrast to their experience of having little social support and few opportunities to discuss losses, thus socially negated losses led to disenfranchised grief (Worden 2001; 2009).

Corr (2002) argues that mourning can be disenfranchised when loss rituals are dismissed or discouraged. Similar to other detained populations (Hendry 2009), participants in this study reported being unable to attend funerals of loved ones as they were detained in hospital or prison. It is worth noting, however, that while participants commented on identifiable rituals associated with bereavement, no other such rituals were identified for other losses (for example, having a child removed or abstract losses such as freedom, future, childhood or adulthood). The process of making sense of loss found in the current study complements existing theories of loss and bereavement. Making sense of loss is the key task in adjusting to a world without the deceased person (Worden 2009), and meaning-making and reconstruction are the key processes that enable individuals to reconstruct a life following loss (Neimeyer 2000).

A clear implication of this study's findings is the importance of therapeutic work around loss with people with ID in a low secure environment, whether this is loss following bereavement or any of the broader losses as outline by Machin (2009) and additional losses associated specifically with being detained in a secure hospital. Blackman (2002) and Watters, Dowling, Hubert and Hollins (2003), Read and

Bowler (2007), McKenzie and Wright (2012) provide examples of how such therapeutic work could be undertaken.

Conclusion

A thoughtful and compassionate approach to working with this client group in this setting is required, which acknowledges the losses experienced throughout life and from being detained, even at the initial assessment stage. Hence, a further implication is considering where loss fits within the ethos and discourses of secure services, and promoting that discourse in a meaningful way. Supporting someone with loss requires sensitivity and compassion (Grey 2010; Machin 2009; Worden 2010). While some discourses in secure care may promote people as victims requiring treatment, there may also be consideration of the dangerousness of individuals and the need for security (Inglis and Dale 2011). Similarly, the effects of dealing with aggressive, violent behaviour and administering physical restraint may leave care staff with negative feelings towards an individual (Howard, Rose and Levenson 2009; Sequeira and Halstead 2002). Consequently it may be difficult for care staff to acknowledge, empathise and be compassionate about someone's loss if they are also dealing with negative emotions towards that person. Developing a discourse with care staff through reflective groups, supervision or team meetings that acknowledge those difficulties and tensions may allow for the person to be heard within the secure environment. However, in this study, not all reported experiences were negative; participants were not completely isolated and did access support from care staff, other professionals and fellow patients. Creative approaches to self-expression can help alleviate distress and produce tangible outcomes (such a drawings, pictures, storytelling or poetry). For those individuals who need specific help and support with their loss, external agencies and independent counsellors can offer that 'safe space' for cathartic conversations.

CHAPTER 15

Supporting children and young people with an intellectual disability and life-limiting conditions

Erica Brown

SUMMARY

A significant proportion of children diagnosed with a life-limiting condition also have an intellectual disability (ID). The aims of this chapter are to explore the meaning and understanding of loss that children and young people hold, to explore a holistic approach to caring with compassion, and to identify good practice initiatives (particularly around communication) within this specific caring context.

Introduction

Amongst the most traumatic events a child's family can experience is when their child's life is threatened. Children are not supposed to die, but they do. Diagnosis of a life-limiting or life-threatening health condition is a turning point for families; their world will never be the same again.

Children's palliative care aims to meet the holistic needs of the child and their family. Improvements in technology and medicine mean that children with life-threatening or life-limiting conditions are surviving longer (Hewitt-Taylor 2005; Kirk 2008) resulting in many children with a diagnosis of a life-limiting or life-threatening condition accessing palliative care services for many years.

Reported figures for the numbers of children in the United Kingdom (UK) who have a diagnosis of a life-threatening or life-limiting condition vary enormously. Notwithstanding, a study by University of Leeds (Fraser *et al.* 2011) estimated the number of children with life-limiting conditions in the UK to be approximately 40,000. Many such children and young people also have IDs and research indicates that the needs of this group are unique (Help the Hospices 2012; Todd 2004). There is almost universal acceptance that professionals should take into account the views of the children and young people who access services. However, the views of this group are often neglected in favour of seeking the views of professionals, carers and families (Franklin and Osbourne 2009; Harcourt, Perry and Waller 2011; Percy-Smith and Thomas 2010). Sparse literature has usually focused on involving children and young people with complex needs in their care, and in particular those aged 16 years and over (Dockrell and Caroll 2009). Although the focus of this chapter concerns children, it is important to recognize that there is increasing numbers of children who will make the transition from children's palliative care to adult care.

Service providers for people with intellectual disabilities have developed a commitment in recent years to holistic care for people from the cradle to the grave (Together for Short Lives 2012; Todd 2006). However, Todd (2006) acknowledges that in addition to sparse literature there is a paucity of research in relation to the quality of care experienced by children and young people with IDs and life-limiting conditions. This contrasts markedly with the growing evidence base for children's palliative care generally, particularly in hospices.

Brown and White (2008) outline several aspects of young people's needs which should be addressed, including past and present achievements, independence, relationships, leisure pursuits and education. Children and young people with palliative care needs and an ID are first and foremost people, regardless of their complexity of health needs. They have needs, likes and dislikes similar to every other child or young person (Percy-Smith and Thomas 2010).

How children and young people understand death

Most of the literature in relation to cognition and how children and young people understand death is dominated by a Piagetian viewpoint. This involves having a conceptual understanding of death as a linear process linked to age, with an end point. Death is understood as a process that happens to all living creatures, caused by a breakdown in the healthy functioning of the body (Bluebond-Langner, Belasco and Goldman 2005; Klatt 1991). Kenyon (2001) defines a number of components for a mature understanding of death, namely:

- an understanding that all functions of life cease at death

- the permanent and irreversible status of death

- the universal nature of death

- causal factors associated with death

- an acceptance by an individual that they will die.

However, Brown (2007) advocates that just as grief is considered to be a complex process with overlapping phases, so it is with understanding death. Brown (2007) concludes that although children may not have a conceptual understanding of their illness, most are aware that something is physically wrong with their body. Furthermore, children and young people facing death have a more mature understanding of death than their healthy peers (Bluebond-Langner 2000; Judd 1995). Herbert (1996) purports that a child or young person often understands they are seriously ill and then they gradually move towards a realization of acute, chronic and fatal sickness. Brown (2007) illustrates this idea well (see Table 15.1). **Stage 1** is dependent on the child observing how other people respond and hearing what they say. After receiving treatment and visiting hospitals/clinics, the child reaches **Stage 2** which may include a period of remission in the illness. After the first relapse, **Stage 3** is reached and, as a result of several more relapses and remissions, the child realizes at **Stage 4** this is the pattern in their life. When the child realizes that someone else has died from the same illness, they parallel their own experience and **Stage 5** is reached.

Table 15.1 Children's understanding of ill health

1	2	3	4	5
My illness is serious	I am taking powerful drugs and they have side-effects	I know why I am having the treatment	I experience relapses and remissions	The pattern of relapses and remissions will end in death

The rights of children and young people to be involved in decisions made on their behalf have been recognized (AAC 2000; ACT 2003; Coad, Carter and Bray 2012), however adults may wish to protect a child from information about their illness (Lester, Chesney and Cookem 2002). Whether a child should be told of the seriousness of their illness remains open to debate, yet Kübler-Ross (1969, p.243), advocated that 'although all patients have the right to know, not all patients have the need to know'. Generally it is believed parents' wishes should be respected regarding how much information should be given to the child.

The impact of life-limiting illness on the non-disabled child

Before discussing how the needs of children who have limited cognition and a life-limiting condition might be best met, it is important to understand the impact of life-limiting or life-threatening illness on the non-disabled child. It has been suggested that the way in which people adjust is largely dependent on how well their primary carers cope, and how open family members are to communicating with one another (Brown 2007). A study in special schools revealed a huge number of individual responses to death, together with inter-related factors which have an impact on the way in which youngsters with special educational needs respond at the time of death and indeed afterwards (Brown 2007). One of these factors is that a life-limiting or a life-threatening condition can impact on a child's or a young person's identity.

Children with life-limiting conditions experience a number of events which are unlikely to be experienced to the same extent by their 'healthy' peer group, including:

- repeated GP, clinic and hospital visits and possible admission to hospital

- repeated absences from school

- long-term treatment/palliative care

- distress and discomfort of medical procedures and possible side-effects of treatment

- chronic or continual episodes of pain

- restricted social interaction or social isolation from their peer group. (Brown 2007, pp.2010–11)

Serious illness in the first year of a baby's life may alter the development of the child's self-awareness. Parents usually find this particularly distressing because they are unable to offer the baby reassurance. During the toddler stage the most frightening aspects of life-limiting illness are likely to include separation anxiety and trauma if invasive procedures have to be undertaken. Although children may have difficulty naming emotions, the intensity of emotions experienced is not dependent on cognitive ability; rather emotions are universal responses to lived experience. Toddlers may regress in previously mastered skills and they may withdraw from primary carers, becoming easily agitated and angry. Examples of the range of emotions experienced are illustrated in Figure 15.1. Typically, young children react angrily (Brown 2012), including breaking toys, lashing out or biting people and refusing to cooperate. Because the child's security is derived from routines, it is extremely important to maintain these as far as possible and to be consistent in approaches to behaviour management.

Figure 15.1 Examples of the range of emotions experienced by young children in response to serious illness

In the middle years, children increase their autonomy, independence and self-esteem. If their illness interferes with their achievements, they may experience repeated frustration and failure. Peer group approval and support are extremely important to children at this age, and spending time with their friends is usually a priority. Many children in this age group will have an increased awareness of the significance of serious illness, and will be developing an understanding of the permanence of death. These children are often aware of the fatal prognosis of their illness, even though they may not have been told. They are acutely aware of adult behaviour and need opportunities to talk about their fears and apprehensions. The child who drew the picture in Figure 15.2 had a younger brother with the same genetic life-limiting condition and was aware that he was likely to die first.

Me next year   Aged 6

Figure 15.2 Understanding of death

Unlike young children, young people generally perceive death as irreversible. Therefore, acceptance of personal death is particularly difficult, because for many children, life is orientated towards the future. But knowing that death is approaching does not mean that children accept the inevitability; they often have great anxiety about the process of dying and may withdraw emotionally as death approaches. Some young people will strive to achieve major accomplishments in an effort to maintain a sense of purpose in the face of impending death. Such young people are usually concerned about the wellbeing of their family and this may extend to aspects of the mental health of their parents and siblings. Figure 15.3 demonstrates the confusion experienced by a young person's family each time his medical condition reaches a crisis situation.

Figure 15.3 An illustration of family confusion and turmoil

Telling bad news

Dilemmas abound around death and telling bad news. Deciding how and when to talk to a child about their illness is one of the hardest decisions professionals have to make (Dunlop 2008; Goldman 2007). Arguably, the extent to which children and young people's experience is meaningful to them is dependent on the agenda for their care, which is more often than not an adult agenda which fails to empower children and young people with complex needs. Feiler and Watson (2011) believe children and young people may be vulnerable to others making assumptions about their needs.

Legislation endorses the importance of effective communication with children, young people and families. The ACT Charter (2004), ICPCN Charter (2008) and IMPaCCT (2007) all purport that information should be appropriate to each person's need. Adult conversations with children with life-limiting conditions is often shrouded in 'mutual pretence' where everyone concerned knows what is happening but nobody talks about the situation (Bluebond-Langner *et al.* (2005). The literature contains a plethora of guidance for those striving to engage children in communication, but there appears to be little published in relation to care for children with complex needs. Shier (2001, p.110) proposes five components for involving children:

- listening to what they communicate

- supporting them in expressing their views

- taking their views into account

- involving children and young people in decision-making processes

- sharing power and responsibility for decision making.

Reciprocal communication

In many ways the communication skills of practitioners determines how effectively children and their families are able to communicate (Brown 2000). However Matthews (2002) suggests there will be few professionals in primary care services with the knowledge and expertise that will enable them to best meet the holistic needs of children with palliative care needs. Persaud (2006) stresses to service providers the importance of a workplace culture that reflects a commitment to enhancing the quality of life experience for children and families.

Active communication involves connecting with the whole 'experience' of the child's world and appreciating the significance of the experience in the context of the child's life (Percy-Smith 2010). Listening to the voices of children is one of the most neglected aspects of research (Grieg, Taylor and MacKay 2007), and Christenson and James (2008) recommend more participatory methods that actively engage children. Roulstone and McLeod (2011) remind readers that there are two main aims for listening to children: to gain greater insight into the impact of complex needs on an individual; and to improve service design and provision so that they are relevant to the needs of children and their families.

Some children may have symbolic understanding and augmented or alternative communication systems can provide effective routes of communication. Systems include objects of reference, signs, together with grammatically spoken sentences, and symbol-based communication. Argyle (1998) asserted that non-verbal communication is reputedly five times more influential than verbal communication and aspects of non-verbal communication include gesture, facial expressions, touch and posture. Regnard *et al.* (2007) found more than twenty changes in behaviour in children with an ID when they encountered distress, and it is likely those who have no verbal language are likely to be more receptive to non-verbal communication (Tuffrey-Wijne and McEnhill 2008). It is therefore vitally important for professionals working directly with children to engage with them however possible (Gonzalez 2005).

Difficulties with communication have been consistently reported as a barrier in supporting adults with IDs at the end of life (Tuffrey-Wijne, Hogg and Curfs 2007), and most people with IDs will encounter some difficulty with communication (Cogher 2005). Iacono and Johnson (2004) define these difficulties as: speech that is either absent or difficult to understand; problems in listeners understanding what has been said; and problems on behalf of the child with the disability expressing themselves because of limited vocabulary and sentence formulation skills. Given that much of the language surrounding death and dying is shrouded in euphemisms and metaphors (Brown 2007), then it is hardly surprising that children with an ID are likely to encounter confusion.

Honest communication

Woolfe (2004) advises that adults should communicate with children when it is clear that the child knows that something is wrong with their body. If a child or young person senses that adults are uncomfortable discussing death then they are more likely to avoid communicating with them (Brown 2007). Therefore it is important that adult fear and anxiety do not get in the way of open and honest communication (National Institute of Health 2006). Sinclair and Franklin (2000, p.283) cite several reasons for helping children and young people in decisions relating to their care, including: upholding democracy and rights; improving service delivery; facilitating decision making; safeguarding; enhancing skills and enhancing emotional wellbeing.

Most definitions of quality of life agree that it 'can only be fully understood from an individual's perspective' (Markham 2011, p.231). Parents and primary carers often have a rich and detailed knowledge of how their child communicates that allows them to make detailed observations of their responses from which they draw inferences about their child's needs (Golbart and Marshall 2004). However parents of children with life-limiting conditions are likely to be experiencing anticipatory grief in relation to the death of their child and the atmosphere at home may be emotionally charged (Brown *et al.* 2013). Ware (2004, p.103) cautions that 'although those who are most familiar with an individual are most likely to interpret their reactions appropriately, they are also likely to be those with the highest degree of emotional involvement'.

Oswin (1991) recognised that most people with an ID did not receive appropriate palliative care and that this was largely due to an assumption that children with an ID did not experience the same emotional responses as others and the combination of a 'double taboo' of ID and 'death' challenging society to the extent that they have been swept under the carpet. Furthermore, grief responses in children with complex needs may be considered as part of abnormal behaviour associated with the ID rather than a universal human response (Brown 2007).

'The learning disability community is sadly underprepared for death and dying, which undermines a claim that concerns stretch from the cradle to the grave' (Todd 2006, p.15) and arguably if the latter is disregarded, there is a risk that the life experience of some children with learning disabilities is 'disenfranchised' (Brown 2007). This may be compounded by identifying how information might be given, when and by whom.

The evidence base

Research into how children with ID react to life-limiting illness is limited and in the main concentrates on adults in long term residential care (Strachan 1981) and PWID are often perceived as a homogeneous group with the result that their needs may be seen to be different to their mainstream peer group (McLoughlin 1986). Subsequently, one of the fundamental dilemmas professionals face is whether (and indeed how) they help children with ID to understand the severity of their condition and that it will end in death (Todd 2004). Carers and professionals needed to be prepared to 'tune' into these needs and the attitudes and skills of practitioners determines how effectively children and young people are able to communicate (Lascelles 2011). Opportunities for the children's workforce to develop their skills and knowledge in communication is pivotal in achieving the best practice outlined in the Equality Act (HM Government Equalities Office 2010). However, the value of listening to children with complex needs is not just to ensure their needs are met through effective service delivery, but also 'to challenge professional assumptions and stereotypes about the lives of this unique group' (Percy-Smith and Thomas 2010, p.42).

It should not be assumed that children with complex needs cannot communicate or are unable to indicate their needs and preferences (Franklin and Sloper 2009); developing purposeful relationships with children and their families is fundamental to ensuring that care remains child centred, sensitive and holistic. Dimensions of care such as ethnicity and cultural and religious practices should be respected (Ali *et al.* 2011; Brown 2012; McLeod 2011). The young person who depicted her beliefs about Muslim burial in Figure 15.4 is acutely aware of the rights and rituals performed by her community, and carers need to be familiar with the beliefs and practices of the families with whom they work.

When I die my soul will go to Allah.
My body will stay in the ground.

Figure 15.4 Understanding spirituality

Conclusion

There is no single way to support children with IDs and their families through their palliative care journey, yet there are avenues open to all of us. We need to travel alongside those who hurt and be open and sensitive to the ways they choose to communicate. Most importantly, we should trust the children and their families to be our guides in order to provide care that is fundamentally supportive and compassionate.

CHAPTER 16

Loss and end-of-life care

Karen Ryan, Suzanne Guerin and Philip Larkin

SUMMARY

Holistic support at the end-of-life is fundamental to the potential for a peaceful or easeful death. This chapter will introduce key factors to end-of-life care and support when the patient has an intellectual disability, identify the factors that may inhibit such care and support and explore best practice initiatives in the form of 'Points of practice' indicators.

Introduction

Palliative care is the active, total care of patients and their families provided by a multidisciplinary team when the patient's disease is no longer responsive to curative treatment. Although the concept of the hospice has been in existence since Roman times, the modern hospice movement evolved from the works of Cicely Saunders, who founded St Christopher's Hospice in 1967. Saunders emphasized the importance of both compassion *and* medical science, and coined the phrase 'total pain', describing it as 'the division of a whole experience into physical, emotional, social and spiritual components' (Saunders and Sykes 1993, pp.6–13). The success of St Christopher's Hospice was remarkable and led to the establishment of a care model where generalist palliative care providers (health and social care providers with basic palliative care skills) and specialist palliative care providers coexist and support each other.

The synergies between palliative care and intellectual disability (ID) have been noted since its inception. Thérèse Vanier described the parallel between the vision of L'Arche (faith communities for the people with IDs) and the hospice movement in the early 1960s as listening very carefully to some very fragile and vulnerable people (Kearney 2000). This resonates with the writing of Saunders, in her descriptions of the presence of one person to another as healing (Clark 2002). Unfortunately, despite these synergies there is evidence that people with an ID experience persistent inequity in palliative care provision. Reports suggest that people with an ID have unmet palliative care needs (Tuffrey-Wijne, Hogg and Curfs 2007) and that the discourse around death and dying, although increasing, may still be described as a 'hidden transition' within the ID community (Todd and Read 2006).

McCallion *et al.* (2012) have commented that the issue of palliative care provision for people with an ID has only come to the fore in recent years. They attribute this neglect to the fact that people with an ID were and, to some extent continue to be, a largely hidden population in general healthcare. Services were largely provided within their own intellectual disabilities services system, ageing was the exception rather than an expectation and there were beliefs that people with IDs themselves were not able or ready to made decisions about their end-of-life care. The relative lack of research in this area has been well documented by Tuffrey-Wijne *et al.* (2007) and presents healthcare professionals with real challenges in practice as they struggle to address inequities and improve outcomes without yet having a detailed understanding of the processes and determinants of care. However, capacity is gradually building within this new field of study and increasingly researchers are addressing the interface between end-of-life care and ID within qualitatively orientated clinical research.

The palliative care needs of people with an ID

People with an ID have the same palliative care needs as the general population but it is acknowledged that they may have additional or special needs relating to specific impairments or the social consequences of impairment. Studies consistently demonstrate that both palliative care and ID staff lack confidence in their abilities to meet the palliative care needs of people with an ID. Palliative care staff consider the provision of care to people with an ID to be 'different' in many ways from the provision of palliative care to the general population, and also find it often to be more 'difficult' (Ryan *et al.* 2010). ID staff feel that they have been inadequately trained or prepared for providing care for service users towards the end-of-life. There are several key factors to consider when providing palliative and end-of-life care to this population, with communication being a predominant feature.

Communication

Impairments of communication pose major challenges for both people with ID and their carers. The assessment, diagnosis and management of healthcare problems are all dependent on the communication of information, and therefore, every stage of healthcare provision is potentially affected by the presence of impairment. Poor communication skills may result in maladaptive behaviours, which pose additional challenges for health professionals and carers and contribute to diagnostic overshadowing.

Points of practice

When communicating with people with ID, conversation should be in simple language and short sentences, appropriate to the person's developmental level. People with an ID often have a short attention span, and it is helpful to recapitulate and summarize previously stated material. This also provides the opportunity to check understanding of what has been discussed. People with an ID may have a limited ability to express emotions verbally and instead express emotions in atypical ways or through behavioural disturbance. Caregivers should recognize these nonverbal methods of communication and respond appropriately. Tuffrey-Wijne has produced web-based guidelines on how to break bad news to people with an ID.[1] In addition Sue Read and colleagues have developed a communication tool kit and an associated interactive tool called 'picTTalk', which aim to support communication with children and adults on sensitive topics.[2]

Symptom assessment and management

Self-report measures are generally considered to be the 'gold standard' of pain management available and this poses challenges for individuals with impairments of communication. The term 'alternative communication' is used to describe the non-verbal signs and behaviours that people use in the place of language (Glennen 1997). Research on the subject of

---

1   This is available at www.breakingbadnews.org.

2   PicTTalk can be freely accessed from www.keele.ac.uk/nursingandmidwifery/research/picttalk/.

alternative communication has tended to focus on the expression of physical pain. In the palliative care setting, however, the concept of 'total' pain reflects the multidimensional nature of suffering, and it can prove difficult to distinguish the expression of physical pain from the expression of other causes of distress.

POINTS OF PRACTICE

While pain assessment tools should be used carefully with people with communication difficulties (in order to ensure that all expressions of distress are not treated with analgesics), tools such as the Disability Distress Assessment Tool (DisDAT) may prove useful support to practice (Regnard *et al.* 2007). Observation-based tools such as the 'Non-communicating Children's pain checklist' can also be helpful when self-report is not possible (Breau and Burkitt 2009).

Truth telling and collusion

Problems around truth telling are not unique to people with an ID because it is a natural instinct for carers to try and protect their loved ones from the knowledge that an illness is incurable. However, carers tend to be particularly concerned about the effects information has on the person with an ID, and often argue that the person 'won't understand' or that 'the truth is too upsetting' (Tuffrey-Wijne 2002). This may be particularly evident when the person with an ID is a child (see Chapter 15). While preparation for loss and change is not an easy option, it is one that can lead to increased emotional growth, self-awareness and empowerment for the individual concerned (Leick and Davidson-Neilson 1991).

POINTS OF PRACTICE

Decisions about truth telling should be made in the same way as they are for the general population, and they should be grounded on ethical principles while considering individual circumstances. When considering individual circumstances, healthcare professionals should assess the person's levels of emotional and conceptual understanding. Family and caregivers should be involved at all stages of the process, and support should be provided for them.

Conceptualization of illness and death

Research shows that PWID do have some understanding of illness and death (McEvoy *et al.* 2012), though there is little research on this among children with ID. It is not clear how this understanding is facilitated by care staff and although staff have endorsed the right of people with an ID to know about the end-of-life, they have provided limited opportunities for people to gain this knowledge in practice (Ryan *et al.* 2011b). Despite the challenging nature of the topic, there is no reason to believe that people with an ID (both adults and children) have less need for information about illness and dying than the rest of the population or that the arguments promoted by professionals, researchers and ethicists in favour of conditional, open awareness are any less valid for people with ID.

POINTS OF PRACTICE

When talking about illness or death, it is important to assess the person's cognitive level and determine whether they are a concrete thinker or capable of abstract thought. Prior experiences of loss, ill-health and death should also be explored, and coping mechanisms identified. The language used should be simple and information should be given in a variety of ways including visual techniques. Healthcare professionals need to be sensitive to non-verbal cues and to actively support the person in understanding their illness and in exploring their feelings.

Issues of capacity, consent and decision making

The right of persons with an ID to make choices about their lives and enjoy legal capacity on an equal basis with others is one of the most significant human rights issues in Europe today. The United Nation Convention on the Rights of Persons with Disabilities (2006) represents a paradigm shift that promotes the empowerment of individuals with disability to control their own lives. However, many adults with an ID are still not involved in decisions about their own general healthcare and decisions that carers make on behalf of people with an ID are often made without proper attention to ethical issues (Holloway 2004; Keywood, Fovargue and Flynn 1999). This is despite multiple research studies demonstrating that a person's self-determination status predicts higher quality of life and that choice-making opportunity is a strong predictor of self-determination (Lachapelle *et al.* 2005; McGuire and McDonnell 2008). Clearly in the case of children with an ID, their status in many contexts as legal minors must be considered and parents/ guardians will play a key role in decision making.

POINTS OF PRACTICE
All health professionals should assume that adult patients can make their own treatment decisions. Patients with mental capacity are able to make their own healthcare decisions based on the options explained to them. If there are concerns about individual patients' decision-making abilities, they should be supported as much as possible by health professionals to help them make a decision. Many people with an ID are able to make their own healthcare decisions if given appropriate support. The use of communication aides, additional time and involvement of family or familiar carers may all support decision making. People with IDs must be assessed before it is decided they lack the capacity to make a decision and before any decisions can be made on their behalf. If it is judged that an individual lacks capacity, then any decision made on behalf of the patient must be made by an appropriately authorized individual and must be in the patient's best interests.

Compassion and collaboration: the way forward

Given some of the challenges to practice presented here, it may help to understand ways forward more clearly by considering a deeper reflection on compassion as a core element of end-of-life care and relationships. Indeed, the practical application of that approach may serve both the palliative care and ID communities to successfully find commonalities.

Compassion: the basis of palliative and end-of-life care
It is unlikely that anyone would challenge the idea that compassion is essential for the delivery of optimal care for dying people. However, as a concept, compassion is often assumed rather than elucidated or explained. In some cases, lack of compassion is levelled at healthcare systems that have failed to meet aspects of quality care, though Courtney (2011) does note that all of the parents in a study of families with children with life-limiting neurodevelopment disabilities described experiences with professionals who were compassionate and supportive.

The idea of people coming to a hospice to die is shifting and has opened debate as to how far palliative care still embraces the original ideals of *'hospitium'* as a place of compassionate care and comfort at end-of-life or if it is a clinical discipline, focusing primarily on symptom interventions through any or all extraneous means. Descriptors of the transition from living to dying (for example curative, chronic and life-limiting, supportive care, palliative care, end-of-life care, terminal care, etc.) suggest that it is no longer clear what is meant in respect to death and dying and, as such, it is subject to criticism (Illhardt 2001; Randall and Downie 2006). This means that the unique contribution of palliative care which may benefit other disciplines (such as ID) can be obscured in a complex dialogue and the place of compassion as enabling people to understand that 'through acceptance of the life one has lived comes acceptance of death' (Breitbart 2008, p.212) may be lost. Of course, this ideal for palliative care holds its own challenges in the ID community where understanding and acceptance may require different indicators.

Compassion reflects a kindness towards all life and an awareness of personal vulnerability in order to support others who are themselves vulnerable (Remen 2000). The etymological definition of 'com' (together with) and 'pati' (to suffer) (Oxford English Dictionary 2004) indicates both the tangible and intangible aspects of palliative care: the ability to be with people at times of suffering and loss. More philosophical and holistic models of practice, some of which derive from medicine, have noted the value of compassion to palliative and end-of-life care (Breitbart 2008; Mount and Kearney 2003).

Nussbaum (2001) considers compassion in three ways which are meaningful to the palliative care/ID interface. First, the suffering undergone by the other person is considered significant. Second, it is largely unmerited and third, could be experienced personally. Gallagher (2009, p.239) considers this when discussing compassion and forgiveness, a language noted in end-of-life care: 'Compassion responds to the pain it can see with its eyes, and its natural expression is the embrace of care'.

The findings of the research studies noted earlier would attest to this, seeking to provide support to the dying person with an ID and their families in the most appropriate way and self-critical of lack of skills to do so. This has also been noted in studies of palliative care professionals in similar roles (Abma 2005; Johns 2004). Linked to this, of course, is the vulnerability of the person with an ID as suggested by Vanier earlier; that the suffering endured in the course of illness is unjust by virtue of all that they have had to contend with in relation to their ID. In terms of impact of compassionate caregiving on the caregiver, Nouwen, McNeill and Morrison's (1982) belief that 'you are the difference you make' points to the work needed when we choose to act in a compassionate way and thus highlights that a compassionate response is not innate as choice is involved. The risk of taking that choice in terms of caregiver stress and burnout are also well documented (Asai *et al.* 2007; Fillion *et al.* 2009; Vachon and Müeller 2009).

In terms of shared learning from palliative care and ID, compassion needs to be seen as action orientated and is meaningless if it does not respond to another's suffering. Action arises from the compassionate presence of someone supporting another's struggle (Nouwen *et al.* 1982; Nussbaum 1996; Vachon and Huggard 2010). As such it resonates with Cicely Saunders' own belief that 'the way care is given can reach the most hidden places' (Saunders 1996, p.1600). The humanity and vulnerability of those we serve are of equal importance to professional competence. A compassionate response to death within the ID community is about believing in one's personal capacity and innate qualities to address the pain and suffering of the other, conscious of what that suffering means to me. Nouwen *et al.* (1982, p.4) describe this as: 'Compassion asks us to go where it hurts, to enter into places of pain, to share in brokenness, fear confusion and anguish... Compassion means full immersion in the condition of being human.'

Although one can look at compassion in greater depth through theological and philosophical treatise, one key element would seem to reflect palliative and end-of-life care well; that is, compassion evokes peacefulness in self and others. In effect 'compassion is contagious' (Barad 2007, p.21). In considering how that contagion might be used to strengthen the links between palliative care and ID, the late Irish philosopher John O'Donohue proposed that that 'no-one was sent into the world without being given the infinite possibilities of the heart' (O'Donohue 2003, p.244). Compassion arises from the ability to share the wisdom in caring for others and knowing how and when to care for oneself (see Chapter 6). Compassion at end-of-life ultimately asks us to consider what caring truly means.

Relational approaches to care and understanding

Compassion in palliative and end-of-life care is based on relationships. It is hard to consider compassion and relationship as separate entities as presented here since compassion assumes the importance of respect for others, the desire to relieve suffering and to be conscious of our responsibility towards the welfare of others (Bergum 2003, 2004). It also assumes a belief that the life of all people holds equal value (Tuffrey-Wijne 2003). For Cicely Saunders, relationship was demonstrated through close engagement with the individual and family (Randall and Downie 2006). Relationship is evoked throughout the palliative and end-of-life care literature, as an essential component of best practice in care (Abma 2005; Brannström *et al.* 2005; Ferrell 2006; Garnet 2003; Johns 2004).

Although relationality is not a new concept and has been addressed in terms of mutual respect and care (Fredricksson 1999; Fredriksson and Eriksson 2001, 2003), the work of Bergum and Dossetor (2005) in considering 'human flourishing' to explore how decisions are made links both to the real engagement needed to understand the real world perspectives of people with IDs and to compassion in the concept of 'Eudaimonia' proposed by Martha Nussbaum (2001). In effect, compassion occurs when we become aware of another's suffering and we are aware of that because of the relationship that develops between persons, both personal and professional. Real decision making is made in partnership, through attentiveness to the other person's perspective. Considering the perspective of the person with an ID at end-of-life, a deeper understanding is best achieved when attention is paid to four dimensions which underpin this relational approach: environment, engagement, embodiment and mutual respect.

Environment refers to the complex relationships which exist in healthcare and the layers of meaning which are attached to them by patients and professionals. For example, negotiating clinical services, appointments, treatments, decisions and so on can be complex and challenging so that decisions made may not be clearly understood. This perspective argues that moving away from 'I' (the professional decision maker) to 'You and I' (the shared decision maker) is a more appropriate way to create understanding and may be particularly useful when considering the advocacy role of the clinical with the person who has ID in negotiating changing goals of care. **Engagement** proposes that decisions are made based on the reality of someone's life, and not just about equity of access. For some people, additional resources are needed for them to achieve the same level of service as another person, simply because their needs and ability to engage are different. Again, there may be learning from this approach in the care of the patient with an ID in terms of decisions around choices for active or palliative care options and place of care at end-of-life. **Embodiment** describes the impact of meaningful relationship on decision making and that this should be taken into account. Where community network is important to someone's health and wellbeing (as in a group home, for example), cognisance of the importance of relationships with family, friends, familiar carers and others may determine correct approaches to care planning at end-of-life. Finally, all three hinge on the premise that *mutual respect* develops when consideration is given to a 'relational space' (Bergum and Dossetor 2005, p.xiii) where global decisions and their implications are shared with all concerned.

Conclusion

The imperative for dialogue and engagement expressed here provides a backdrop to the complex picture of end-of-life care for people with an ID. It calls for a recognition of dignity and respect and shifts the balance of power from a hierarchical model to one of shared goals and objectives. The ideal may be as yet one step too far in the general healthcare arena but could offer a model of best practice for the ID community in creating partnerships with the palliative care practitioners to improve and consolidate approaches to care which are meaningful and sustainable in the current healthcare environment.

CHAPTER 17

Living with shattered dreams
A parent's perspective

Mandy Parks

SUMMARY

This chapter considers a parental perspective of life following the diagnosis of a child with a disability, a concept previously described as 'living with shattered dreams' (Parks 2012). Three main themes will be highlighted which have influenced adaptations within (and to) the family dynamics. Whilst this chapter will include themes that may well have been expressed previously in the literature, since much has been written about families whose children have intellectual disabilities, this chapter will bring the unique parental and family perspective and provide a living experience of loss within the family context.[1]

Introduction

A key quality of being a nurse is compassion for patients and their families and how this is reflected in the care and support delivered, in whatever specialism of nursing. Caring for patients with an intellectual disability (ID) in mainstream health services may challenge organisations and those professionals within it who may not be overly familiar with this client group. When a child or young person with an ID is in hospital, care should encompass the whole family, and compassion remains crucial in appreciating the impact that this health crisis has on those who love and support them.

---

1   Consent from family members and carers has been given to incorporate their personal reflections and my grateful thanks go to them for sharing their thoughts with me.

I'm dedicating this chapter to Alicia Parks, since she is the central hub from which to unpack these issues, and an understanding of her condition is crucial. Exploring the family dynamics when living with Alicia and her severe disabilities will illustrate well the rollercoaster journey of everyday life experienced. The prevailing demands of having a disabled child impacts variably on the family in terms of independence, freedom, holiday choices, marriage and grief as we struggle to come to terms with the inherent losses.

This, for me, resonates well with the oscillation process so ably described by Stroebe and Schutt (2001). Living with the trials and tribulations of disability hourly/daily/weekly, we (as a family) move through living comfortably with the loss associated with Alicia's condition and then suddenly find ourselves plunging down into the depths of despair as ill health threatens yet again.

Three main themes will be explored in relation to the family experience, which have influenced adaptations within (and to) the family dynamics:

1. the prevailing impact of loss, and ongoing adaptations associated with the transition, whilst living with a child/adolescent with a deteriorating health condition

2. recognizing the learning associated with coming to terms with such losses

3. the potential impact on generic healthcare professionals caring and supporting children and young people.

These themes produce focal points that illustrate how we live our daily lives and are a stark reminder of the constant battles faced by the whole family. In identifying the very real inherent challenges faced by us all, as individuals and as a family, this chapter will provide evidence to support best practice approaches, influencing and enhancing the key skills of health professionals when dealing with young people with additional and complex health needs. It will also highlight the current and future challenges around loss and support provided in a dynamic, ever changing health and social care context. As Parks (2012) highlights, nothing can prepare parents for the turmoil that begins when their child is diagnosed with a disability, but compassionate care can help to ease this turmoil.

Impact of loss

Giving birth to children who are significantly different can shatter life's dreams (Bowman 2001) as parents and siblings have to reconsider life plans, dreams and aspirations. Living with shattered dreams as Bowman (2001) suggests can cause families to lose hope, leading them to question their abilities and reconfigure ambitions and goals. Personal accounts of experiences of caring for children with multiple and profound disabilities and the subsequent impact on families are rare (Parks 2012), therefore this chapter supports existing literature, adding a different dimension to inform awareness and understanding of the very harsh reality of living with, and caring for, a child with a life-limiting condition.

Fundamentally the psychological, emotional and physical movement between health crisis situations, whilst trying to retain a central focus on living well, and reflecting on what used to be our lives, can be torturous. Being faced with the untimely companion of impending death has not given us, as a family, the chance to ever live life to the full, as we constantly try to keep positive to survive turmoil surrounded by our daughter and her disabilities, and continue to live with our shattered dreams. The sense of profound isolation is often overwhelming but is something I have learned to live with. The confrontation of reality, the remembrance of where we came from and the ambitions we had, to not knowing where we are going and constantly living in transition is a daily struggle. However, being in this situation has become a way of life, not just for our own relationship, but in our connections with our children and grandchildren.

Becoming a parent

I had long wanted children and a husband with whom I could enjoy sharing the trials and tribulations of family life. When Neil and I first met we were full of enthusiasm; we enjoyed travelling and had plans to walk around Europe. Our first memorable trip was to Austria with Sam, our daughter, where we saw amazing waterfalls and incredible sights which we vowed we would return to with subsequent children.

For 12 years we yearned for Alicia, became top of the list for IVF, but I fell pregnant naturally after many intrusive and investigative tests, and in 1999 we were blessed with the arrival of our daughter. I had a healthy pregnancy and a short labour and Alicia entered our world weighing 5 pounds 5 ounces; no baby bonnet fitted her, her head circumference being 27.5cm. We were sent home with no indication that she was 'different' in any way. Six weeks later, her paediatric routine appointment raised concerns that she did not fix and follow with her eyes, indicating she may be blind. As the weeks progressed, blood and urine tests confirmed Alicia was born with Cytomegalovirus (CMV).

CMV is a common but little known virus, which is thought to be a major cause of congenital infection and disease, thus leading to permanent birth defects (Kadambari *et al.* 2011; Nozawa *et al.* 2009). From our perspective, Alicia was asymptomatic at birth, as then we had no knowledge of symptomatic signs of CMV. Information from clinical staff could have defined that she was Intrauterine Growth Retarded (in the womb), with microcephaly being a key symptom, indicating the need for further diagnostic tests and immediate treatment immediately. Alicia developed multiple and profound disabilities including cerebral palsy, cortical blindness, severe global developmental delay and spastic quadriplegia. Being bound to a wheelchair, totally reliant on her family and carers, she is nevertheless a precious gift that we would not have chosen, but this was not our choice and has led us on a very hard road no parent would choose to travel (Parks 2012). However difficult this journey has been, the experience has made us different (but better) people in many respects, not least as experts in knowing and understanding our daughter.

Prior to Alicia's birth, we had our daughter, Sam, for 13 years. On reflection, our spontaneous lifestyle was fulfilled, enthusiastic and enjoyable and free from any real anxiety. Following Alicia, Sebastian arrived healthy but has sadly had no experience of life without his disabled sister, and has conscientiously been given a planned and adapted lifestyle to suit his disabled sister's needs throughout his childhood. Whilst providing a safe, warm, nurturing environment we also recognize our own failures when trying to provide for our young man.

Living with loss and change

As there are many grief models associated with death and loss when expressing the parental and family perspective, it becomes difficult to adopt a framework where death is not the central feature, but where loss and change are prevalent and continuous. The Stroebe and Shutt (2001) oscillation model of grief conceptualizes well the constant features of adaptation as we swing from living and coping well, to swinging towards the struggles, the overwhelming feeling of sadness and the realization of the future and what is yet to come.

When remembering our years of carefree living prior to having Alicia and acknowledging the fact that our eldest and youngest had such different lifestyles, we appreciate that one form of loss is paramount: the loss of freedom. This is highlighted especially when comparing our life with Sam to that with Alicia, and emphasizes the loss in adaptation after she was born. For example, simply taking Sam out in the car we could park when and where we chose. With Alicia, we have to consider where to shop and when to go; we become anxious regarding where to park our large, adapted vehicle to ensure ease of access for the wheelchair. We worry about comments from misinformed people as they ask me again 'You have legs – why are you in that space?' or say 'This space is for disabled people'. The freedom to spontaneously decide to go shopping seems a luxury to us, but is an everyday event for many other families.

Like shopping, holidays are now different. With Sam they were carefree; we had the luxury of being able to go anywhere and choose any place to visit, any property to stay in. Nowadays, we have to look for a place to visit that is easily accessible and plan meticulous doses of medicines. When flying we have to pre-board before everyone else which singles us out as problematic or different. We now hire a minibus abroad to accommodate Alicia's wheelchair and the entire luggage we require, which incurs further expense. Occasionally a carer accompanies us as Alicia requires two people for lifting; therefore our holidays do not always feel private and personal.

Whilst recognizing the lifestyle that Sam grew up with and comparing it with Sebastian's, with all its proactive planning, lack of spontaneity and a focus on his sister for her associated endless hospital and hospice visits, I only hope that some of the quality time we have given him has been enough to encourage him to be confident and has reassured him that we have tried to provide him with a secure upbringing.

Direct payments enable us to employ carers to support Alicia at home, which is invaluable but comes with a cost. Becoming an employer and understanding the law when hiring staff has caused much heartache. Purchasing our own care has allowed us some freedom to choose, but it is also very labour intensive and time consuming constantly interviewing prospective people. We have lost our privacy, which is one of the biggest impacts of loss on the family dynamics. The opportunity for Sebastian to be a child and run free just as Sam did is difficult; he has sadly encountered a harsher spoken Mum and Dad. The reality of having a disabled child in the home has altered our family dynamics at its basic level and has made for frustrated parenting. This frustration is also combined with sleep deprivation. This is, for me, the hardest physical effect of caring for Alicia. The time and energy required to provide care and support to her as she is wholly dependent on us for everything is not only repetitive but exhausting. The daily routine begins at 6.00 a.m. with her personal hygiene needs. Dressing a child who is doubly incontinent with severe physical disabilities remains challenging. Taking this situation for a day is manageable, but continuing with sleep deprivation day after day is not an easy road.

Learning from loss

Following Alicia's birth, we changed as people. I became besotted, dedicated and seemingly obsessed in providing our child with the right to survive and live with as good a quality life as feasibly possible. I never thought I would feel like that; it was not planned, it was a natural, parental instinct. Neil is also dedicated, besotted and a hardworking father. Yet over time he has found it difficult to express how he feels and with his frustrations comes a man scorned with a life he did not expect or desire.

Despite this, whilst encouraging Alicia's vision to develop, we were provided with opportunities to learn about visual impairment. The use of pen torches and finger puppets taught us how much we learn through our eyes. We learned physiotherapy routines to try to prevent muscle stiffness; we were introduced to numerous appointments gathering multidisciplinary knowledge and new experiences. Sadly, we did not really see our eldest child, Sam, being overlooked whilst our tiny, vulnerable daughter was so helpless and needy.

Being Alicia's parent has made me much more aware of (and compassionate to) others and I have developed better skills around (for example) empathy, while Sam shows less compassion and tolerance for others nowadays, as she tends to critically compare other people's lives with ours. She feels that if they can walk or do not have much to 'be sad' about they should motivate themselves.

The impact of loss on my personal life has been profound, I feel as though I have lost my identity as a wife to my husband. Whilst I do not particularly like whom I've become, I feel that Alicia has had to come first and everything (and everyone) else second. My marriage has suffered through our constant battles around support and care for Alicia's changing health status, which have drained our energy levels over the years. We have fought constantly for remedial items such as continence nappies or argued to prove that adaptations to our home were necessary, causing immense sadness. My husband feels he has no choice but to provide 'care' for Alicia either in a personal way or by entertaining her so she does not get frustrated as she tries to communicate her needs. The lack of freedom and worries for our family financially is additional pressure. He appreciates other families suffer in many different ways, but as Alicia has such complex health needs, the combined lack of compassion from others and the ongoing support needed make his situation harder.

Thirteen years later, our marriage is still unified but generally strained; we do have togetherness but often in hospitals. We have limited time to support each other, which feels extremely sad. Our discussions are around what is best for Alicia and we also give as much time as we can to help Sebastian at his new school. Sam now has her own family, a daughter of four years and a new baby boy. We are happy grandparents and I cannot begin to realize what I actually wish for them, or what I may miss in the future. This constantly caring life has definitely not allowed me to reflect on these issues as yet.

Battling the system

Both Neil and I are tired of the constant battle to prove we need support in an environment in which we feel professionals do not have more experience. Whilst we were not originally the professionals in this situation, we naively expected our road to be easier, especially when Alicia was initially diagnosed, and professionals advocated to just 'ask' for support. I feel disappointed and am distraught with the insensitive system that requires constant proof that Alicia cannot walk. Over the years, I have received numerous flippant remarks and healthcare decisions that have at times shattered our family's hopes, fears and dreams. We are starting to break and the cracks are becoming larger, which feels sad and defeatist, but realistic. In the early years we had boundless eager energy; perhaps we are not broken, just empty and drained as constant care and support inevitably takes it toll. Of course we are growing older, as are our children.

As we have become more confident in Alicia's progress and our understanding about her disability, we have taught medical staff how to deal with her condition and its deteriorating impact. We do try to nurture a relaxed attitude but sometimes being assertive is the only way to obtain the necessary equipment or the surgical procedure that Alicia desperately needs.

Recently we were advised that Alicia had suddenly developed severe scoliosis within a short period of time. An X-ray confirmed a curvature so bad that her lung was compromised and her rib cage had twisted and was pressing down on her hip. Functionally, she had begun to deteriorate and required medications to relieve her breathing status. Waking regularly during the night to listen to her breathe, we were scared. On waking Alicia would often be cyanosed; we would rush to her room in fear of her being dead, performing mouth-to-mouth resuscitation to stimulate her breathing. We cried daily for nearly eight months, eventually paying for a private consultation to explore the most appropriate healthcare options. It was agreed that spinal surgery was the only option as soon as possible, to minimize Alicia ending up in a permanent 'c' shaped wheelchair. We had various appointments to establish the suitability for this major surgery, one particular day resulting in five appointments. A few weeks later we were given a date for Alicia's surgery.

At 10.50 a.m. on the day of admission the procedure was cancelled, as there was no bed available in intensive care and no staff nurse available for after care. Having spent 12 months preparing for this, we were devastated and in shock. Everything was now on hold: my work was on hold and my husband had been given two weeks compassionate leave that had to be subsequently cancelled. We couldn't envisage what to do if this would be a regular occurrence as feasibly identified by the consultant. Alicia was not categorized as a sick child, and it was stipulated during this particular time of year that bed priorities were for very poorly children. Whilst fully appreciative of the need for prioritization, our family was in a dilemma. My husband could not get any more time off work and the uncertainty around organizing ongoing support for Sebastian was becoming problematic. We were physically drained from worrying about Alicia's epilepsy and her increasing breathing difficulties. Our carers were fearful to be with Alicia on their own because of her deteriorating condition and were leaving.

The surgery finally went ahead. My big girl needed this surgery and we look back with sadness to think of how difficult and strained this recent journey has been. The benefits of this surgery have been overwhelming; she looks better, smiles, does not tire easily, eats more easily and is more comfortable. She is beginning to sleep longer which gives us recuperation time and requires no orthotic body brace at present.

Positivity and progress

The positivity and outcomes that have fulfilled our lives remain important. Despite Alicia's disabilities and perceived frailty, she has remained strong. Surviving surgical procedures such as de-rotation of both hips and major spinal surgery, she continues to teach us so many valuable lesson throughout this difficult journey. We have been able to confront reality and fears, acknowledging them and talking them through together. Writing this chapter has been cathartic whilst raising many issues for me, but such reflections remind us how far we have come and our ability as a family to cope.

Sibling perspectives

From Sam's perspective, she sees that it is hard for her parents to relax as she feels they live in a constant state of anxiety and with the constant disappointment of being let down. She recently admitted that she left home partly to escape the pressure involved in Alicia's care and because having a sibling of six years old made her feel unable to associate with the trials and tribulations they both brought. Nowadays, as a parent herself, she wants to be part of the family once again, admitting that she misses her mum and dad. She wants to do what she wanted to do at 19 years old but did not then have the necessary adult knowledge for, which has torn her apart. Sebastian wrote a poem when he was just nine years old.

> ### My sister,
> ### by Sebastian
>
> Ali is a person that people can't bare
> Which gets really annoying when people stop and stare.
> Disabled people like Ali are born every day
> Which gets really sad when it blows your wishes away.

> Ali can't talk you hear her through a cry,
> Which you can understand but only if you try
> Ali can't walk
> She can't even stride
> But when I'm there to help her it fills me with pride.

Powerful words and very profound for such a young boy; it reduced me to tears. This has had a huge effect on him and I did not know he felt this way until I read it.

Regularly being brought back into the reality of loss highlights the prevailing impact on us all of living with Alicia. Achievements and milestones from the other children remind us of all the ordinary, simple things that Alicia cannot (and will never) achieve.

Impact on healthcare professionals

As a parent, we are obviously biased regarding the health needs of our daughter. As a nurse myself, I hope that I provide care and compassion for all the patients and families within my care and that they feel their anxieties and fears are heard and understood. I encourage families to be open to discussion, to be honest. Furthermore, I treat them with respect.

The impact that Alicia has on health professionals is unknown as requested feedback following appointments is rare. I actively support the local university by teaching student nurses, providing insight into family life with a child/young person with a deteriorating health condition and the wider impact it has on the family.

Conclusion

Death is an untimely companion, and facing the prospect of death every day is a reminder of what was, is now, and what could have been. It remains profoundly sad. We constantly fight the acceptance that we may lose Alicia, grieving her loss whilst she is still here. We cannot conceive how empty our lives will be when the time comes for Alicia to leave us. Undoubtedly the chasm that will be created will be immense. We will have to consider what other new roles we need to learn for the future.

Neil cannot think about losing Alicia, despite the challenges she brings. Our coping strategies have been to accept the changes in our family dynamics and stay focused. I am very strong and resilient; my energy is my optimism and family relationships are extremely important to me. Knowing the expectation to fail is high according to the statistics, staying together is my goal. This in turn makes me wonder why more is not done to help families stay together, in what feels like the toughest job.

Healthcare professionals are at the forefront of change for services and are beginning to encompass intellectual disabilities with all its challenges. Healthcare professionals hold the key to ensuring that families like us are supported and heard. Communication is crucial for families to be able to express themselves meaningfully and for professionals, at whatever level, to be holistic in their approach and to understand that sometimes a child or young person cannot speak, but has other ways in which they express themselves. It is vital for families to be given time, understanding and compassion in order for them to articulate themselves, in whatever fashion they need, to be able to cope in living with their shattered dreams.

In identifying our stressors of loss and restoration, the Dual Process model helps us to analyse our actions and in turn, this model acknowledges that through our adaptive behaviours we are able to recognize and confront our fears and feelings sometimes, but other times we have to avoid the grieving of such losses and that this is a perfectly natural process in coping. We didn't choose to have daughter with a profound disability, but we would never choose to be without her.

CHAPTER 18

Research, inclusivity and marginalised groups

Sue Read

SUMMARY

Research involving people with an intellectual disability (PWID) cannot be described as easy because it has not been done enough as yet. The aims of this chapter are to briefly introduce the concept of research and its particular importance in relation to healthcare practice; explore the challenges to meaningfully engaging marginalised groups across the research continuum; introduce research methodologies that may be conducive to inclusive research; and finally to identify research areas within the loss, dying, death and bereavement context for future considerations.

Introduction

Research is described as being:

> Compiled of two syllables *re* and *search*. The dictionary defines the former as a prefix meaning again, anew…and the latter as a verb meaning to examine closely and carefully, to test and try, or to probe. Together they form a noun describing a careful, systematic, patient study and investigation into some field of knowledge…to establish facts or principles. (Grinnell 1993, p.4)

More recently, Polit and Beck (2010, p.4) define it as 'systematic enquiry that uses disciplined methods to answer questions and solve problems. The ultimate goal of research is to develop, refine, and expand a body of knowledge.' In its simplest form, research can be described as 'finding out work', and health research incorporates the exploration of a wide range of issues, topics and themes incorporating the systematic and rigorous collection of data on clinical applications, organisations, service delivery, health outcomes and nursing/patient/family attitudes, knowledge and perceptions (Parahoo 1997).

Research remains fundamentally important across the health spectrum for a number of practical, socio economic, demographic and scientific reasons, namely because of:

- technological advances

- ageing populations

- treatment developments

- scientific advances

- complexity of healthcare needs

- escalating healthcare costs

- raised public expectations of healthcare services

- developing services

- introducing and managing change

- providing effective and efficient care – the best care possible

- emphasis on evidence based practice.

Remaining responsive and proactive to demographic trends is crucial to maintaining high quality standards and promoting optimum healthcare for all. Healthcare professionals are increasingly expected to understand and conduct research, and to base their professional practice on emerging evidence from research, adopting an evidence-based practice approach (EBP) to care delivery (Polit and Beck 2010).

Sackett (1997) describes EBP as the 'conscientious, explicit and judicious use of current best evidence in making decisions about the care of individuals or groups of patients', and healthcare professionals are adopting a critical, clinical decision-making approach to promote best practice outcomes (Salmond 2007). However, whether as a research consumer (e.g. participating in journal clubs, reading research journals, attending research conferences or helping others to solve clinical problems based on rigorous research); a producer and participant of research (e.g. by helping to develop ideas for a clinical study, assisting researchers or leading a study); or as a research lead, many healthcare professionals remain actively engaged across the whole continuum of research activities (Polit and Beck 2010).

Approaches to research

An individual's assumptions, concepts, values, practices and personal experiences all have the potential to influence and affect the way that reality is viewed, what Cresswell and Clark see as 'world views' or research paradigms (2007, p.21). Such paradigms may inform one's attraction to, and selection of, particular research methods, which are an important, fundamental consideration when conducting research across the different research populations in healthcare (Lindop 2006).

Research design involves translating research ideas and questions into plausible research projects, and the principle task is that of selecting appropriate research strategies and data collection methods to satisfy the fundamental aims of the research and its inherent questions/hypotheses. There are a variety of established research methods at the researchers' disposal, depending on the nature of the research, its aims and anticipated outcomes.

Research methods

Qualitative research incorporates 'Research that produces findings not arrived at by statistical procedures or other means of quantification' (Strauss and Corbin 1998, p.11), and is often perceived as the 'soft' side of research. Qualitative researchers are concerned with how people understand their experiences, presenting the uniqueness of each participant's individual situation (idiographic). They focus on explaining and understanding people's experiences and taking an insider's (emic) perspective, using their subjectivity (Watson *et al.* 2008), which is often inductive and exploratory (Janesick 2000). Qualitative researchers use narratives, documents and biographical data collection methods including (for example) ethnography, observation, semi-structured interviews, focus groups and case studies. Visual methodologies (Rose 2007) including the use of video, film and pictures (Heath, Hindmarsh and Luff 2010) and sensory ethnography (Pink 2009) are becoming popular with qualitative researchers, particular within the social sciences. 'It has long been recognised that visual media, including photography, film and more recently video, provide unprecedented opportunities for social science research' (Heath *et al.* 2010, p.2), and may also have much to offer health researchers.

In contrast, quantitative researchers adopt a positivist/empiricist paradigm incorporating reductionist, determinist, deductive (experiments) or inductive approaches. Quantitative methods are focused on the measurement and quantification of behaviour, attitudes and events and researchers are concerned with the *objective* measurement of reality where measurement (of frequency, intensity, etc.) can be compared, contrasted and illustrative. Such approaches are concerned with obtaining the most valid and reliable measurement.

However, incorporating both qualitative and quantitative research methods together also has great merits, with such triangulation of approaches combining the outcomes of numerical data with rich and illustrative texts. Mixed methods research is rooted in the social and behavioural sciences (Gray 2007) and is recognised by many as the third major approach or paradigm (Johnson *et al.* 2007). Mixed methods research includes data collection triangulation and/or data analysis triangulation.

Because of the very nature of the varying health contexts, research conducted within the healthcare population often includes vulnerable people, largely as a result of their healthcare status. However, some patients may be considered to be more vulnerable than others because of (for example) complex health diagnosis, or a pre-existing health diagnosis (such as having an intellectual disability) or because of multiple co-morbidities. Careful consideration may need to be addressed when involving sensitive or vulnerable populations in any research.

Research involving sensitive populations or vulnerable people

A vulnerable adult can be described as someone:

> Who is or may be in need of community care services by reason of mental or other disability, age or illness; and who is or may be unable to take care of him or herself, or unable to protect him or herself against significant harm or exploitation. (DH 2000, pp.8–9)

A person's vulnerability will always depend on their circumstances and environment, and each case must be considered individually. A bereaved person or a person with a life-limiting condition may be perceived as vulnerable, particularly if there are additional health needs (such as, for example, having an ID, mental health condition, or dementia) which may compound their understanding of treatment, options, decision making and of what is happening around them. Research involving sensitive populations has been described as 'when the people being studied are powerless or disadvantaged, where there is an opportunity for people to feel exploited or degraded, or when the subject matter is related to personals experience' (Owen 2001, p.656).

Any research involving PWID cannot be described as easy because it has not been done often enough as yet (Read and Corcoran 2009). There is steady trickle of research literature emerging where PWID have been collaborating in research (e.g. Atkinson 2004; Bigby and Frawley 2010; McClimens 2008), actively co-researching with others (e.g. Read and Bowler 2007; Tuffrey-Wijne and Butler 2009), leading the research (e.g. White and Morgan 2012) and purposely directing the methodological routes of research (Read *et al.* 2013). However, research directly involving PWID in the sensitive topics of death, dying and bereavement is particularly difficult to conduct because of the sensitive nature of the topic and the potential vulnerabilities of the population, but is slowly emerging (e.g. Read and Bowler 2007; Tuffrey-Wijne and Butler 2009).

Challenges to meaningful engagement
In 2005, the English Department of Health (DH) recognised:

> [The] fundamental shift in the nature of healthcare professionals' relationship with patients and the public, resulting in a move from a service that does things to and for its patients to one which is patient led, where the service works with patients to support them with their health needs; thus promoting a collaborative approach to care delivery. (DH 2005, p.3)

Within research, this included enabling service users to have a louder voice in research that focuses on them, where research is increasingly seen as 'must do activity' (Beresford 2000); and where service users' views are included in the design, conduct, analysis and reporting of health and social research (DH 2005).

Fox, Martin and Green (2007) describe service users as people who use health, education or social services; informal (unpaid) carers and parents; and organisations that represent service users' interests. Ways of being involved in research include the user or carer as a consultant, as a collaborator or as controlling the research (see INVOLVE at www.invo.org.uk).

Some people may be doubly disadvantaged when it comes to being involved in research from a health or social care perspective, because of compounding, existing predisposed conditions. Marrow *et al.* (2012) identifies a number of what they describe as 'seldom heard' groups in the research literature:

- people with physical disabilities

- deaf communities

- blind and partially sighted communities

- people with mental health issues

- black, minority ethnic groups

- people with ID.

Research is an important aspect of everyday life, has a flexible application, and does not have to be hierarchical and conducted purely by academics, although it is often perceived as such (Read and Corcoran 2009). People with an intellectual disability have a right to be involved in research, whether that right is by design or status, if that research incorporates issues that they can meaningfully contribute to and it can be a vehicle for listening and promoting meaningful consultation with PWID (Read and Corcoran 2009). The challenges to including PWID and their meaningful engagement in research are well documented. The intellectual disability itself (see Chapter 1) can incorporate a whole host of communication issues, but equally the values, beliefs and attitudes of the researchers themselves (i.e. wanting to involve PWID) remain crucial.

Ethical and methodological issues around understanding, anonymity, consent and roles (Stalker 1998); clarification of power, control and ownership of research (Nind 2008) and indeed levels of involvement, all require careful and early consideration and discussion to avoid exploitation and tokenism of any research collaborator.

To promote clarity around inclusivity and emancipation, Nind (2008) recommends researchers ask some of Barton's (1999) earlier fundamental questions:

- Who is this work for?

- What right do we have to undertake it?

- What responsibilities come with it?

The nature and quality of the relationship between researcher and participants remains fundamentally important and Walmsley (2004) recommends the negotiation and establishment of agreed terms of engagement together with protocols to focus on how rapport is established and the identification of agreed boundaries to be maintained throughout the research study. The inherent language used amongst research communities is often complex, involving somewhat alien concepts that are often notoriously difficult to spell or pronounce and do not easily translate into clear words and pictures (Nind 2008). Nind's review paper (2008) is an excellent resource, and is recommended for further reading around the challenges to engagement for this population. In summary, the concept of inclusive research practice involves:

- preparation:
  - research protocols
  - consent protocols
  - relationship building
  - wanting to involve

- consent/capacity:
  - engagement protocols
  - transport
  - access
  - environments
  - using clear words and pictures in all documents and consent forms

- communication:
  - ○ active not passive
  - ○ using clear words and pictures in all documents and consent forms
  - ○ creative approaches to meaningful engagement
- resources
- collaborative working.

Such practical considerations are important, and will influence the research methods selected for effective engagement.

Research methods conducive to inclusive research

Selecting the appropriate research method is one of the most important parts of the research process. Before identifying methods of involvement for any disabled person in research, it is important to recognise that the level of involvement adopted should be meaningful, proportionate and appropriate to each particular research project (Office for Disability Issues 2011). Involving PWID in the continuum of research (from consultation, through collaboration or via user controlled) can include a raft of research methods, such as:

- participatory action research
- interviews
- focus groups
- case studies
- narratives
- biographies
- life story approaches.

Common approaches include participatory or emancipatory research. Participatory research involves utilising the experiences of PWID themselves and partnership working and predominantly uses qualitative methods (Walmsly 2004), whereas emancipatory research aims to facilitate the empowerment of disabled people and their organisations through the research process, requiring researchers to have their knowledge and skills at the disposal of disabled people (Office for Disability Issues 2011). Emancipatory research can include qualitative and/or quantitative research methods.

While these aforementioned research methods are well established, involving PWID may mean adapting existing methods to suit their particular needs. For example, focus groups can be a useful method to help people to talk together, share their experiences and focus upon a particular identified issue. The focus group discussion is usually audiotaped, transcribed verbatim and analysed in accordance with the aims of the research. When facilitating a focus group for PWID this may mean translating the focus group questions, writing them down and adding pictures and words as the discussion progresses on large flip chart paper (see Figure 18.1). Primarily these serve as aides-memoires for the participants throughout the focus group discussion, but they can also be photographed and become further research data that also demonstrates how the researcher has attempted to fully engage with PWID within the research process. Involving PWID in research may also involve adapting consent forms to include words and/or pictures.

Figure 18.1 Recording a focus group discussion

Clearly engaging PWID in research requires careful and deliberate consideration prior to any involvement, and can prove time consuming and challenging. However, the merits of doing so far outweigh these challenges, as the Office for Disability Issues reminds us that:

Involving disabled people throughout the research process…
from the start will lead to better outcomes and will help you to
meet your objectives…enabling disabled people to participate
in your research will improve the quality of your data by
reducing the risk of excluding groups of interest. (Office for
Disability Issues 2011, p.10)

Exploring future research within loss, dying and death

The theories underpinning therapeutic care and support for PWID
experiencing loss, dying and bereavement are substantial and broad
reaching, as witnessed within this text. However, the evidence base
that informs these theories in relation specifically to PWID is variable,
with empirical findings inconsistent and lacking in many areas, as also
identified throughout this text. This book has raised numerous ideas
for future research across the spectrum of loss, death and dying which
it now feels appropriate to identify, whilst acknowledging that this is
only a flavour of research that could be undertaken.

Death never occurs in a vacuum, but within a social context, and
that context is crucial in enabling what support is provided and by
whom. For PWID diagnosed with life-limiting conditions, much will
depend upon those caring for (and around) them, as they are often
reliant on so many people for so much in their lives. This social context
will be pivotal in orchestrating and coordinating appropriate holistic
end-of-life care, particularly around the role of place, space and people
(personal and professional). We have much yet to learn from generic
hospice research around these issues of place and space (Moore *et al.*
2013) in relation to this client population when identifying what is
important to meaningful end-of-life care and support. One particular
space or context that currently lacks any notable evidence base is the
concept of loss within the forensic or medium secure environment.
Whilst Chapter 14 incorporates one of a handful of research studies
around this area, collaborative, international studies that provide
strategic direction around loss within assessments and encapsulates
therapeutic interventions is desperately required for this marginalised
population to provide consistency of support and guidance.

Ascertaining the person's preference for place of death is not
always clear and straightforward, as those caring for the dying person
with an intellectual disability (ID) will attest to. From a research,
operational perspective, we still have much to explore regarding the

expectations of PWID as the end of their life approaches and how we practically identify this. Holistic care incorporates parents and families, and there is still much to discover here and a strong evidence base particularly around therapeutic interventions will enhance an easeful death. From a managerial and strategic perspective, the identification of realistic strategic approaches to collaborative working that promotes empowerment of patients with an ID in their care and treatment remains fundamental to ongoing development around this sensitive area of care. Any approaches need to be underpinned by a strong evidence base to inform such strategies.

Whilst there is now general acceptance that PWID do grieve, there is little empirical evidence regarding what interventions work best, for whom, by whom and under what circumstances. There are numerous resources available to support therapeutic grief work, but no evidence as to whether (for example) stories or pictures (whether cartoons, photographs or cue cards) work well for certain bereaved PWID. There is a plethora of evidence around complicated grief generally, but relatively little in relation to PWID and its prevalence, impact and outcomes. A relatively new and developing concept in the grief world is that of resilience (see Chapter 7) and this provides opportunities to adapt and translate such ideas across to supporting PWID.

Recognising that PWID are living longer, and may be exposed to conditions associated with an ageing population, the longer term, enduring impact on families (parents and siblings) needs scrutinising, as families too are ageing alongside their children. Issues surrounding families (Chapter 12) and the potential for carer fatigue (Chapter 9) lack empirical evidence to underpin this longer term impact.

Such ideas for future research provide a brief flavour of areas that could be addressed within the realm of loss, dying and bereavement with the ID population, but of course are not exclusive and are directly related to many of the themes included within this text.

Conclusion

People with an ID have important thoughts and ideas to share with professionals; we simply need to establish the mechanisms to listen effectively and to promote opportunities for engagement within the world of research. The very act of involving people suggests they have something to offer that is valuable and worthwhile and research that proactively involves PWID is likely to be useful and fit for purpose.

For genuine involvement of PWID in research to become a meaningful reality, researchers must fully engage with the importance of the challenges and the need for additional considerations that enable active participation, particularly when the research areas are around the sensitive topics of loss, dying, end-of-life care and bereavement. Whilst research can be a vehicle for listening and meaningful consultation with PWID (Read and Corcoran 2009), it also has the capacity to enhance and inform the evidence base for the various professions.

It feels a fitting end to this book (having previously consolidated what we know about loss, dying and death in the preceding 17 chapters) to identify the areas on which we need to concentrate our future research endeavours. Indeed, all my professional life it has felt that the more that is discovered, the more it highlights the need to know more. Long may the quests continue.

Conclusion

Sue Read

Grief is a social activity, and the social contexts in which people with an intellectual disability (PWID) live, work, relax and eventually die are likely to be multiple and varied. Nonetheless, these myriad contexts remain crucial in enabling and shaping how members of this marginalised group experience loss, death and bereavement and subsequently manage emergent responses. The social networks of people surrounding those with IDs may be variably functioning as gatekeepers, filtering out information, knowledge and opportunities that may be deemed inappropriate or difficult before even involving the person with an ID themselves.

Sometimes dealing with death and dying may be perceived as too difficult for a person with an ID to deal with, and such individuals then miss opportunities to say goodbye to their loved ones and fail to learn the social etiquette involved (funerals for example) and about coping with loss and death. Such missed opportunities to share the pain and sorrow when a whole family or community stops for a while and weeps as it mourns their dead can be shared opportunities for learning. This learning can be about loss, about life, about death, about moving on, about sadness, about compassion and about resilience and growth. We cannot deny PWID the opportunities to learn about coping with loss, dying and death; how else did we ourselves learn about it?

Whilst we can try our best to protect and safeguard PWID from all manner of harm and abuse, we can never truly protect them from the sadness and pain of loss. Well-meaning people may try to deliberately avoid discussing feelings associated with loss with PWID; some may even decide to deliberately withhold information about death and dying and some may even be less than truthful regarding loss in the lives of this group of marginalised people. Involving PWID in loss, death and bereavement can be challenging and may be fraught with difficulties, but it can be done, as this book so ably and sensitively shows.

People with an ID can teach us so much about what's important in life, about unconditional love, about stigma, difference and indifference; they can teach us so much about humility and respect. They can also teach us much about loss, death and dying, if only we gave them the opportunity.

A lifetime of living means a lifetime of loss, of journeys where individuals can learn and become stronger in coping with these losses. Following the death of someone close, people may not always know the truth, indeed they may not be informed about the death, but they miss people who no longer visit, despite what well-meaning carers tell them about their loved ones. As one young man told me once, when I asked where he thought his mother was: 'She must be dead, she loved me so much, she would never not visit me for so long for any other reason.' These words were spoken some two years after the death of his mother, after the care staff had been reluctant to tell him because of his history of challenging behaviours. This man truly was having to 'make sense of nonsense'.

This book was introduced with a quote from Bonanno, which I repeat here:

> *If we understand the different ways people react to loss,*
> *we understand something about what it means to be*
> *human…something about the way we experience life*
> *and death, love and meaning, sadness and joy.*

(Bonanno 2009, p.3)

Understanding and appreciating the different ways that people react to loss and providing good support for bereavement and loss rely heavily on compassion for the person with an ID. Developing sensitive, thoughtful and realistic opportunities for genuine involvement and engagement, based on a foundation of mutual trust and respect, and emphasising person-centred, holistic care throughout, will nurture a healthy response to loss, dying and death.

People with an ID can teach us much about being human, as many have done so splendidly in this book, as their experiences have been woven within the fabric of every page. People with an ID can also show empathy and compassion to others. We simply need to reciprocate and show them empathy and compassion too.

References

Abrahams, B. S. and Geschwind, D. H. (2008) 'Advances in autism genetics: On the threshold of a new neurobiology.' *Nature Reviews Genetics 9*, 341–355.

Abma, T. A. (2005) 'Struggling with the fragility of life: A relational-narrative approach to ethics in palliative nursing.' *Nursing Ethics 12*, 4, 337–348.

ACT (Association for Children with Life-threatening or Terminal Conditions and their Families) (2003) *A Guide to the Development of Children's Palliative Care Services.* Bristol: ACT.

ACT (Association for Children with Life-threatening or Terminal Conditions and their Families) (2004) *The ACT Charter for Children with Life-Threatening or Terminal Conditions and their Families.* Bristol: ACT.

Agnew, A., Manktelow, R., Taylor, B. J., and Jones, L. (2009) 'Bereavement needs assessment in specialist palliative care: A review of the literature.' *Palliative Medicine 24*, 46–59.

Ainsworth, M. D. S. (1963) 'The Development of Mother-Infant Interaction among the Ganda.' In B. M. Foss (ed) *Determinants of Infant Behaviour.* London: Methuen.

Ainsworth, M. D. S., Bell, S. M. and Stayton, D. J. (1974) 'Infant-Mother Attachment and Social Development: Socialization as a Product of Reciprocal Responsiveness to Signals.' In M. Richards (ed) *The Integration of a Child into a Social world.* Cambridge: Cambridge University Press.

Ainsworth, M. D. S., Blehar, M. C., Waters, E. and Wall, S. (1978) *Patterns of Attachment: A Psychological Study of the Strange Situation.* Hillsdale, NJ: Erlbaum.

Ali, Z., Fazil, Q., Bywaters, P., Wallace, L. and Singh, G. (2011) 'Disability, ethnicity and childhood: A critical review of research.' *Disability and Society 16*, 7, 949–968.

Allison, H. G. (2001) *Support for the Bereaved and Dying in Services for People with Autism Spectrum Disorders.* London: National Autistic Society.

Alquraini, T. (2012) 'Critical components of successful inclusion of students with severe disabilities: Literature review.' *International Journal of Special Education 27*, 1, 42–59.

Ambalu, S. (1997) 'Communication.' In J. O'Hara and A. Sperlinger (eds) *Adults with Learning Disabilities: A Practical Approach for Health Professionals.* Chichester: John Wiley and Sons.

American Academy of Pediatrics (AAC) (2000) 'Palliative care for children.' *Paediatrics 106,* 2, 351–7.

American Psychiatric Association (2012) *Diagnostic and Statistical Manual of Mental Disorders (DSM-5).* Arlington: American Psychiatric Association.

Argyle, M. (1998) *Bodily Communication.* London: Methuen.

Arthur, A. R. (2003) 'The emotional lives of people with learning disability.' *British Journal of Learning Disabilities 31,* 25–30.

Asai, M., Morita, T., Akechi, T., Sugawara, Y., Fujimori, M., Akizuki, N., Nakano, T. and Uchitomi, Y. (2007) 'Burnout and psychiatric morbidity among physicians engaged in end-of-life care for cancer patients: A cross-sectional nationwide survey in Japan.' *Psycho-Oncology, 16,* 421–428.

Asperger, H. (1944) 'Die "Autistischen Psychopathen" im Kindesalter.' *Nervenkrankheiten 117,* 76–136. Cited in U. Frith (1989) *Autism, Explaining the Enigma.* Oxford: Blackwell.

Atkinson, D. (2004). 'Research and empowerment: Involving people with learning difficulties in oral and life history research.' *Disability and Society 19,* 7, 691–702.

Attig, T. (1996) *How we Grieve: Relearning the World.* New York: Oxford University Press.

Attig, T. (2011) *How We Grieve: Relearning the World* (2nd ed). New York: Oxford University Press.

Attwood, T. (2006) *The Complete Guide to Asperger's Syndrome.* London: Jessica Kingsley Publishers.

Barad, J. (2007) 'The understanding and experience of compassion: Aquinas and the Dalai Lama.' *Buddhist-Christian Studies 27,* 11–29.

Baron-Cohen, S. (2008) *Autism and Asperger Syndrome.* Oxford: Oxford University Press.

Barry, L., Kasl, S. and Prigerson, H. (2002) 'Psychiatric disorders among bereaved persons: The role of perceived circumstances of death and preparedness for death.' *American Journal of Geriatric Psychiatry 10,* 447–457.

Barton, L. (1999) 'Developing an Emancipatory Research Agenda: Possibilities and dilemmas.' In P. Clough and L. Barton (eds) *Articulating with Difficulty: Research Voices in Inclusive Education.* London: Sage.

Bates, P. and Davis, F. A. (2004) 'Social capital, social inclusion and services for people with learning disabilities.' *Disability and Society 19,* 3, 196–207.

Bauminger, N. and Shulman, C. (2003) 'The development and maintenance of friendship in high-functioning children with autism.' *Journal of Child Development 7,* 2, 447–456.

Becker, G. (1997) *Disrupted Lives: How People Create Meaning in a Chaotic World.* Berkeley: University of California Press.

Bekkema, N., deVeer, A. J. E., Hertogh, C. M. P. M. and Francke, A. L. (2013) 'Respecting autonomy in the end-of-life care of people with intellectual disabilities: A qualitative multiple-case study.' *Journal of Intellectual Disability Research* [Epub ahead of print]. Doi: 10.1111/jir/12023

Benderix, Y. and Sivberg, B. (2007) 'Siblings' experiences of having a brother or sister with autism and mental retardation: A case study of 14 siblings from five families.' *International Pediatric Nursing 22*, 410–418.

Beresford, P. (2000) 'Service users' knowledge and social work theory: Conflict or collaboration.' *British Journal of Social Work 30*, 4, 489–504.

Bergum, V. (2003) 'Relational pedagogy. Embodiment, improvisation and interdependence.' *Nursing Philosophy 4*, 121–128.

Bergum, V. (2004) 'Relational Ethics in Nursing.' In J. Storch, P. Rodney, and R.Starzomski (eds) *Toward a Moral Horizon: Nursing Ethics for Leadership and Practice*. Toronto: Prentice Hall.

Bergum, V. and Dossetor, J. (2005) *Relational Ethics. The Full Meaning of Respect*. Maryland: University Publishing Group.

Berube, M. (1996) *Life As We Know It: a Father, a Family, and an Exceptional Child*. New York: Pantheon Books.

Bhaumik, S., Watson, J., Barrett, M., Raju, B., Burton, T. and Forte, J. (2011) 'Transition for teenagers with intellectual disability: Carers' perspectives.' *Journal of Policy and Practice in Intellectual Disabilities 1*, 53–6.

Bicknell, J. (1983) 'The psychopathology of handicap.' *British Journal of Medical Psychology 56*, 167–178.

Bigby, C. (2010) 'A five-country comparative review of accommodation support policies for older people with intellectual disability.' *Journal of Policy and Practice in Intellectual Disabilities 7*, 1, 3–15.

Bigby, C. and Frawley, P. (2010) 'Reflections on doing inclusive research in the "making life good in the community" study.' *Journal of Intellectual and Developmental Disability 35*, 2, 53–61.

Bion, W. R. (1963) *Elements of Psycho-Analysis*. London: Heinemann.

Blackman, N. (2002) 'Grief and intellectual disability: A systemic approach.' *Journal of Gerontological Social Work 38*, 253–63.

Blackman, N. (2003) *Loss and Learning Disability*. London: Worth Publishing.

Blackman, N. (2012a) *The Use of Psychotherapy in Supporting People With Intellectual Disabilities Who Have Experienced Bereavement*. PhD dissertation: University of Hertfordshire.

Blackman, N. (2012b) 'Bereavement and people with intellectual disabilities: A critical review of the literature'. Paper presented at the Tosinvest Award at the International Association of Scientific Research into Intellectual Disability Congress, Halifax, Canada.

Blackman, N., and Curen, R. (2013) 'Psychoanalytical Approaches in Practice'. In P. Heslop and A. Lovell (eds) *Understanding and Working with People with Learning Disabilities who Self-injure*. London: Jessica Kingsley Publishers.

Blackman, N. and Todd, S. (2005) *Caring for People with Learning Disabilities who are Dying*. London: Worth Publishing.

Bluebond-Langner, M. (2000) *In the Shadows of Illness: Parents and Siblings of the Chronically Ill Child*. Princetown: Princetown University Press.

Bluebond-Langner, M., Belasco, J. and Goldman, A. (2005) 'Involving Children with Life-Shortening Illnesses in Decisions about Participating in Clinical Research: A Proposal for Shuttle Diplomacy and Negotiation.' In E. Kodish (ed) *Ethics and Research with Children: a Child-based Approach*. New York: OUP.

Boelan, P., van den Bout, J. and de Keijser, J. (2003) 'Traumatic grief as a disorder distinct from bereavement-related depression and anxiety: A replication study with bereaved mental healthcare patients.' *American Journal of Psychiatry 160*, 1229–1241.

Bogdashina, O. (2005) *Communication Issues in Autism and Asperger Syndrome: Do we Speak the Same Language?* London: Jessica Kingsley Publishers.

Bonanno, G. A. (2009) *The Other Side of Sadness: What the New Science of Bereavement Tells Us About Life After Loss*. New York: Basic Books.

Bonell-Pascual, E., Hulne-Dickens, S., Hollins, S., Esterhuyzen, A., Sedgwick, P., Abdelnoor, A. and Hubert, J. (1999) 'Bereavement and grief in adults with learning disabilities: a follow-up study.' *British Journal of Psychiatry 175*, 4, 348–350.

Boss, P. (1999) *Ambiguous Loss: Learning to Live With Unresolved Grief*. Cambridge: Harvard University Press.

Boss, P. (2006) *Loss, Trauma, and Resilience: Therapeutic Work With Ambiguous Loss*. New York: W.W. Norton & Company.

Boss, P. (2011) *Loving Someone who has Dementia*. San Francisco: Jossey-Bass.

Boström, P. K., Broberg, M. and Hwang, P. (2009) 'Parents' descriptions and experiences of young children recently diagnosed with intellectual disability.' *Child: Care, Health and Development 36*, 1, 93–100.

Botsford, A. L., and King, A. (2010) 'End-of-life Policies and Practices.' In S. L. Friedman and D. T. Helm (eds) *End-of-life Care for Children and Adults with Intellectual and Developmental Disabilities*. Washington DC: American Association on Intellectual and Developmental Disabilities.

Bouras, N. and Holt, G. (eds) (2010) *Mental Health Services for Adults with Intellectual Disability: Strategies and Solutions*. Hove: Psychology Press.

Bowlby, J. (1960) 'Grief and mourning in infancy and early childhood.' *Psychoanalytic Study of the Child 15*, 9–52.

Bowlby, J. (1979) *The Making and Breaking of Affectional Bonds*. London: Tavistock.

Bowlby, J. (1980) *Attachment and Loss, Vol. 3: Loss, Sadness and Depression*. New York: Basic Books.

Bowman, T. (2001) *Finding Hope when Dreams Have Shattered*. Minneapolis St Paul: Bowman.

Braddock, D., Emerson, E., Felce, D., and Stancliffe, R. J. (2001) 'Living circumstances of children and adults with mental retardation or developmental disabilities in the United States, Canada, England and Wales, and Australia.' *Mental Retardation and Developmental Disabilities 7*, 115–121.

Bradshaw, J. (2013a) 'Communication and Interviewing.' In. E. Chaplin, L. Underwood and S. Hardy (eds) *An Introduction to Autism Spectrum Conditions*. Brighton: Pavilion Publishing.

Bradshaw, J. (2013b) 'Commentary on "Communication is the key: improving outcomes for people with learning disabilities".' *Tizard Learning Disability Review 18*, 3, 141–145.

Brannström, M., Brulin, C., Norberg, A., Boman, K. and Strandberg, G. (2005) 'Being a palliative nurse for persons with severe congestive heart failure in advanced homecare.' *European Journal of Cardiovascular Nursing 4*, 4, 314–323.

Breau, L. M. and Burkitt, C. (2009) 'Assessing pain in children with intellectual disabilities.' *Pain Research and Management 14*, 2, 116–120.

Breitbart, W. (2008) 'Thoughts on the goals of psychosocial palliative care.' *Palliative and Supportive Care 6*, 211–212.

Brickell, C. and Munir, K. (2008) 'Grief and its complications in individuals with intellectual disability.' *Harvard Review of Psychiatry 16*, 1, 1–12.

British Association for Counselling and Psychotherapy. Available at www.bacp.co.uk, accessed on 2nd January 2014.

Brown, E. (ed) (2000) *Baseline Assessment and Target Setting for Pupils with Profound and Multiple Learning Difficulties*. London: David Fulton.

Brown, E. (2007) *Supporting the Child and the Family in Paediatric Palliative Care*. London: Jessica Kingsley.

Brown, E. (2012) 'Around the Time of Death: Culture, Religion and Ritual.' In A. Goldman, R. Hain and S. Liben (eds) *Oxford Textbook of Palliative Care for Children* (2nd ed). Oxford: OUP.

Brown, E. and White, K. (2008) 'The Transition from Paediatric Palliative Care to Adult Services.' In R. Gatrad, E. Brown and A. Sheikh (eds) *Palliative Care for South Asians: Muslims, Hindus and Sikhs*. London: Quay Books.

Brown, E., Kaur, J., Patel, R. and Coad, J. (2013) 'The interface between South Asian culture and palliative care for children, young people, and families – a discussion paper.' *Issues in Comprehensive Paediatric Nursing 1*, 1–24.

Brown, G. W. and Harris, T. O. (1989) 'Life Events and Measurement.' In G.W. Brown and T. O. Harris (eds) *Life Events and Illness*. New York: Guildford Press.

Brown, H., Burns, S. and Flynn, M. (2003) 'Please don't let it happen on my shift! Supporting staff who are caring for people with learning disabilities who are dying.' *Tizard Learning Disability Review 8*, 2, 32–41.

Brown, I. and Brown, R. I. (2003) *Quality of Life and Disability: An Approach for Community Practitioners*. London: Jessica Kingsley.

Brown, J. and Beail, N. (2009) 'Self-harm among people with intellectual disabilities living in secure service provision: A qualitative exploration.' *Journal of Applied Research in Intellectual Disabilities 22*, 503–513.

Brown, S. D. and Stoudemire, G.A. (1983) 'Normal and pathological grief.' *Journal of the American Medical Association 250*, 378–382.

Burgess, D. C., Burgess, M. A., and Leask, J. (2006) 'The MMR vaccination and autism controversy in United Kingdom 1998–2005: Inevitable community outrage or a failure of risk communication?' *Vaccine 24*, 18, 3921–3928.

Burton, J. W. (1993) *Conflict Resolution Theory and Practice: Integration and Application*. Manchester: Manchester University Press.

California Coalition for Compassionate Care (2007) *Thinking Ahead. My Life at the End. Workbook and DVD*. Available at www.coalitionccc.org/thinking-ahead.php, accessed on 19 November 2013.

Carney, T. (2013) 'Participation and service access rights for people with intellectual disability: A role for law?' *Journal of Intellectual and Developmental Disability 38*, 1, 59–69.

Carter, E. (2012) 'What matters most: families, disabilities, and compelling congregational supports.' Plenary presentation at 2012 Summer Institute on Theology and Disability, Chicago, Illinois. Accessed on 19/11/13 at http://bethesdainstitute.org/Theology2012Presentations.

Cartlidge, D. and Read, S. (2010) 'Exploring the needs of hospice staff when supporting people with an intellectual disability: A UK perspective.' *International Journal of Palliative Nursing 16*, 2, 93–98.

Caruso, G. A. and Osburn, J. A. (2011) 'The origins of and best practices in the principle of normalisation and social role valorization.' *Journal of Policy and Practice in Intellectual Disabilities 8*, 3, 191–196.

Centers for Disease Control and Prevention (2012) 'Prevalence of autism spectrum disorders – autism and developmental disabilities monitoring network, 14 sites, United States, 2008.' *CDC Morbidity and Mortality Weekly Reports 61*, 3, 1–19.

Centre for Economic Performance's Mental Health Policy Group (2006) *The Depression Report: A New Deal for Depression and Anxiety Disorders (Layard Report)*. Accessed on 19/11/13 at http://cep.lse.ac.uk/textonly/research/mentalhealth/DEPRESSION_REPORT_LAYARD.pdf

Chaison, J. (1996) "Hearing the Whole Story." In S. Gordon, P. Benner and N. Noddings (eds) *Caregiving: Readings In Knowledge, Practice, Ethics, and Politics*. Philadelphia: University of Pennsylvania Press.

Charmaz, K. (2006) *Constructing Grounded Theory: A Practical Guide Through Qualitative Analysis*. Thousand Oaks, CA: Sage.

Chiovitti, R. and Piran, N. (2003) 'Rigour and grounded theory research.' *Journal of Advanced Nursing 44*, 4, 427–435.

Christenson, P. and James, A. (eds) (2008) *Research with Children: Perspectives and Practices*. London: Falmer.

Clark, D. (ed) (2002) *Cicely Saunders – Founder of the Hospice Movement. Selected Letters 1959–1999*. Oxford: Oxford University Press.

Clayton, P. (2010) 'From insecure attachment to (partial) inter-subjectivity (fearful aloneness to safely being with others).' *Journal of Learning Disabilities and Offending Behaviour 1*, 1, 33–43.

Cleiren, M. (1992) *Bereavement and Adaptation: A Comparative Study of the Aftermath of Death*. London: Hemisphere.

Cleveland. D. W. and Miller, N. (1977) 'Attitudes and life commitments of older siblings of mentally retarded adults: An exploratory study.' *Mental Retardation 15*, 38–41.

Coad, J., Carter, B. and Bray, L. (2012) 'Home-based care for special healthcare needs: Community children's nursing services.' *Nursing Research 61*, 4, 260–268.

Cocking, A. and Astill, J. (2004) 'Using literature as a therapeutic tool with people with moderate and borderline learning disabilities in a forensic setting.' *British Journal of Learning Disabilities 32*, 1, 16–23.

Cogher, L. (2005) 'Communication and People with Learning Disabilities.' In G. Grant, P. Goward, M. Richardson and P. Ramcharan (eds) *Learning Disability: A Life-cycle Approach to Valuing People.* Maidenhead: OUP.

Conboy-Hill, S. (1992) 'Grief, loss and people with learning disabilities.' In A. Waitman and S. Conboy-Hill (eds) *Psychotherapy and Mental Handicap.* London: Sage.

Cooper, S. A., Smiley, E., Morrison, J., Williamson, A and Allan, L. (2007) 'Mental ill-health in adults with intellectual disabilities: Prevalence and associated factors'. *British Journal of Psychiatry 190*, 27–35.

Cooperrider, D., Sorensen, P.F., Whitney, D. and Yeager, T.F. (eds) (2000) *Appreciative Inquiry: Rethinking Human Organization Toward a Positive Theory of Change.* Champaign, IL: Stipes Publishing L.L.C.

Corr, C. (2002) 'Revisiting the Concept of Disenfranchised Grief' In K. Doka (ed) *Disenfranchised Grief: New Directions, Challenges, and Strategies for Practice.* Champaign, IL: Research Press.

Courtney, E. (2011) *Exploring the Palliative Care Needs and Delivery of Services to Young Children with Life-limiting Neurodevelopmental Disabilities and their Families: A Mixed Methods Study.* Unpublished PhD thesis submitted to the School of Nursing, Dublin City University, Ireland.

Cresswell, J. W. and Clark, V. (2007) *Designing and Conducting Mixed Methods Research.* London: Sage.

Crichton, J. H. M. (2009) 'Defining high, medium, and low security in forensic mental healthcare: The development of the Matrix of Security in Scotland.' *Journal of Forensic Psychiatry and Psychology 20*, 3, 333–353.

Crick, L. (1988) 'Facing grief.' *Nursing Times 84*.28, 61–62.

Cropanzano, R., Weiss, H. and Elias, S. (2003) 'The Impact of Display Rules and Emotional Labor on Psychological Well-being at Work.' In P. Perrewé and D. Ganster (eds) *Emotional and Physiological Processes and Positive Intervention Strategies (Research in Occupational Stress and Well-being, Volume 3).* Bingley: Emerald Group Publishing Limited.

Cummins, R. A. and Lau, A. L. D. (2003) 'Community integration or community exposure? A review and discussion in relation to people with an intellectual disability.' *Journal of Applied Research in Intellectual Disabilities 16*, 2, 145–157.

Davys, D., Mitchell, D. and Haigh, C. (2011) 'Adult sibling experience, roles, relationships and future concerns – a review of the literature in learning disabilities. *Journal of Clinical Nursing 20*, 2837–2853.

Dennison, T. and Mee, S. (2011) 'Personal Narrative and Life Story.' In H. Atherton and D. Crickmore (eds) *Learning Disabilities: Towards Inclusion.* London: Churchill Livingston Elsevier.

Department of Health (2000) *No Secrets: Guidance on Developing and Implementing Multi-Agency Policies and Procedures to Protect Vulnerable Adults from Abuse.* London: Department of Health.

Department of Health (2001a) *Valuing People: A New Strategy for Learning Disability for the 21st Century.* London: Department of Health.

Department of Health (2001b) *Family Matters: Counting Families In.* London: Department of Health.

Department of Health (2005) *Research Governance Framework for Health and Social Care* (2nd ed). London: The Stationery Office.

Department of Health (2008) *The End of Life Care Strategy – Promoting High Quality Care at the end of Life.* London: Department of Health.

Department of Health (2009) *Valuing Employment Now: Real Jobs for People with Learning Disabilities.* London: Department of Health.

Department of Health (2010) *High Secure Design Guide Overarching Principles.* London: Department of Health.

Department of Health (2012a) *Transforming Care: A National Response to Winterbourne View Hospital.* London: Department of Health.

Department of Health (2012b) *Compassion in Practice. Nursing, Midwifery and Care staff. Our Vision and Strategy.* London: Department of Health.

Deutsch, H. (1937) 'Absence of grief.' *Psychoanalytic Quarterly 6,* 12–22.

Devine, E. C. (1992) 'Effects of psychoeducational care for adult surgical patients: A meta-analysis of 191 studies.' *Patient Education and Counselling 19,* 129–142.

Di Blasi, Z., Harkness, E., Ernst, E., Georgiou, A. and Kleijnen, J. (2001) 'Influence of context effects on health outcomes: A systematic review.' *The Lancet 357,* 757–762.

Disability Rights Commission (2006) *Equal Treatment: Closing the Gap. A Report into the Inequalities in the Physical Health Experienced by People with Mental Health Problems and Learning Disabilities.* London: DRC.

Dockrell, J. and Carroll, C. (2009) 'Leaving special school: Post 16 outcomes of young people with specific language impairment.' *European Journal of Special Needs Education 25,* 131–147.

Dodd, P., Dowling, S. and Hollins, S. (2005a) 'A review of the emotional, psychiatric and behavioural responses to bereavement in people with intellectual disabilities.' *Journal of Intellectual Disability Research 49,* 537–543.

Dodd, P., Guerin, S., McEvoy, J., Buckley, S., Tyrrell, J. and Hillery, J. (2008) 'A study of complicated grief symptoms in people with intellectual disabilities.' *Journal of Intellectual Disability Research 52,* 5, 415–425.

Dodd P., McEvoy J., Guerin S., McGovern E., Smith E. and Hillary J. (2005b) 'Attitudes to bereavement and intellectual disabilities in an Irish context.' *Journal of Applied Research in Intellectual Disabilities 18,* 237–243.

Doka, K. J. (ed.) (1989) *Disenfranchised Grief: Recognising Hidden Sorrow.* New York: Lexington.

Doka, K. J. (ed) (2002) *Disenfranchised Grief: New Directions, Challenges and Strategies for Practice.* Champaign, Illinois: Research Press.

Doody, M. A., Hastings, R. P., O'Neill. S. and Grey, I. M. (2010) 'Sibling relationships in adults who have siblings with or without intellectual disabilities.' *Research in Developmental Disabilities 31*, 224–231.

Dowling, S., Hubert, J. and Hollins, S. (2003) 'Bereavement interventions for people with learning disabilities.' *Bereavement Care 22*, 2, 19–21.

Dowling, S., Hubert. J., White. S. and Hollins, S. (2006) 'Bereaved adults with intellectual disabilities: A combined randomized controlled trial and qualitative study of two community-based interventions.' *Journal of Intellectual Disability Research 50*, 4, 277–287.

Duffy, S. (2003) *Keys to Citizenship. A Guide to Getting Good Support for People with Learning Disabilities.* Birkenhead: Paradigm Consultancy and Development Agency Ltd.

Dunlop, S. (2008) 'The dying child: Should we tell the truth?' *Paediatric Nursing 20*, 828–31.

Ellem, K. A. and Wilson, J. (2010) 'Life story work and social work practice: A case study with ex-prisoners labelled as having an intellectual disability.' *Australian Social Work 63*, 1, 67–82.

Elliott, D. (1995) 'Helping people with learning disabilities to handle grief.' *Nursing Times 91*, 43, 27–29.

Elliott, D. (2003) 'Loss and Bereavement.' In M. Jukes and M. Bollard (eds) *Contemporary Learning Disability Practice.* Wiltshire: Quay Books.

Emerson, P, (1977) 'Covert grief reactions in mentally retarded clients.' *Mental Retardation 15*, 6, 46–47.

Emerson, E., Hatton, C., Robertson. J., Baines, S., Christie A. and Glover, G. (2013) *People with Learning Disabilities in England 2012.* Lancaster: Improving Health and Lives: Learning Disabilities Observatory.

Emerson, E., Hatton, C., Robertson, J., Roberts, H., Baines, S. and Glover, G. (2011) *People with Learning Disabilities in England 2010.* Durham: Improving Health and Lives, Learning Disability Observatory.

Emerson, E., Moss, S. and Kiernan, C. (1999) 'The Relationship between Challenging Behaviour and Psychiatric Disorders in People with Severe Developmental Disability.' In N. Bouras (ed.) (1999) *Psychiatric and Behaviour Disorders in Developmental Disabilities and Mental Retardation.* Cambridge: Cambridge University Press.

Erikson, E. H. (1980) *Identity and the Lifecycle: A Reissue.* New York: W. W. Norton.

Farrell, B., Vande Vusse, A. and Ocobock, A. (2012) 'Family change and the state of family sociology.' *Current Sociology 60*, 3, 283–301.

Feiler, A. and Watson, D. (2011) 'Involving children with learning and communication difficulties: The perspectives of teachers, speech and language therapists and teaching assistants.' *British Journal of Learning Disabilities 39*, 2, 113–20.

Ferrell, B. R. (2006) 'Understanding the moral distress of nurses witnessing medically futile care.' *Oncology Nursing Forum 33*, 5, 922–930.

Figley, C. R (1995) *Compassion Fatigue: Secondary Traumatic Stress Disorder from Treating the Traumatized.* New York: Brunner/Mazel.

Fillion, L., Duval, S., Dumont, S., et al. (2009) 'Impact of a meaning-centered intervention on job satisfaction and on quality of life among palliative care nurses.' *Psycho oncology 18*, 1300–1310.

Fitchett, G. (2002) *Assessing Spiritual Needs: A Guide for Caregivers.* Lima: Academic Renewal Press.

Folkman, S. (2001) 'Revised Coping Theory and the Process of Bereavement.' In M. Stroebe, R.O. Hansson, W. Stroebe, and H. Schut (eds) *Handbook of Bereavement Research.* Washington: American Psychological Association.

Forrester-Jones, R. (2013) 'The road barely taken: Funerals and people with intellectual disabilities.' *Journal of Applied Research in Intellectual Disabilities 26*, 243–256.

Forrester-Jones, R. and Broadhurst, S. (2007) *Autism and Loss.* London: Jessica Kingsley Publishers.

Fox, M., Martin, P. and Green, G. (2007) *Doing Practitioner Research.* London: Sage.

Francis, R. (2013) *The Mid Staffordshire NHS Foundation Trust Inquiry.* London: The Stationery Office.

Franklin, A. and Osbourne, C. (2009) *Independent Reviewing Officers Communicating with Children with Complex Communication Needs. An Investigation for DCFS.* London: The Children's Society.

Franklin, A. and Sloper, P. (2009) 'Supporting the participation of disabled children and young people in decision making.' *Children and Society 23*, 3–15.

Fraser, L., Miller, M., Aldridge, J., McKinney, P., Parslow, R. and Hain, R. (2011) *Life-limiting Conditions in Children in the UK. National and Regional Prevalence in Relation to Socioeconomic Status and Ethnicity'* Leeds: University of Leeds and Children's Hospices UK.

Fredriksson, L. (1999) 'Modes of relating in a caring conversation: A research synthesis on presence, touch and listening.' *Journal of Advanced Nursing 30*, 1167–76.

Fredriksson, L. and Eriksson, K. (2001) 'The patient's narrative of suffering – a path to health? An interpretive research synthesis on narrative understanding.' *Scandinavian Journal of Caring Science 15*, 3–11.

Fredriksson, L. and Eriksson, K. (2003) 'The ethics of the caring conversation.' *Nursing Ethics 10*, 138–47.

Freud, S. (1917) 'Mourning and Melancholia.' In J. Strachey (ed and trans) *Standard Edition of the Complete Psychological Works of Sigmund Freud.* London: Hogarth Press.

Frith, U. (2001) 'Mind blindness review and the brain in autism.' *Neuron 32*, 6, 969–979.

Froggatt, K., Wilson, D., Justice, C., MacAdam, M., Leibovici, K., Kinch, J. and Choi, J. (2006) 'End-of-life care in long-term care settings for older people: A literature review.' *International Journal of Older People Nursing 1*, 1, 45–50.

Gallagher, P. (2009) 'The grounding of forgiveness: Martha Nussbaum on compassion and mercy.' *American Journal of Economics and Sociology 68*, 1, 231–252.

Garbutt, R. (2011) 'Advocacy.' In H. Atherton and D. Crickmore (eds) *Learning Disabilities: Towards Inclusion* (6th ed). London: Churchill Livingston Elsevier Learning Disabilities.

Garnet, M. (2003) 'Sustaining the cocoon: The emotional inoculation produced by complementary therapies in palliative care.' *European Journal of Cancer Care 12*, 129–136.

Gaventa, W. (1996) 'Re-imaging the Role of Clinical Training for Hospital Chaplaincy and Pastoral Care: Moving Beyond the Institutional Walls to the Community.' In R. Anderson (ed) *A Look Back: The birth of the Americans with Disabilities Act.* Binghamton: Haworth Press.

Gaventa, W. (2006) 'Defining and Assessing Spirituality and Spiritual Supports: Moving from Benediction to Invocation.' In H. Switzky and S. Greenspan (2006) *What is Mental Retardation? Ideas for an Evolving Disability in the 21st century.* Washington, D.C.:AAMR.

Gaventa, W. (2008) 'Rekindling commitment: Reflections from a pastoral educator enmeshed in direct support professional workforce development and person centered supports.' *Journal of Intellectual Disability Research 52*, 7, 598–607.

Gaventa, W. (2010a) 'Learning from People with Disabilities: How to ask the Right Questions.' In H. Reinders (ed) *The Paradox of Disability: Responses to Jean Vanier and L'Arche Communities from Theology and the Sciences.* Grand Rapids: Wm. Eerdmans Publishing Co.

Gaventa, W. (2010b) 'Spirituality Issues and Strategies: Crisis and Opportunity.' In S. Friedman and D. Helm (eds) *End-of-life Care for Children and Adults with Intellectual Disabilities.* Washington: AAIDD.

Gaventa, W. (2012) 'Building communities of care at the end of life when there don't seem to be any: Lessons from people with intellectual disabilities.' *The Forum. Association of Death Education and Counselling 38*, 1, 26–29.

Gaventa, W. (2013a) 'Resources in developmental disabilities and coping with grief, death and dying.' Accessed on 13/11/13 at http://rwjms.umdnj.edu/boggscenter/projects/end_of_life.html

Gaventa, W. (2013b) 'Ideas from your peers: Strategies for supporting grief, loss, and end of life issues compiled from strategy planning groups at the Boggs Centre's grief, loss, and end of life workshops.' Accessed on 1/11/13 at http://rwjms.umdnj.edu/boggscenter/projects/end_of_life.html

Gerhardt, S. (2004) *Why Love Matters: How Affection Shapes a Baby's Brain.* London: Brunner-Routledge.

Ghaziuddin, M. (1988) 'Behavioural disorders in the mentally handicapped. The role of life events.' *British Journal of Psychiatry 152*, 683–686.

Gilbert, S. M. (2006) *Death's Door: Modern Dying and Ways of Grieving.* New York: W.W. Norton & Co.

Gilbert, P. (2009) *The Compassionate Mind.* London: Constable and Robinson.

Gilrane-McGarry, U. and Taggart, L. (2007) 'An exploration of the support received by people with intellectual disabilities who have been bereaved (Review).' *Journal of Research in Nursing 12*, 2, 129–144.

Glennen, S. L. (1997) 'Introduction to Augmentative and Alternative Communication.' In S. L. Glennen and D. C. DeCoste (eds) *Handbook of Augmentative and Alternative Communication.* San Diego: Singular Publishing Group.

Golbart, J. and Marshall, J. (2004) 'Pushes and pulls on the parents of children using AAC.' *Augmentative and Alternative Communication 20*, 4, 194–208.

Goldman, A. (2007) 'An overview of paediatric palliative care.' *Medical Principles and Practices 16*, 1, 46–7.

Gonzalez, N. (2005) *I am my Language: Discourses of Women and Children in the Borderlands.* Arizona: University of Arizona Press.

Gore, N. and Dawson, D. (2009) 'Mental disorder and adverse life events in a forensic intellectual disability service.' *British Journal of Forensic Practice 11*, 1, 8–13.

Gotto, G. S., Calkins, C.F., Jackson, L., Walker. H. and Beckmann, C. (2010) *Accessing Social Capital: Implications for Persons with Disabilities. A National Gateway to Self-Determination.* Funded by the US Department of Health and Human Services: Administration on Developmental Disabilities. Accessed on 3/1/14 at www.aucd.org/ngsd.

Gray, D. E. (2007*) Doing Research in the Real World* (2nd ed). London: Sage.

Greene, R. (2002) 'Holocaust survivors: A study in resilience.' *Journal of Gerontological Social Work 37*, 3–18.

Grey, R. (2010) *Bereavement, Loss and learning Disabilities: A Guide for Professionals and Carers.* London: Jessica Kingsley Publishers.

Grieg, A., Taylor, J. and MacKay, T. (2007) *Doing Research with Children* (2nd ed) London: Sage.

Grinnell, R. M. (1993) *Social Work Research and Evaluation* (4th ed). Itasca, IL: F.E.Peacock.

Grove, N. and Park, K. (2008) *Odyssey Now* (2nd ed). London: Jessica Kingsley.

Gunaratnam, Y. and Oliviere, D. (eds) (2009) *Narrative and Stories in Healthcare: Illness, Dying and Bereavement.* Oxford: Oxford University Press.

Hackett, A. and Palmer, S. (2010) 'An investigation into the perceived stressors for staff working in the hospice service.' *International Journal of Palliative Nursing 16*, 6, 290–296.

Hanh, T. N. (1987) *Being Peace.* Berkeley: Parallax Press.

Harcourt, D., Perry, P. and Waller, T. (eds) (2011) *Researching Young Children's Perspectives: Debating the Ethics and Dilemmas of Educational Research with Children.* Abingdon: Routledge.

Harper, D. C. and Wadsworth, J.S. (1993) 'Grief in adults with mental retardation: preliminary findings.' *Research in Developmental Disabilities 14*, 313–330.

Harrison, A. (2001) 'The mental health needs of patients in physical care settings.' *Nursing Standard 15*, 51, 47–54.

Hawkins, J. (2002) *Voices of the Voiceless: Person Centred Approaches and People with Learning Disabilities.* Hertfordshire: PCCS Books Ltd.

Healthcare Commission (2006) *Joint Investigation into Services for People with Learning Disabilities at Cornwall Partnership NHS Trust.* London: Healthcare Commission.

Healthcare Commission (2007) *Investigation into the Service for People with Learning Disabilities Provided by Sutton and Merton Primary Care Trust.* London: Healthcare Commission.

Heath, C., Hindmarsh, J. and Luff, P. (2010) *Video in Qualitative Research: Analysing Social Interaction in Everyday Life.* London: Sage.

Hegge, M. J. (2012) 'Ethical Issues in the Care of Individuals with Autism Spectrum Disorders.' In E. Giarelli and M. Gardner (eds) *Nursing of Autism Spectrum Disorder. Evidence-Based Integrated Care across the Life Span.* New York: Springer Publishing Company.

Heller, T. and Arnold, C. K. (2010) 'Siblings of adults with developmental disabilities: Psychological outcomes, relationships and future planning.' *Journal of Policy and Practice in Intellectual Disabilities 7*, 1, 16–25.

Help the Hospices (2012) *Towards Excellence in Hospice Care – Widening Access to Palliative Care for People with Learning Disabilities – Guidance and Resources for Professionals.* London: Help the Hospices.

Henderson, R. and Pochin, M. (2001) *A Right Result? Advocacy, Justice and Empowerment.* London: Policy Press.

Hendry, C. (2009) 'Incarceration and the tasks of grief: A narrative review.' *Journal of Advanced Nursing 65*, 2, 270–278.

Herbert, M. (1996) *Supporting Bereaved and Dying Children and their Parents.* Leicester: British Psychological Society.

Heslop, P., Blair, P., Fleming, P., Hoghton, M., Marriott, A. and Russ, L. (2013) *Confidential Inquiry into Preamture Deaths of people with Learning Disabilities* (CIPOLD). University of Bristol: Norah Fry Research Centre. Accessed on 10/1/14 at www.bris.ac.uk/cipold/fullfinalreport.pdf.

Hewitt-Taylor, J. (2005) 'Caring for children with complex and continuing health needs.' *Nursing Standard 19*, 42, 41–47.

Hill, E. L. (2004) 'Evaluating the theory of executive dysfunction in autism.' *Developmental Review 24*, 189–233.

Hilsman, G. (1997) 'Spiritual pathways: One response to the current standards challenge'. *National Association of Catholic Chaplains Newsletter. Vision VII*, 7, 8–9.

HM Government Equalities Office (2010) *Equality Act 2010.* Available at www.legislation.gov.uk/ukpga/2010/15/contents, accessed on 10 January 2014.

Hinds, J. D. (2007) "My Turn: 'I'm Sorry' Shouldn't Be the Hardest Words" *Newsweek*, May 28. 2013.

Hobson, B. (2012) *Exploring the Loss Experiences of People with Intellectual Disabilities in a Low Secure Environment.* Unpublished Doctoral Thesis, Staffordshire and Keele Universities, UK.

Hobson, B. and Rose, J. (2008) 'The mental health of people with intellectual disabilities who offend.' *The Open Criminology Journal 1*, 1, 2–18.

Holland, T., Clare, I. and Mukhopadhyay, T. (2002) 'Prevalence of "criminal offending" by men and women with intellectual disability and the characteristics of "offenders": Implications for research and service development.' *Journal of Intellectual Disability Research 46*, 6–20.

Hollins, S. and Esterhuyzen, A. (1997) 'Bereavement and grief in adults with learning disabilities.' *British Journal of Psychiatry 170*, 497–502.

Hollins, S., and Tuffrey-Wijne, I. (2009) *Am I Going to Die? (Books Beyond Words Series)*. London: RCPsych Publications and St George's University.

Holloway, D. (2004) 'Ethical dilemmas in community learning disabilities nursing: What helps nurses resolve ethical dilemmas that result from choices made by people with learning disabilities?' *UK Journal of Learning Disabilities 8*, 3, 283–298.

Horowitz, M. (1997) *Stress Response Syndromes*. Northvale, NJ: Aronson.

Howard, R., Rose, J. L. and Levenson, V. (2009) 'The psychological impact of violence on staff working with adults with intellectual disabilities.' *Journal of Applied Research in Intellectual Disabilities 22*, 538–548.

Howe, D. (1993) *On Being a Client: Understanding the Process of Counselling and Psychotherapy*. London: Sage.

Howlin, P. (2004) *Autism and Asperger Syndrome: Preparing for Adulthood* (2nd ed). London: Routledge.

Iacono, T. and Johnson, H. (2004) 'Patients with disabilities and complex communication needs.' *Family Physician 33*, 8, 585–9.

ICPCN (International Children's Palliative Care Network) (2008) *The ICPCN Charter of Rights for Life Limited and Life Threatened Children*. Accessed on 4/12/13 at www.icpcn.org/icpcn-charter/.

Illhardt, F. J. (2001) 'Scope and Demarcation of Palliative Care.' In H. Ten Have and R. Janssens (eds) *Palliative Care in Europe: Concepts and Policies*. Oxford, UK: IOS.

IMPACT (2007) 'Standards for paediatric palliative care in Europe.' *European Journal of Palliative Care 14*, 3, 2–7.

Inglis, P. A. and Dale, C. (2011) 'Justifications of detainment – from ideology to practice.' *Journal of Learning Disabilities and Offending Behaviour 1*, 1, 44–57.

INVOLVE. A national advisory group that supports greater public involvement in NHS, public health and social care research. Available at www.invo.org.uk, accessed on 30 December 2013.

Isherwood, T., Burns, M., Naylor, M. and Read, S. (2007) '"Getting into trouble": A qualitative analysis of the onset of offending in the accounts of men with learning disabilities.' *Journal of Forensic Psychiatry and Psychology 18*, 2, 221–234.

James, N. (2011) 'Working with Families.' In: H. Atherton and D. Crickmore (eds) *Learning Disabilities: Towards Inclusion*. London: Churchill Livingston.

Janesick, V. (2000) 'The Choreography of Qualitative Research Design: Minuets, Improvisations, and Crystallization.' In N. K. Denzin and Y. S. Lincoln (eds) *The Handbook of Qualitative Research*. Thousand Oaks, California: Sage.

Jeffreys, J. S. (2011) *Helping Grieving People – When Tears are not Enough. A Handbook for Care Providers* (2nd ed). East Sussex: Routledge.

Jennings, E. (1996) "For Charlotte with Down's Syndrome" from *In the Meantime* Manchester (UK): Carcanet Press Limited.

Jennings, S. (2005) *Creative Storytelling with Adults at Risk.* Bicester: Speechmark.

Jennings, S. (2013) *Using Storytelling to Support Children and Adults with Special Needs: Transforming Lives through Storytelling.* London: Routledge.

Johns, C. (2004) *Being Mindful, Easing Suffering: Reflections on Palliative Care.* London: Jessica Kingsley.

Johnson, J, G., First, M, B., Block, S., Vanderwerker, L.C., Zivin, K., Zhang, B. and Prigerson, H. G. (2009) 'Stigmatization and receptivity to mental health services among recently bereaved adults.' *Death Studies 33*, 8, 691–771.

Johnson, N., Backlund, E., Sorlie, P., and Loveless, C. (2000) 'Marital status and mortality: The national longitudinal mortality study.' *Annals of Epidemiology, 10*, 4, 224–238.

Johnson, R. B., Onwuegbuzie, A. J. and Turner, L. A. (2007) 'Towards a definition of mixed methods research.' *Journal of Mixed Methods Research 1*, 2, 112–33.

Joseph, S. and Linley, P. A. (2006) *Positive Therapy.* Hove: Routledge.

Judd, D. (1995) *Give Sorrow Words – Working with a Dying Child.* London: Free Association Books.

Kadambari, S., Williams, E., Luck, S., Griffiths, P., and Sharland, M. (2011) 'Evidence based management guidelines for the detection and treatment of congenital CMV.' *Early Human Development 87*, 723–728.

Kauffman, J. (2005) *Guidebook on Helping Persons with Mental Retardation Mourn.* Amityville, NY: Baywood Publishing Company.

Kearney, M. (2000) *A Place of Healing: Working with Nature and Soul at the End of Life.* New Orleans, LA: Spring Journal Books.

Kellehear, A. (2012) *Compassionate Cities: Public Health and End-of-life Care.* Oxfordshire: Routledge.

Kenyon, B. (2001) 'Current research in children's conceptions of death: A critical review.' *Omega Journal of Death and Dying 43*, 1, 63–91.

Kerr, M., Fraser, W. and Felce, D. (1996) 'Primary healthcare for people with a learning disability.' *British Journal of Learning Disabilities 24*, 1, 2–8.

Keywood, K., Fovargue, S. and Flynn, M. (1999) *Best Practice? Healthcare Decision-making by, with and for Adults with Learning Disabilities.* Manchester: NDT.

Killick, J. and Schneider, M. (2010) *Transforming Personal Material: Writing Yourself.* London: Continuum International Publishing Group.

Kingsbury, L. A. C. (2009) *People Planning Ahead: A Guide to Communicating Healthcare and End-of-life Wishes.* Washington DC: American Association on Intellectual and Developmental Disabilities.

Kingsbury, L. A. C. (2010) 'Use of Person-centred Planning for End-of-life Decision Making.' In S. L. Friedman and D. T. Helm (eds) *End-of-life Care for Children and Adults with Intellectual and Developmental Disabilities.* Washington DC: American Association on Intellectual and Developmental Disabilities.

Kingsley, E. P. (c1987) *Welcome to Holland.* Accessed on 27/5/14 at www.our-kids.org/archives/Holland.html.

Kirk, S. (2008) 'Transitions in the lives of young people with complex healthcare needs.' *Child: Care, Health and Development 34*, 5, 567–75.

Kirkpatrick, P. (2013) "Altered Self: Medical Directive." In *Odessa: Poems*. Minneapolis: Milkweed Editions.

Kitching, N. (1987) 'Helping people with mental handicaps cope with bereavement: A case study with discussion.' *Mental Handicap 15*, 60–65.

Klass, D., Silverman, P .R. and Nickman, S. L. (2006) Continuing Bonds: New Understanding of Grief. (2nd edition) London: Taylor and Franics.

Klass, D., Silverman, P. R. and Nickman, S. L. (1996) *Continuing Bonds: New Understandings of Grief* (1st ed) London: Taylor and Francis.

Klatt, K. (1991) 'In search of a mature understanding of death.' *Death Studies 15*, 2, 177–87.

Klein, M. (1940) 'Mourning and its Relation to Manic-depressive States.' In E. Jones (ed) *Contributions to Psychoanalysis*. London: Hogarth Press.

Koenig, O. (2012) 'Any added value? Co-constructing life stories of and with people with intellectual disabilities.' *British Journal of Learning Disabilities 40*, 3, 213–221.

Kristjanson, L., Lobb, E., Aoun, S. and Monterosso L. (2006) *A Systematic Review of the Literature on Complicated Grief*. Churchlands, Western Australia: WA Centre for Cancer and Palliative Care, Edith Cowan University.

Kübler-Ross, E. (1969) *On Death and Dying*. New York: Touchstone.

Lachappelle. Y., Wehmeyer, M. L., Haelewyck, M. C., Courbois, Y., Keith, K. D., Schalock, R., Verdugo, M. A. and Walsh, P. N. (2005) 'The relationship between quality of life and self-determination: An international study.' *Journal of Intellectual Disability Research 49*, 740–744.

Landrigan, P. J. (2010) 'What causes autism? Exploring the environmental contribution.' *Current Opinion in Paediatrics 2*, 219–225.

Lannen, P., Wolfe, J., Prigerson, H.G. and Onelov, E. (2008) 'Unresolved grief in a national sample of bereaved parents: Impaired medical and physical health 4–9 years later.' *Journal of Clinical Oncology 26*, 5870–5876.

Lascelles, L. (2011) 'Tuning in to Children with Speech and Language Impairment.' In S. Roulstone and S. McLeod (eds) *Listening to Children and Young People with Speech, Language and Communication Needs*. Guildford: J and R Press.

Latham, A. and Prigerson, H. (2004) 'Suicidality and bereavement: Complicated grief as psychiatric disorder presenting greatest risk for suicidality.' *Suicide and Life Threatening Behaviour 34*, 4, 350–362.

Lavin, C. (2002). 'Individuals with Developmental Disabilities.' In: K.J. Doka, (ed) *Disenfranchised grief: New directions, challenges and strategies for practice*. Illinois: Research Press.

Leick, N. and Davidson-Neilson, M. (1991) *Healing Pain*. London: Routledge.

Leslie, A. and Roth, D. (1993) 'What autism teaches us about meta representation.' In S. Baron-Cohen, H. Tager-Flusberg and D.J. Cohen (eds) *Understanding Other Minds: Perspectives from Autism*. Oxford: Oxford University Press.

Lester, P., Chesney, M. and Cookem, M. (2002) 'When the time comes to talk about HIV: Factors associated with diagnostic and emotional distress in HIV-infected children.' *Journal of Acquired Immune Deficiency Syndromes 31*, 307–17.

Lewer, A. and Harding, C. (2013) 'Communication is the key: Improving outcomes for people with learning disabilities.' *Tizard Learning Disability Review 18*, 3, 132–140.

Lewis, C. S. (1961) *A Grief Observed*. London: Faber and Faber Ltd.

Light, J. (1989) 'Toward a definition of communication competence for individuals using augmentive and alternative communication systems.' *Augmentive and Alternative Communication 5*, 2, 137–144.

Light, J. (1997) '"Communication is the essence of human life": Reflections on communicative competence.' *Augmentative and Alternative Communication 13*, 2, 61–70.

Lindemann, E. (1944) 'Symptomology and management of acute grief.' *American Journal of Psychiatry 101*, 141–148.

Linden, W. (1996) 'Psychosocial interventions for patients with coronary artery disease. A meta-analysis.' *Archives of Internal Medicine 156*, 745–753.

Lindop, E. (2006) 'Research, palliative care and learning disability.' In S. Read (ed) *Palliative Care for People with Learning Disability*. London: Quay Books.

Long, R. (2005) *Loss and Separation*. London: David Fulton Publishers.

Lord, C. and Bailey, A. (2002) 'Autism Spectrum Disorders.' In M. Rutter and E. Taylor (eds) *Child and Adolescent Psychiatry* (4th ed). Oxford: Blackwell Publishers.

Lord, C. and Jones, R. (2012) 'Annual research review: Re-thinking the classification of autism spectrum disorders.' *Journal of child Psychology and Psychiatry 53*, 5, 490–509.

Lord, J. and Hutchison, P. (1993) 'The process of empowerment: Implications for theory and practice.' *Canadian Journal of Community Mental Health 12*, 1, 5–22.

Luckerson, R., Coulter, D. L., Polloway, E. A., Reiss, S., Shalock, R. I., Snell, M. E., Spialink, D. M. and Stark, J. (1992) *Mental Retardation: Definition, Classification and Systems of Support*. Washington DC: American Association on Mental Retardation.

Lutfiyya, Z. M. and Schwartz, K. D. (2010) 'Applying the Dignity-conserving Model.' In S. L.Friedman and D. T. Helm (eds) *End-of-life Care for Children and Adults with Intellectual and Developmental Disabilities*. Washington DC: American Association on Intellectual and Developmental Disabilities.

MacHale R. and Carey, S. (2002) 'An investigation of the effects of bereavement on mental health and challenging behaviour in adults with learning disability.' *British Journal of Learning Disabilities 30*, 3,113–117.

MacHale, R., McEvoy, J. and Tierney, E. (2009) 'Caregiver perceptions of the understanding of death and need for bereavement support in adults with intellectual disabilities.' *Journal of Applied Research in Intellectual Disabilities 22*, 6, 574–581.

Machin, L. (1998) *Looking at Loss: Bereavement Counselling Pack* (2nd ed). Brighton: Pavilion Publishing.

Machin, L. (2001) *Exploring a Framework for Understanding the Range of Response to Loss: A Study of Clients Receiving Bereavement Counselling.* Unpublished Doctoral Thesis: Keele University, UK.

Machin, L. (2007a) *The Adult Attitude to Grief Scale as a Tool of Practice for Counsellors Working with Bereaved People.* Unpublished report for Age Concern, Tameside and Keele University.

Machin, L. (2007b) 'Resilience in Bereavement: Part 1.' In B. Monroe and D. Oliviere (eds) *Resilience in Palliative Care.* Oxford: Oxford University Press.

Machin, L. (2009) *Working with Loss and Grief: A New Model for Practioners* (1st ed.). London: Sage.

Machin, L. (2014) *Working with Loss and Grief: A New Model for Practitioners* (2nd ed). London: Sage.

Machin, L. and Spall, R. (2004) 'Mapping grief: A study in practice using a quantitative and qualitative approach to exploring and addressing the range of response to loss.' *Counselling and Psychotherapy Research 4*, 1, 9–17.

Maes, B. (2012) '*Palliative Care for Persons with Profound Intellectual and Multiple Disabilities.*' Paper presented at the 14th World Congress of the International Association for the Scientific Study of Intellectual Disability, Halifax, Nova Scotia, Canada.

Main, M. and Goldwyn, R. (1984) 'Predicting rejection of her infant from mother's representation of her own experience: Implications for the abused-abusing intergenerational cycle.' *Child Abuse and Neglect 8*, 2, 203–217.

Mairs, N. (1997) "Letting Go." *The Christian Century, 114*, 31, 1014.

Manning, C. (2010) '"My memory's back!" Inclusive learning disability research using ethics, oral history and digital storytelling.' *British Journal of Learning Disabilities 38*, 3, 160–167.

Manson, J. (2012) *Core Spiritual Questions: A Clinical Pastoral Education Reflection.* New Brunswick: The Elizabeth M. Boggs Center on Developmental Disabilities.

Markham, C. (2011) 'Designing a Measure to Explore the Quality of Life for Children with Speech, Language and Communication Needs.' In S. Roulstone and S. McLeod (eds) *Listening to Children and Young People with Speech, Language and Communication Needs.* Guildford: J and R Publishing.

Marrow, E., Boaz, A. Brearley, S. and Ross, F. (2012) Handbook of service user involvement in nursing and healthcare research. London: Wiley-Blackwell.

Martin, D. K., Emanuel, L. L. and Singer, P. A. (2000) 'Planning for the end of life.' *The Lancet 356*, 1672–1676.

Martison, I., Deck., E. and Adams, D. (1992) 'Ritual and Mourning Customs.' In J. Littlewood (ed) *Aspects of Grief: Bereavement in Adult Life.* London: Tavistock Routledge.

Maslach, C. (1982) *Burnout: The Cost of Caring.* Englewood Cliffs, NJ: Prentice Hall.

Maslow, A. (1973) *The Farther Reaches of Human Nature.* Harmondsworth: Penguin.

Matthews, D. (2002) 'Learning disabilities: The need for better health care.' *Nursing Standard 16,* 39, 40–1.

McCallion, P., McCarron, M., Fahey-McCarthy, E. and Connaire, K. (2012) 'Meeting the End of Life Needs of Older Adults with Intellectual Disabilities.' In E. Chang (ed) *Contemporary and Innovative Practice in Palliative Care.* Croatia: InTech.

McClimens, A. (2008) 'This is my truth, tell me yours: Exploring the internal tensions within collaborative learning disability research.' *British Journal of Learning Disabilities 36,* 4, 271–276.

McDermott, O., Prigerson, H. and Reynolds, C. (1997) 'Sleep in the wake of complicated grief symptoms: an exploratory study.' *Biological Psychiatry 41,* 6, 710–716.

McEvoy, J., Guerin, S., Dodd, P. and Hillery, J. (2010) 'Supporting adults with an intellectual disability during experiences of loss and bereavement: Staff views, experiences and suggestions for training.' *Journal of Applied Research in Intellectual Disabilities 23,* 585–596.

McEvoy, J., MacHale, R. and Tierney, E. (2012) 'Concept of death and perceptions of bereavement in adults with intellectual disabilities.' *Journal of Intellectual Disability Research 56,* 191–203.

McEvoy, J., Reid, Y. and Guerin S. (2002) 'Emotion recognition and concept of death in people with learning disabilities.' *British Journal of Learning Disabilities 48,* 83–89.

McGinn, M. K., Shields, C., Manley-Casimir, M., Grundy, A. L. and Fenton, N. (2005) 'Living ethics: A narrative of collaboration and belonging in a research team.' *Reflective Practice: International and Multidisciplinary Perspectives 6,* 4, 551–567.

McGuire, J. and McDonnell, J. (2008) 'Relationships between recreation and levels of self-determination for adolescents and young adults with disabilities.' *Career Development for Exceptional Individuals 31,* 3, 154–163.

McKnight, J. (1985) *John Deere and the Bereavement Counselor.* Fourth Annual E. F. Schumacher Lectures, October 1984, New Haven, Connecticut.

McLeod, S. (2011) 'Listening to Children and Young People with Speech, Language and Communication Needs: Who, Why and How?' In S. Roulstone and S. McLeod (eds) *Listening to Children and Young People with Speech, Language and Communication Needs.* Guildford: J and R Publishing.

McLoughlin, J. (1986) 'Bereavement in the mentally handicapped.' *British Journal of Hospital Medicine 36,* 4, 256–60.

Medina, J. (2006) *Speaking from Elsewhere: A New Contextualist Perspective on Meaning, Identity and Discursive Agency.* Albany: State University of New York Press.

Mencap (2004) *Treat me Right!* London: Mencap.

Mencap (2007) *Death by Indifference.* London: Mencap.

Mencap (2012) *Death by Indifference: 74 Deaths and Counting.* London: Mencap.

Mencap (2013a) *What is a Learning Disability?* Accessed on 3/1/14 at www.mencap.org.uk/all-about-learning-disability/about-learning-disability.

Mencap (2103b) *Communicating with People with a Learning Disability: A Guide.* Available at www.mencap.org.uk/all-about-learning-disability/information-professionals/communication, accessed on 20 June 2014.

Mental Capacity Act (2005). London: The Stationery Office Limited.

Mental Health Act (2009) London: The Stationery Office Limited.

Minnis, H., Fleming, G. and Cooper, S. (2010) 'Reactive attachment disorder symptoms in adults with intellectual disabilities.' *Journal of Applied Research in Intellectual Disabilities 23*, 4, 398–403.

Moss, S. (2010) *PAS-ADD Mental Health Assessments for People with Intellectual Disability.* Brighton: Pavilion Publishing.

Moore, A. J., Carter, B., Hunt, A., and Sheikh, K. (2013) '"I am closer to this place" – Space, place and notions of home in lived experiences of hospice day care.' *Health and Place 19*, 151–8.

Mount, B. and Kearney, M. (2003) 'Healing and palliative care: Charting our way forward.' *Palliative Medicine 17*, 657–658.

Moyson, T. and Roeyers, H. (2012) '"The overall quality of my life as a sibling is all right, but of course, it could be better". Quality of life of siblings of children with intellectual disability: The siblings' perspective.' *Journal of Intellectual Disability Research 56*, 1, 87–101.

Muhle, R., Trentacoste, S. V. and Rapin, I. (2004) 'The genetics of autism.' *Paediatrics 113*, 5, 472–86.

Murdock, G. P. (1949) *Social Structure.* New York: The MacMillan Company.

Murray, G. C., McKenzie, K. and Quigley, A. (2000) 'An examination of the knowledge and understanding of health and social care staff about the grieving process in individuals with a learning disability.' *Journal of Learning Disabilities 4*, 1, 77–90.

Nadarajah, J., Roy, A., Harris, T. O. and Corbett, J. A. (1995) 'Methodological aspects of life events research in people with learning disabilities: A review and initial findings.' *Journal of Intellectual Disability Research 39*, 47–56.

Naseef, R. A. (2013) *Autism in the Family: Caring and Coping Together.* Baltimore: Paul A. Brookes Publishing Company.

National Autistic Society (2013) *What is Autism?* Accessed on 20/10/13 at www.autism.org.uk/about-autism/autism-and-asperger-syndrome-an-introduction/what-is-autism.aspx

National Health Service Act (2006). London: HMSO.

National Institute of Health (2006) *Talking to Children about Death: Patient Information.* Bethesda: CCNIH.

Neff, K. D. (2003) 'The development and validation of a scale to measure self-compassion.' *Self and Identity 2*, 3, 223–250.

Neimeyer, R.A. (2000) 'Searching for the meaning of meaning: Grief therapy and the process of reconstruction.' *Death Studies 24*, 541–558.

Nichols, K. (1993) *Psychological Care in Physical Illness.* London: Chapman and Hall.

Nichols, K. (2003) *Psychological Care for Ill and Injured People.* Maidenhead: Open University Press.

Nind, M. (2008) *Conducting Qualitative Research with People with Learning, Communication and Other Disabilities: Methodological Challenges.* Southampton: National Centre for Research Methods.

Nouwen, H. J. M., McNeill, D. and Morrison, D. (1982) *Compassion – A Reflection on the Christian Life.* New York: Doubleday.

Nozawa, N., Fang-Hoover, J., Tabata, T., Maidji, E. and Pereira, L. (2009) 'Cytomegalovirus-specific, high-avidity IgG with neutralizing activity in maternal circulation enriched in the foetal bloodstream.' *Journal of Clinical Virology 46*, 4, 58–63.

Nussbaum, M. C. (1996) 'Compassion: The basic social emotion.' *Social Philosophy and Policy 13*, 27–58.

Nussbaum, M. (2001) *Upheavals in Thought: The Intelligence of Emotions.* Cambridge: Cambridge University Press.

O'Connor, M. (2012) 'Immunological and neuroimaging biomarkers of complicated grief.' *Dialogues Clinical Neuropsychology 14*, 2, 141–148.

O'Donohue, J. (2003) *Divine Beauty: The Invisible Embrace.* London: Bantam Press.

O'Hara, J. and Sperlinger, D. (1997) *Adults with Learning Disabilities. A Practical Approach for Health Professionals.* Chichester: Wiley.

O'Kelly, E. and O'Kelly, C. (2006) *Chasing Daylight: How my Forthcoming Death Transformed my Life.* London: Mcgraw Hill.

O'Nians, R. (1993) 'Support in Grief.' *Nursing Times 89*, 50, 62–64.

Office for Disability Issues (2011) *Involving Disabled People in Social Research: Guidance by the Office for Disability Issues.* London: UK Stationery Office.

Office for National Statistics (2012) *Families and Households – 2012.* Accessed on 17/12/14 at www.ons.gov.uk/ons/rel/family-demography/families-and-households/2012/index.html, accessed on 17/12/13.

Oswin, M. (1981) *Bereavement and Mentally Handicapped People.* London: King's Fund Report KFC 81/234.

Oswin, M. (2000) *Am I Allowed to Cry?* (2nd ed). London: Souvenir Press.

Owen, S. (2001) 'The practical, methodological and ethical dilemmas of conducting focus groups with vulnerable clients.' *Journal of Advanced Nursing 36*, 5, 652–8.

Palletti, R. (2008) 'Recovery in context: Bereavement, culture, and the transformation of the therapeutic self.' *Death Studies 32*, 1, 17–26.

Palliative Care Australia (n.d.) *Guidelines for a Palliative Care Approach in Residential Aged Care: End of life Care.* Accessed on 4/12/13 at http://agedcare.palliativecare.org.au/Portals/35/EndofLife/EndOfLifeCareResource.pdf

Parahoo, K. (1997) *Nursing Research: Principles, Process and Issues.* Basingstoke: Macmillan.

Parkes, C. M. (1996) *Bereavement Studies of Grief in Adult Life* (3rd ed). London: Routledge.

Parkes, C. M. (2006) *Love and Loss: The Roots of Grief and its Complications.* London: Routledge.

Parkes, C. M. and Weiss, R. S. (1983) *Recovery from Bereavement.* New York: Basic Books.

Parks, M. (2012) 'Caring for a child with profound disabilities: A mother's story.' *Learning Disability Practice 15*, 5, 27–30.

Percy-Smith, B. and Thomas, N. (eds) (2010) *A Handbook of Children's and Young People's Participation: Perspectives from Theory and Practice*. London: Routledge.

Persaud, M. (2006) 'Historical Perspectives – Care for People with Learning Disabilities over the Past Century.' In S. Read (ed) *Palliative Care for People with Learning Disabilities*. London: Quay Books.

Petalas, M. A., Hastings, R. P., Nash, S., Hall, L. M., Joannidi, H. and Dowey, A. (2012) 'Psychological adjustments and sibling relationships in siblings of children with autism spectrum disorders: Environmental stressors and the broad autism phenotype.' *Research in Autism Spectrum Disorders 1*, 6, 546–555.

Polit, D. F. and Beck, C. T. (2010) *Essentials of Nursing: Appraising Evidence for Nursing Practice*. Philadelphia: Lippincott, Williams and Wilkins.

Pink, S. (2009) *Doing Sensory Ethnography*. London: Sage.

Poston, D. and Turnbull, A. (2004) 'Role of spirituality and religion in family quality of life for families of children with disabilities'. *Education and Training in Developmental Practice 39*, 2, 95–108.

Priest, H. (2012) *An Introduction to Psychological Care in Nursing and the Health Professions*. London: Routledge.

Priest, H. and Gibbs, M. (2004) *Mental Health Care for People with Learning Disabilities*. Oxford: Elsevier/Churchill Livingstone.

Prigerson, H., Shear K., Jacobs S., Reynolds, C. and Maciejewski, P. (1999) 'Consensus criteria for traumatic grief: A preliminary empirical test.' *British Journal of Psychiatry 174*, 67–73.

Prigerson H. G., Vanderwerker L. C. and Maciejewski, P. K. (2008) 'Complicated Grief as a Mental Disorder: Inclusion in DSM.' In M. Stroebe, R. Hansson, H. Schut and W. Stroebe (eds) *Handbook of Bereavement Research and Practice: 21st Century Perspectives*. Washington DC: American Psychological Association Press.

Puchalski, C. (2013) *The FICA Spiritual History Tool*. Accessed on 4/12/13 at http://smhs.gwu.edu/gwish/clinical/fica/spiritual-history-tool.

Raji, O. and Hollins, S. (2003) 'How far are people with learning disabilities involved in funeral rites?' *British Journal of Learning Disabilities 31*, 42–45.

Randall, F. and Downie, R. S. (2006) *The Philosophy of Palliative Care: Critique and Reconstruction*. Oxford: Oxford University Press.

Read, S. (1996) 'How counselling services can help deal with loss and change.' *Nursing Times 92*, 38, 40–41.

Read, S. (1999) 'Creative Ways of Working when Exploring the Bereavement Counselling Process.' In N. Blackman (ed) *Living with Loss*. Brighton: Pavilion Publishing.

Read, S. (2001) 'A year in the life of a bereavement counselling and support service for people with learning disabilities.' *Journal of Learning Disabilities 5*, 1, 19–33.

Read, S. (2005a) 'Palliative care for people with learning disabilities: Recognizing pitfalls and exploring potential.' *International Journal of Palliative Nursing 11*, 1, 15–20.

Read S. (2005b) 'Loss, bereavement and learning disability: Providing a continuum of support.' *Learning Disability Practice 8*, 1, 31–37.

Read, S. (2006) 'Communication in the Dying Process.' In S. Read (ed) *Palliative Care for People with Learning Disability*. London: Quay Books.

Read, S. (2007*) Bereavement Counselling for People With Learning Disabilities*. London: Quay Books.

Read, S. (2008) 'Loss, bereavement, counselling and support: An intellectual disability perspective.' *Grief Matters 11*, 2, 54–59.

Read, S. (2010) '*When Someone you Know has Died...*' United Kingdom: Faculty of Health, School of Nursing and Midwifery, Keele University.

Read, S. (2011) 'End of Life.' In H. Atherton and D. Crickmore (eds) *Learning Disabilities: Towards Inclusion* (6th ed). London: Churchill Livingston Elsevier.

Read, S. and Bowler, C. (2007) 'Life story work and bereavement: Shared reflections on its usefulness.' *Learning Disability Practice 10*, 4, 10–15.

Read, S. and Corcoran, P. (2009) 'Research: A vehicle for listening and promoting meaningful consultation with people with an intellectual disability.' *British Psychological Society Qualitative Methods in Psychology Bulletin 8, 29–37.*

Read, S. and Elliott, D. (2003) 'Death and learning disability: A vulnerability perspective.' *Journal of Adult Protection 5*, 1, 5–14.

Read, S. and Morris, H. (2008) *Living and Dying with Dignity: The Best Practice Guide to End of-life Care for People with a Learning Disability.* London: Mencap.

Read, S. Nte, S., Corcoran, P. and Stephens, R. (2013) 'Using action research to design bereavement software: Engaging people with intellectual disabilities for effective development.' *Journal of Applied Research in Intellectual Disabilities 26*, 3, 195–206.

Realpe, A. and Wallace, L. M. (2010) *What Is Co-production?* Coventry University: The Health Foundation.

Regnard, C., Reynolds, J., Watson, B., Matthews, D., Gibson, L. and Clarke, C. (2007) 'Understanding distress in people with severe communication difficulties: Developing and assessing the Disability Distress Assessment Tool (DisDAT).' *Journal of Intellectual Disability Research 51*, 4, 277–92.

Reindal, S. M. (1999) 'Independence, dependence, interdependence: Some reflections on the subject and personal autonomy.' *Disability and Society 14*, 3, 353–367.

Reiss, S., Levitan, G. W. and Szyszko, J. (1982) 'Emotional disturbance and mental retardation: Diagnostic overshadowing.' *American Journal of Mental Deficiency 86*, 567–574.

Remen, R. N. (1996) *Kitchen Table Wisdom: Stories That Heal.* New York: Riverhead Books.

Remen, R. N. (2000) *My Grandfather's Blessings*. New York: Riverhead Books.

Reynolds, C., Miller, M., Pasternak, R., Frank, E., Perel, J. and Cornes, C. (1999) 'Treatment of bereavement related major depressive episodes in later life: A controlled study of acute and continuation treatment with nortryptiline and interpersonal psychotherapy.' *American Journal of Psychiatry 156*, 2, 202–208.

Roberts, B. and Hamilton, C (2010) '"Out of the darkness into the light". A life-story from Ireland.' *British Journal of Learning Disabilities 38*, 2, 127–132.

Roberts, S. (ed) (2011) *Professional Spiritual and Pastoral Care: A Practical Clergy and Chaplain's Handbook.* Woodstock, VT: Skylight Paths Publishing.

Rogers, C. R. (1961) *On Becoming a Person.* London: Constable.

Rogers, C. R. (1980) *A Way of Being.* Boston: Houghton Mifflin.

Rose, G. (2007) *Visual Methodologies: An Introduction to the Interpretation of Visual Materials* (2nd ed). London: Sage.

Rosenblatt, P. C. (1996) 'Grief that does not end.' In D. Klass, P. R. Silverman and S. L. Nickman (eds) *Continuing Bonds: New Understandings of Grief.* Washington DC: Taylor and Francis.

Roulstone, S. and McLeod, S. (2011) *Listening to Improve Services for Children and Young people with Speech, Language and Communication Needs.* Guildford: J and R Press.

Ryan, K., Guerin, S., Dodd, P. and McEvoy, J. (2011a) 'End-of-life care for people with intellectual disabilities: Paid carer perspectives.' *Journal of Applied Research in Intellectual Disabilities 24*, 3, 199–207.

Ryan, K., Guerin, S., Dodd, P. and McEvoy, J. (2011b) 'Communication contexts about illness, death and dying for people with intellectual disabilities and life-limiting illness.' *Palliative and Supportive Care 9*, 201–208.

Rumi, M. J. (2007) 'The Guest House.' In N. Astley and P. Robertson-Pearce (eds) *Soul Food: Nourishing Poems for Starved Minds.* Tarset, Northumberland: Bloodaxe Books Ltd.

Ryan, K., McEvoy, J., Guerin, S. and Dodd, P. (2010) 'An exploration of the experience, confidence and attitudes of staff to the provision of palliative care to people with intellectual disabilities.' *Palliative Medicine 24*, 6, 566–72.

Sackett, D. L. (1997) 'Evidence-based medicine.' *Seminars in Perinatology 21*, 1, 3–5.

Salmond, S. (2007) 'Advancing evidence based practice: A primer.' *Orthopaedic Nursing 26*, 2, 114–125.

Saunders, C. (1996) 'Into the valley of the shadow of death: A personal therapeutic journey.' *British Medical Journal 7072*, 313, 1599–1601.

Saunders, C. and Sykes, N. (eds) (1993) *The Management of Terminal Malignant Disease* (3rd ed). London: Edward Arnold.

Schaffer, H. R. (1958) 'Objective observations of personality development in early infancy.' *British Journal of Medical Psychology 31*, 174–183.

Schalock, R. L. (1997) 'The conceptualization and measurement of quality of life: Current status and future considerations.' *Journal of Development Disabilities, 5*, 1–21.

Schuengel, C. and Van Ijzendoorn, M. (2001) 'Attachment in mental health institutions: A critical review of assumptions, clinical implications, and research strategies.' *Attachment and Human Development 3*, 3, 304–323.

and Butler, G. (2009) 'Co-researching with people with learning
experience of involvement in qualitative data analysis.' *Health*
13, 174–184.

and McEnhill, L. (2008) 'Communication difficulties and
isability in end of life care.' *International Journal of Palliative*
189–94.

Hogg J. and Curfs, L. (2007) 'End-of-life and palliative care
intellectual disabilities who have cancer or other life-limiting
w of the literature and available resources.' *Journal of Applied*
ellectual Disabilities 20, 331–344.

mbly (2006) Convention on the Rights of Persons with
RES/61/106, Annex I. Accessed on 4/12/13 at www.refworld.
0cd212.html.

ble (n.d) *Ratifications and Signatories of the Convention and its*
ol. Accessed on 4/12/13 at www.un.org/disabilities/countries.
ndpid=166.

d Huggard, J. (2010) 'The Experience of the Nurse in End-of-
21ˢᵗ Century: Mentoring the Next Generation.' In B. R.Ferrell
eds) *Oxford Textbook of Palliative Nursing* (3ʳᵈ ed). New York:
ity Press.

d Müeller, M. (2009) 'Burnout and Symptoms of Stress.' In
d H. Chochinov (eds) *Handbook of Psychiatry in Palliative*
York: Oxford University Press.

Bereavement Narratives: Continuing Bonds in the Twenty-first
: Routledge.

., Stroebe, M., Schut, H., Stroebe, W. and van den Bout,
ating processes in bereavement: The role of rumination,
interpretations, and deliberate grief avoidance.' *Social*
cine 71, 9, 1669–1676.

, S., Beery, L., Jacobs, S. and Prigeron, H. (1998) 'The
ital quality and attachment styles on traumatic grief and
ms.' *Journal of Nervous and Mental Disease 186*, 9, 566–

nd Maes, B. (2005) 'Reminiscence in ageing people with
ities: An exploratory study.' *British Journal of Developmental*
3–16.

nd Maes, B. (2008) 'A review of critical, person-centred
aches to reminiscence work for people with intellectual
v).' *International Journal of Disability, Development and*
8–60.

d Maes, B. (2009) 'The effect of reminiscence group work
self-esteem and mood of ageing people with intellectual
of Applied Research in Intellectual Disabilities 22, 1, 23–33.
s, S., Parkes, C. and Prigerson, H. (2006) 'An exploration
een separation anxiety in childhood and complicated grief
of Nervous and Mental Disease 194, 2, 121–123.

Schultz, C. L. and Harris, D. L. (2011) 'Giving Voice to Non-finite Loss and Grief in Bereavement.' In R. A. Neimeyer, D. L. Harris, H. R. Winokuer and G. F. Thornton (eds) *Grief and Bereavement in Contemporary Society; Bridging Research and Practice*. London: Routledge.

Seligman, M. E. P. and Csikszentmihalyi, M. (2000) 'Positive psychology: An introduction.' *American Psychologist 55*, 5–14.

Sepúlveda, M., Marlin, A., Yoshida, T. and Ullrich, A. (2002). 'Palliative care: The World Health Organization's global perspective.' *Journal of Pain and Symptom Management 24*, 2, 91–96.

Sequeira, H. and Halstead, S. (2002) 'Control and restraint in the UK: Service user services.' *Learning Disability Practice 7*, 12–15.

Shear K., Frank E., Houck P and Reynolds C. (2005) 'Treatment of complicated grief: A randomized controlled trial.' *Journal of the American Medical Association 293*, 2601–2608.

Sheir, H. (2001) 'Pathways to participation: Openings and obligations.' *Children and Society 15*, 2, 107–17.

Silverman, G., Johnson, J. and Prigerson, H. (2001) 'Preliminary explorations of the effects of prior trauma and loss on risk for psychiatric disorders in recently widowed people.' *Israel Journal of Psychiatry and Related Sciences 38*, 202–215.

Sim, J., Machin, L. and Bartlam, B. (2013) 'Identifying vulnerability in grief: Psychometric properties of the Adult Attitude to Grief scale.' (DOI10.1007/s11136-013-0551-1

Simons, R. (1987) *After the Tears: Parents Talk about Raising a Child with a Disability*. New York: Harcourt Brace Jovahovich.

Simon, N. M., Thompson, E. H., Pollack, M. H. and Shear M. K. (2007) 'Complicated grief: a case series using escitalopram.' *American Journal of Psychiatry 164*, 1760–1761.

Sinason, V. (1992) *Mental Handicap and the Human Condition*. London: Free Association Books Ltd.

Sinclair, R. and Franklin, A. (2000) *Young People's Participation. Quality Protects Research Briefing No 3*. London: Department of Health.

Skills for Care (2013) *New Qualifications for the Adult Social Care Sector*. Accessed on 17/12/13 at www.skillsforcare.org.uk/Document-library/Qualifications-and-Apprenticeships/Adult-social-care-qualifications/Qualifications-in-adult-social-care---overview-leaflet.pdf.

Smith, C. (1994) 'Building a Hospice: A Personal Viewpoint' In W. Kornburm and C. Smith (eds) *The healing experience: Readings on the social context of healthcare*. Englewood Cliffs, NJ: Prentice Hall.

Socialist Health Association (1969) *Report of the Committee of Enquiry into Allegations of Ill-treatment of Patients and other Irregularities at Ely Hospital Cardiff (Cmnd 3975)*. London: HMSO. Accessed on 11/1/13 at www. sochealth.co.uk/national-health-service/democracy-involvement-and-accountability-in-health/complaints-regulation-and-enquries/report-of-the-committee-of-inquiry-into-allegations-of-ill-treatment-of-patients-and-other-irregularities-at-the-ely-hospital-cardiff-1969.

Solomon, A. (2012) *Far From the Tree: Parents, Children and the Search for Identity.* New York: Scribner.

Sooben, R. D. (2010) 'Antenatal testing and the subsequent birth of a child with Down syndrome: A phenomenological study of parents' experiences.' *Journal of Intellectual Disabilities 14*, 79 –94.

Speece, M. W. and Brent, S. B. (1984) 'Children's understanding of death: A review of three components of the death concept.' *Child Development 55*, 1671–1686.

Stalker, K. (1998) 'Some ethical and methodological issues in research with people with learning difficulties.' *Disability and Society 13*, 1, 5–19.

Stamm, B. H. (ed) (1999) *Secondary Traumatic Stress: Self care Issues for Clinicians, Researchers, and Educators* (2nd ed). Lutherville: Sidran Press.

Stefanelli, H. (2006) 'Is your advocacy service up to scratch?' *Community Living 20*, 2, 20–21.

Stoddart, K. P., Burke, L. and Temple, V. (2002) 'Outcome Evaluation of Bereavement Groups for Adults with Intellectual Disabilities.' *Journal of Applied Research in Intellectual Disabilities 15*, 1, 28–35.

Strachan, J. (1981) 'Reactions to bereavement: A study of a group of hospital residents.' *Apex 9*, 1, 20–1.

Strauss, A. and Corbin, J. (1998) *Basics of Qualitative Research Techniques and Procedures for Developing Grounded Theory* (2nd ed). Thousand Oaks, CA: Sage.

Stroebe, M. and Schut, H. (1999) 'The dual process model of coping with bereavement: Rationale and description.' *Death Studies 23*, 197–224.

Stroebe, M. and Schutt, H. (2001) 'Meaning Making in the Dual Process Model of Coping with Bereavement.' In R.A. Neimeyer (ed) *Meaning Reconstruction and the Experience of Loss*. Washington, DC: American Psychological Association.

Stroebe, M. S., Folkman, S., Hansson, R. O. and Schut, H. (2006) 'The prediction of bereavement outcome: Development of an integrative risk factor framework.' *Social Science and Medicine 63*, 2440–2451.

Stroebe, R. O. Hansson, W. Stroebe, and H. Schut (eds) (2001) *Handbook of Bereavement Research*. Washington: American Psychological Association.

Stroebe, M., van Son, M., Stroebe W., Kleber, R., Schut, H., and van den Bout, J. (2001) 'On the classification and diagnosis of pathological grief.' *Psychiatric Services 52*, 1069–1074.

Strohmer, D. C. and Prout, H. T. (eds) (1994) *Counselling and Psychotherapy With Persons With Mental Retardation and Borderline Intelligence*. Brandon, Vermont: Clinical Psychology Publishing Company.

Stuart, M. (1997) *Looking Back, Looking Forward: Reminiscence with People with Learning Difficulties*. London: Pavilion.

Sutcliffe J. and Simons K. (1993) *Self-advocacy and Adults with Learning Difficulties: Contexts and Debates*. The Open University Press, Leicester: The National Institute of Adult Continuing Education.

Taggart, L., Trousdale-Kenne[...] 'Examining the support [...] plans for a relative with [...] *Disabilities 16*, 3, 217–23[...]

Taylor, J. L., Greenberg, J. S., [...] adults with mild intellect[...] outcomes.' *Journal of Fa[...]

The Editors (2010) 'Retractio[...] colitis, and pervasive de[...] 9713, 445.

The Marie Curie Palliative C[...] for the Dying Patient ([...] liverpool-care-pathway[...]

Thompson, N. (2002) *Loss[...] London: Palgrave Mac[...]

Tinbergen, N. and Tinber[...] *Cure*. London: Routle[...]

Todd, S. (2004) 'Death [...] disability services.' *Le[...]

Todd, S. (2006) 'A Troubl[...] In S. Read (ed) *Palli [...] Quay Books.

Todd, S. (2009) 'The A[...] Research.' In S. Ear[...] *Dying: A Reader*. M[...]

Todd, S. and Read S. (2[...] of death and disab[...] *19*, 252.

Todd, S. and Read, S.[...] *Journal of Child H[...]

Together for Short Li[...] togetherforshortli[...]

Tolstoy, L. (2005) *The [...]

Trivedi, D., Goodmar[...] V. (2013) 'The [...] living in the con[...] *Community 21*, [...]

Tuffrey-Wijne, I. (2[...] disabilities: A [...] 222–32.

Tuffrey-Wijne, I. ([...] disabilities: A l[...]

Tuffrey-Wijne, I. ([...] *Learning Disa[...]

Tuffrey-Wijne, I. [...] difficulties: [...] *Expectations [...]

Tuffrey-Wijne, I. [...] intellectual [...] *Nursing 14, [...]

Tuffrey-Wijne I., [...] for people wi[...] illness: A revi[...] *Research in In[...]

UN General Ass[...] Disabilities, A[...] org/docid/468[...]

United Nations En[...] *Optional Proto[...] asp?navid=12a[...]

Vachon, M. L. S. an[...] life Care in the [...] and N. Coyle ([...] Oxford Univers[...]

Vachon, M. L. S. an[...] W. Breitbart an[...] *Medicine*. New [...]

Valentine, C. (2008)[...] *Century*. Londo[...]

Van Der Houwen, [...] J. (2010) 'Med[...] threatening grie[...] *Science and Medi[...]

Van Doorn, C., Kas[...] influence of mar[...] depressive sympt[...] 573.

Van Puyenbroeck, J. a[...] intellectual disabi[...] *Disabilities 51*, 1, [...]

Van Puyenbroeck, J. a[...] and clinical appr[...] disabilities (Revie[...] *Education 55*, 1, 4[...]

Van Puyenbroeck, J. an[...] on life satisfaction[...] disabilities.' *Journa[...]

Vanderwerker, L., Jacob[...] of associations betw[...] in later life.' *Journa[...]

Wadensten, B., Conden, E., Wahlund, L. and Murray, K. (2007) 'How nursing home staff deal with residents who talk about death.' *International Journal of Older People Nursing 2*, 4, 214–249.

Wakefield, A. J., Murch, S. H., Anthony, A., Linnell, J., Casson, D. M., Malik, M., Berelowitz, M., Dhillon, A. P., Thomson, M. A., Harvey, P., Valentine, A., Davies, S. E. and Walker-Smith, J. A. (1998) 'Ileal-lymphoid-nodular hyperplasia, non-specific colitis, and pervasive developmental disorder in children.' *Lancet 28*, 351 (9103), 637–41.

Walmsley, J. (2004) 'Involving users with learning difficulties in health improvement: Lessons from inclusive learning disability research.' *Nursing Inquiry 11*, 1, 54–64.

Walter, T., Hourizi, R., Moncur, W. and Pitsillides, S. (2012) 'Does the internet change how we die and mourn? Overview and analysis.' *OMEGA 64*, 4, 275–302.

Ward, B. (1989) *The Good Grief Guide. Exploring Feelings, Loss and Death with the Under 11's: A Holistic Approach. Volume 2.* Middlesex: Good Grief.

Ware, J. (2004) *Creating a Responsive Environment.* London: David Fulton.

Watchman, K. (2005) 'Practitioner raised issues and end-of-life care for adults with Down syndrome and dementia.' *Journal of Policy and Practice in Intellectual Disabilities 2*, 2, 156–162.

Watson, R., McKenna, H., Cowman, S. and Keady, J. (2008) *Nursing Research: Design and Methods.* London: Churchill Livingstone.

Watters, L., McKenzie, K. and Wright R. (2012) 'The impact of staff training on the knowledge of support staff in relation to bereavement and people with an intellectual disability.' *British Journal of Learning Disabilities 40*, 3, 194–200.

Webb, J. and Whitaker, S. (2012) 'Defining learning disability.' *Psychologist 25*, 6, 440–443.

Webber, R., Bowers, B. and McKenzie-Green, B. (2010) 'Staff responses to age-related health changes in people with an intellectual disability in group homes.' *Disability and Society 25*, 6, 657–671.

Wehmeyer, M. L. and Bolding, N. (2001) 'Enhanced self-determination of adults with intellectual disability as an outcome of moving to community-based work or living environments.' *Journal of Intellectual Disability Research 45*, 5, 371–383.

Westgate Pesola, R. J. (2008) 'Poetry emotion or effective literacy practices for individuals with intellectual disabilities.' *Teaching Exceptional Children Plus 4*, 5, 1–14. Accessed on 2/12/13 at http://files.eric.ed.gov/fulltext/EJ967488.pdf

White, E. L. and Morgan, M. F. (2012) 'Yes! I am a researcher. The research story of a young adult with Down syndrome.' *British Journal of Learning Disabilities 40*, 2, 101–108.

Wiese, M., Dew, A., Stancliffe, R. J., Howarth, G. and Balandin, S. (2013) 'If and when?: Experiences of community living staff engaging older people with intellectual disability to know about dying.' *Journal of Intellectual Disability Research 57*, 10, 980–92.

Wiese, M., Stancliffe, R. J., Balandin, S., Howarth, G. and Dew, A. (2012) 'End-of-life care and dying: Issues raised by staff supporting older people with intellectual disability in community living services.' *Journal of Applied Research in Intellectual Disabilities 25*, 6, 571–583.

Wilks, T. (2012) *Advocacy and Social Work Practice.* Oxford: Open University Press.

Williams, J. G., Higgins, J. P. T. and Brayne, C. E. G. (2006) 'Systematic review of prevalence studies of autism spectrum disorders.' *Archives of Disease in Childhood 91*, 1, 8–15.

Wilson-Barnett, J. (1976) 'Patients' emotional reactions to hospitalization: An exploratory study'. *Journal of Advanced Nursing 1*, 351–358.

Wing, L. (1981) 'Language, social and cognitive impairments in autism and severe mental retardation.' *Journal of Autism and Developmental Disorders*, 10, 31–44.

Wing, L. and Gould, J. (1979) 'Severe impairments of social interaction and associated abnormalities in children: Epidemiology and classification.' *Journal of Autism and Developmental Disorders 9*, 1, 11–29.

Wing, L., Gould, J. and Gillberg, J.C. (2011) 'Autism spectrum disorders in the DSM-V: Better or worse than the DSM-IV?' *Research in Developmental Disabilities 32*, 768–773.

Wing, L., Leekam, S. R., Libby, S. J., Gould, J. and Larcombe, M. (2002) 'The Diagnostic Interview for Social and Communication Disorders: Background, inter-rater reliability and clinical use.' *Journal of Child Psychology and Psychiatry 3*, 3, 307–325.

Woolfe, L. (2004) 'Should parents speak with a dying child about impending death?' *The New England Journal of Medicine 351*, 1251–3.

Worden, J. W. (1991) *Grief Counselling and Grief Therapy: A Handbook for the Mental Health Practitioner.* New York: Springer.

Worden, W. (2001) Grief Counselling and Grief Therapy: A Handbook for the Mental Health Practitioner (2nd ed). East Sussex: Routledge.

Worden, W. (2010) *Grief Counselling and Grief Therapy: A Handbook for the Mental Health Practitioner* (4th ed).). New York: Springe Publ. Com., LLC.

World Health Organisation (2001) *The World Health Report 2001: Mental Health: New Understandings, New Hope.* Geneva: WHO.

World Health Organisation (2010) *International Classification of Diseases 10th Revision* (ICD-10). Geneva: WHO.

World Health Organisation and the World Bank (2011) *World Report on Disability.* Accessed 4/12/13 at www.who.int/disabilities/world_report/2011/en/index.html.

Yacoub, E. (2010) 'Low security: Patient characteristics which lead to an offer of admission and staff perceptions in a unit for people with intellectual disability.' *Advances in Mental Health and Intellectual Disabilities 4*, 25–34.

Contributors

Professor Owen Barr is Head of School at the School of Nursing, University of Ulster.

Dr Noelle Blackman PhD is CEO of Respond and a research fellow at the University of Hertfordshire, UK.

Ted Bowman is a family and grief educator who works with organizations in Minnesota, USA, in other states, and annually in Scotland and England. Ted is also an adjunct professor at both the University of Minnesota (Family Education) and the University of Saint Thomas (Social Work).

Erica Brown is Senior Lecturer in Early Childhood at the Institute of Education, University of Worcester, UK.

Patsy Corcoran is the Reach Coordinator at Asist in Stoke on Trent, UK.

Mary Carr, a woman with intellectual disabilities, is a member of Reach in Stoke on Trent, UK.

Dr Philip Dodd is Consultant Psychiatrist/Director of Psychiatry at St. Michael's House, Dublin; Clinical Senior Lecturer at the University of Dublin, Trinity College; and Senior Lecturer at the Centre for Disability Studies, School of Psychology, University College Dublin, Ireland.

Dr Rachel Forrester-Jones is Reader in Health, Community and Social Care at the Tizard Centre, UK.

Professor Bill Gaventa is Director of Community and Congregational Supports at the Elizabeth M. Boggs Center on Developmental Disabilities, and Associate Professor at UMDNJ Robert Wood Johnson Medical School, Georgia, USA.

Mike Gibbs is Lecturer in Learning Disability Nursing at the School of Nursing and Midwifery, Keele University, UK.

Dr Suzanne Guerin is Director of the University College Dublin Centre for Disability Studies and a Senior Investigator with All Ireland Institute of Hospice and Palliative Care.

Dr Ben Hobson is a clinical psychologist in the National High Secure Learning Disability Service, Rampton Hospital, UK.

Professor Phil Larkin is Professor of Clinical Nursing (Palliative Care/ Head of Discipline Children's Nursing/Director of Clinical Academic Partnership, UCD School of Nursing, Midwifery and Healthcare Systems, and Our Lady's Hospice and Care services, University College Dublin, College of Health Sciences, Dublin and Chair, All Ireland Institute for Hospice and Palliative Care.

Dr Linda Machin is Honorary Research Fellow at Keele University, UK.

Mandy Parks is the parent of a daughter with severe disabilities from Cheshire, UK.

Dr Helena M. Priest is Senior Lecturer in Psychology at Keele University and Research Director for Staffordshire and Keele Doctorate in Clinical Psychology at Staffordshire University, UK.

Professor Sue Read is Professor of Learning Disability Nursing at the School of Nursing and Midwifery, Keele University, UK.

Dr Karen Ryan is Consultant in Palliative Medicine at St Francis Hospice, Dublin and Mater Hospital Senior Investigator, All Ireland Institute of Hospice and Palliative Care, Ireland.

Michele Wiese is a research associate at the University of Sydney, Australia.

Subject Index

Sub-headings in *italics* indicate figures.

Author Index